MARINES IN THE SPANISH-AMERICAN WAR
1895-1899
Anthology and Annotated Bibliography

Compiled and Edited by

Jack Shulimson

Wanda J. Renfrow

Lieutenant Colonel David E. Kelly,
U.S. Marine Corps Reserve

Evelyn A. Englander

HISTORY AND MUSEUMS DIVISION
HEADQUARTERS, U.S. MARINE CORPS
WASHINGTON, D.C.

1998

PCN 19000314400

Foreword

In this the 100th anniversary of the Spanish-American War, the History and Museums Division decided to take another look at this so-called "Splendid Little War" which had such large implications, not only for the nation at large, but also for the Marine Corps. Rather than another history, the Division decided to make available in one volume some of the rich historical literature about the Marine participation in the war. This anthology, like almost all of the works published by the History and Museums Division, is the result of a team effort. Dr. Jack Shulimson, who heads the History Writing Unit, selected the articles and made the necessary revisions. Ms. Wanda Renfrow of the History Writing Unit copy edited the material and prepared the text for printing. Ms. Evelyn Englander, the librarian of the History and Museums Division, and Lieutenant Colonel David Kelly, USMCR, a member of Marine Corps Reserve Individual Mobilization Augmentee Detachment, prepared the selected bibliography of the war and collected most of the illustrations. Lieutenant Colonel Kelly also prepared the chronology and listing of the Medal of Honor recipients. Air Force Academy Cadet First Class Craig Prather assisted in the preparation of the chronology and participated in the final review.

While the editors altered none of the text in the published articles to conform with division guidelines, they made certain stylistic revisions for clarity in some of the unpublished material. Because of their length, both the Commandant's Annual Report for 1898 and James Holden-Rhodes' chapter on the Spanish-American War were much condensed.

The editors are indebted to the personnel of the Editing and Design section, Mr. Robert E. Struder, Mrs. Cathy A. Kerns, and Mr. W. Stephen Hill for their assistance and advice in the final preparation.

M. F. MONIGAN
Colonel, U.S. Marine Corps
Director of Marine Corps History and Museums

Introduction

The modern Marine Corps owes its genesis to the Spanish-American War when the United States entered the world stage. In this the 100th anniversary year of the war with Spain, the History and Museums Division decided upon a new publication about the Marine Corps participation in the conflict. At first, the thought was to write a new history, but upon examination of the historical literature of the war, we discovered a trove of new writings (and some old) that deserved further exploitation. The upshot is this anthology.

The Director Emeritus of the Division, Brigadier General Edwin H. Simmons, Jr., USMC (Ret), in his revised history, *The United States Marines: A History*, 3d Edition, U.S. Naval Institute Press, 1998, provides a brief overview of the Marines in the Spanish-American War. In the chapter reprinted here, "The Spanish-American War," Simmons opens his narrative with the sinking of the U.S. battleship *Maine* with Private William Anthony, the Marine orderly, entering the cabin of Captain Charles Sigsbee, saluting smartly, and then stating, "Sir, I beg to report that the Captain's ship is sinking." The author covers succinctly the formation and deployment of the 1st Marine Battalion, Marines with Dewey in the Philippines, the 1st Battalion at Guantanamo, the defeat of the Spanish fleet in Santiago Bay, and the taking of Guam. He then ends with Admiral Dewey's lament that only if he had 5,000 Marines he could have captured Manila.

Lieutenant Colonel David Kelly, USMCR, a member of the Marine Corps Reserve Individual Mobilization Augmentee Detachment, and a high school history teacher in civilian life, is the author of "The Marines in the Spanish-American War, A Brief History." This was originally to be published by itself, but now has been incorporated into the anthology. In this study, Kelly provides a descriptive account of the Marine participation in the war from the steadiness of Marine Private William Anthony on board the *Maine* to the final review of the Marine battalion as it paraded before President William McKinley in Washington. He touches in passing upon the heroics of the Marines and sailors involved in the cutting of the cable south of Cuba, the taking of Cavite Island in the Philippines, the role of Marines on board ship, and especially emphasizes the rapid deployment of the Marine battalion and its establishment of an advance base for the Navy on Guantanamo. According to Kelly, "The War with Spain gave the Marines the opportunity to show the Navy and, more importantly, the nation, the many roles that Marines were in a unique position to fill as the United States became a world power."

Colonel Allan R. Millett, USMCR (Ret), the General Raymond E. Mason, Jr. Professor of Military History at The Ohio State University, in his seminal history, *Semper Fidelis, the History of the United States Marine Corps*, provides a more analytical account of the war. According to Millett, the Navy had an excellent idea of the requirements it needed in a war with Spain, but the role of the Marine Corps was not so clear. He also disputes the claim of the Marine

Corps Commandant Charles Heywood that Marines manning the secondary guns on board the Navy warships played a vital role in the two major sea battles, Manila Bay and Santiago Bay. Still, the Marines were there on board ship during these actions. Marines also helped in destroying cable stations and cutting cables, capturing a lighthouse, and taking Cavite in the Philippines, Apra in Guam, and Ponce in Puerto Rico. All of these activities received a favorable press and the Marine Corps basked in its public approval. Moreover, while the Navy was initially unsure how it was to use Huntington's Marine battalion, it was ready for action when the call came. While the battalion's action at Guantanamo may have been "a minor skirmish of no consequence to the course of the war," it would have "incalculable importance for the Marine Corps," especially at a time when the Army was still in Florida. Even more significantly, the experience of the battalion "suggested to some Navy and Marine officers that the Corps might indeed have an important role to play in the New Navy."

Dr. Jack Shulimson's "Marines in the Spanish-American War" first appeared in James Bradford, editor, *Crucible of Empire*, published by the Naval Institute Press, 1993. This article, based upon Shulimson's larger work, *The Marines Search For A Mission, 1880-1898*, Kansas University Press, 1993, focuses on how the war with Spain delineated the Marine mission and its future relationship with the Navy in the new century. Like Millett, Shulimson, who heads the History Writing Unit at the Marine Corps Historical Center, notes the detailed Navy war plans against Spain and also emphasizes the vagueness of the Marine mission. Most of the wartime emergency funding of the Marine Corps reflected the traditional Marine roles, yet the Navy very quickly called for the formation of a Marine battalion to serve with the fleet. While treating the general scope of the war, including service legislation and the integration of new officers, the main theme becomes the newly formed Marine battalion and its establishment of a naval advance base at Guantanamo. In some variance from Millett, Shulimson views the Guantanamo campaign as having more significance than a "minor skirmish." Until reinforced by some Cuban troops and guides who provided much needed intelligence, the Marine battalion at one time even considered abandoning their position and reembarking. The seizure of the Cuzco Well with the aid of the Cubans secured the advance base. Shulimson also stresses the major differences between the Navy and Army at Santiago about attacking the Morro and Socapa Heights overlooking and commanding the entry into Santiago Bay. The Navy wanted the Army reinforced by Marines to make a ground assault on the heights; the Army wanted the Navy ships to run pass the heights and support the Army campaign against Santiago City. While the destruction of the Spanish fleet and the surrender of the Spanish Army garrison at Santiago made this a moot point, Navy commanders took as a lesson from this experience that they could not depend upon the Army to secure land-based sites for naval purposes. For this the Navy required its own land force which it already had in the Marine Corps.

Dr. James F. Holden-Rhodes, Senior Policy Analyst in the Office of the Secretary, Department of Public Safety, State of New Mexico, is the author of "Crucible of the Corps" which is condensed from his uncompleted biography of

Henry Clay Cochrane. Cochrane as a major served as the executive officer of the 1st Marine Battalion on Guantanamo. Like Shulimson, Holden-Rhodes holds that the struggle for Guantanamo was a near thing. He refers to Bowman McCalla's autobiography and Henry Cochrane's diary to support the contention that the Marines were ready to evacuate their foothold on Cuban territory. Holden-Rhodes believes that the Guantanamo battle was the linchpin for the entire Cuban campaign. He asserts that if the Marine battalion had been forced off Guantanamo there would have been much larger consequences including the delay and possible abandonment of the Army's larger Santiago operation.

Trevor K. Plante, an archivist with the National Archives, is the author of "New Glory to Its Already Gallant Record, The First Marine Battalion in the Spanish-American War," published in the Spring, 1998 issue of *Prologue, the Journal of the National Archives*. Plante also insists upon the importance of the Guantanamo campaign and like the previous authors observes that the 1st Battalion was a glimpse of the Marine Corps of the future. While providing a more or less traditional interpretation of the battalion experience, he does employ some new documentation from the Bureau of Naval Personnel, Record Group 24 and Records of Naval Operating Forces, North Atlantic Station, Correspondence with Commanders of Vessels, 1897-99, Record Group 313, all in the National Archives.

Novelist Stephen Crane's impressionistic eyewitness account "The Red Badge of Courage Was His Wig-Wag Flag" describes the Marine attack on the Cuzco Well. During the course of the advance, a "spruce young sergeant of Marines, erect, his back to the showering bullets, solemnly and intently wig-wagging to the distant [U.S. Navy warship] *Dolphin*" directed naval gunfire support for the Marines. The Marines gained the high ground and took the Spanish troops under a deadly crossfire. After the successful mission, the Marines returned to their original lines where they were met by the Sergeant of the Guard: "Sergeant of the Guard! Saintly man! Protector of the Weary! Coffee! Hardtack! Beans! Rest! Sleep! Peace!"

One of the most important primary sources for the Marine experience in the Spanish-American War is the 1898 annual report of the then Colonel Commandant of the Marine Corps, Charles Heywood. The excerpts of Heywood's rather voluminous report reprinted in this volume include the organizing and outfitting of the Marine battalion, the limited wartime expansion of the Corps, and a description of the role of Marines on board ship. Additionally there are copies of correspondence from Lieutenant Colonel Robert Huntington, the commander of the Marine battalion, and Marine Captain George Elliott, who led the attack on Cuzco Well, as well as comments by Commander Bowman H. McCalla, the naval commander at Guantanamo, relating to the actions ashore. While obviously pleased with the success of the Marine battalion in Cuba, Colonel Heywood still placed a heavy stress upon the Marines serving with the secondary batteries on board ship which he still viewed as the primary mission of the Corps.

The final article in this series is the unpublished report by Colonel Robert R. Hull, USMC (Ret), a former senior communications officer, who described his

1997 visit to Guantanamo and the results of his team's field research at the scene to identify the key sites and terrain features of the 1898 activity there. According to Hull, with the use of metal detectors and a close study of the ground, his group reached a consensus on the location of the principal areas occupied by the battalion including Elliott's route to the Cuzco Well.

In addition to the articles listed above, there are three appendices: a select bibliography, a chronology of the war, and a listing of Spanish-American War Marine Medal of Honor holders. The editors and the History and Museums Division wish to thank the Naval Institute Press; Trevor K. Plante; Professor Allan R. Millett; Simon and Schuster; Dr. James F. Holden-Rhodes; University Press of Kansas; Colonel Robert R. Hull, USMC (Ret); Brigadier General Edwin H. Simmons, USMC (Ret), Director Emeritus, History and Museums Division; and the University Press of Virginia for their permission to publish the articles in this anthology.

Table of Contents

Appendices

Illustrations

Maps

Marines In The Spanish-American War

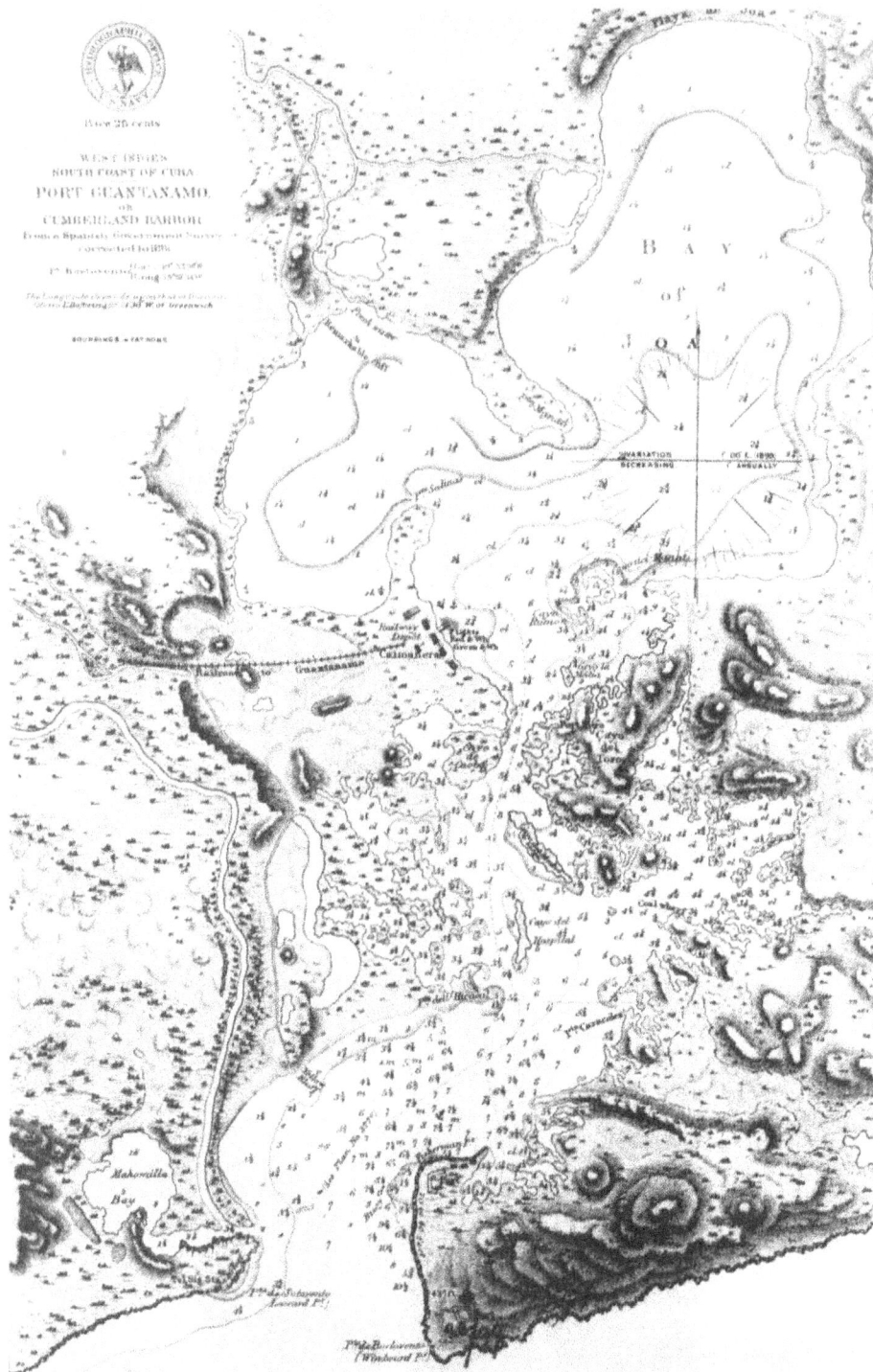

The contemporary map shown above carried the following handwritten inscription: "The original survey appears hereon but as corrected by the survey made by the 'Columbia' in 1894." This chart was published in June 1898.

Excerpted from *The United States Marines: A History*, 3d Edition, U.S. Naval Institute Press, 1998, and reprinted with permission of the author and publisher.

The Spanish-American War
by Brigadier General Edwin Howard Simmons,
USMC (Retired)
Director Emeritus, Marine Corps History and Museums

There was a sharp report and then a heavier explosion deep in the bowels of the armored cruiser *Maine* as she rode at anchor in Havana's harbor on the night of 15 February 1898. Capt. Charles Sigsbee, interrupted in the writing of a letter to his wife, left his cabin, went out into the smoke-filled passageway, and stumbled into his Marine orderly.

"Sir," said Pvt. William Anthony, drawing himself up to attention and saluting, "I beg to report that the Captain's ship is sinking."

The *Maine* had come into the harbor on 25 January. Spanish reception had been cool but correct. Now 232 seamen and twenty-eight marines were dead. 1st. Lt. Albertus W. Catlin, the senior marine, was unharmed. Like his captain, he had been in his stateroom writing a letter home when the explosion occurred. Although no definitive evidence, then or now, connected the Spanish with the sinking, the cry went up, "Remember the *Maine!*" On 19 April, Congress passed a resolution of intervention. Three days later, President McKinley informed the neutral nations that a state of war existed between the United States and Spain.

On 27 April Col. Cmdt. Heywood ordered a Marine battalion formed, and five days later it sailed from Brooklyn for Key West aboard the ex-banana boat USS *Panther*. The five rifle companies had the new Lee rifle, a bolt-action .236-caliber weapon using smokeless powder. There was also an artillery company equipped with a battery of four 3-inch landing guns. The commanding officer was Lt. Col. Robert W. Huntington, who had been with Reynolds as a lieutenant at First Manassas and in the Carolinas.

In the Pacific, Commodore George Dewey, commanding the Asiatic Squadron, caught Adm. Patricio Montojo's elegant but antique squadron at anchor off Sangley Point, the southwestern lip of Manila Bay, as dawn broke 1 May. He gave his famous order to the captain of his flagship Olympia, "You may fire when you are ready, Gridley."

Battle stations for the marines in Dewey's five cruisers were the rapid-fire guns of the secondary batteries. For two hours the Americans blazed away, retired for breakfast, then came back and finished the job. Seven Spanish ships were destroyed, three land batteries silenced, 381 Spanish sailors were dead and many wounded. Dewey had two officers and six men, none of them marines, slightly hurt.

Two days later, on 3 May, the Marine detachment from the protected cruiser *Baltimore*, under 1st. Lt. Dion Williams, landed and raised the flag over Cavite station. But there were still thirteen thousand Spanish troops in Manila itself and a kind of uneasy standoff was maintained until sufficient Army troops could arrive to take the city.

In Washington, on 4 May, the Naval Appropriation Act brought the Marine Corps up to a permanent authorized strength of 3,073 men, plus a wartime augmentation of forty-three lieutenants and 1,580 men. One of the new lieutenants, commissioned on 20 May, was a Pennsylvania Quaker named Smedley D. Butler, age 18 (or maybe 16—there is a suspicion that he added two years to his age). He had an inside track to the new commissions. His father was a member, and later chairman, of the House Naval Affairs Committee.

In the Caribbean, by the end of May, Rear Adm. William T. Sampson had bottled up the Spanish fleet under Adm. Pascual Cervera in Santiago de Cuba, but he needed an advance base close by from which to coal his blockaders. "Can you not take possession of Guantanamo, occupy as a coaling station?" asked the secretary of the Navy. "Yes," said Sampson. "Send me Huntington's Marine battalion."

On 7 June the *Panther* chugged out of Key West with Huntington's battalion on board. Meanwhile, the protected cruiser *Marblehead* was shelling Guantanamo, defended by a single decrepit gunboat and a reported seven to nine thousand Spaniards. Some of Sampson's fleet marines had gone ashore to reconnoiter. On 10 June, Huntington's battalion landed inside Guantanamo Bay, forty miles from Santiago. There was no opposition at the beach. First Spanish reaction came at midnight and for the next three days Huntington was sniped at and harassed, losing his men by ones and twos. Crux of the matter seemed to be Cuzco Well, the Spanish water supply (water supply at semiarid Guantanamo has always been a consideration).

On 14 June, Huntington sent out two companies of marines, along with sixty to seventy Cuban guerrillas, to take the well. The dispatch boat *Dolphin* was to provide naval gunfire support. Sun and heat caused more casualties than Spanish bullets and command eventually devolved upon Capt. George F. Elliott. The *Dolphin's* shells began dropping on the marines' position. Lean, cadaverous Sgt. John H. Quick went up on a ridge line to wigwag an adjustment. The estimated five hundred Spanish defenders were routed. The marines counted up and found their own casualties to be six killed, sixteen wounded.

There was no further fighting of consequence at Guantanamo. On 3 July, Admiral Cervera elected to come out of Santiago. The victory was even more lopsided than Manila Bay. Cervera's four armored cruisers and three destroyers were no match for Commodore Winfield Scott Schley's five battleships and armored cruiser. Every Spanish ship was sunk or surrendered.

In the Pacific, on 21 June, the protected cruiser *Charleston* had approached Guam and fired twelve rounds with its 3-pounders at old (and abandoned) Fort Santa Cruz. A Spanish officer came out in a small boat with apologies; he had no powder with which to return the "salute," and had to be informed that a state of war existed between Spain and the United States. 1st. Lt. John Twiggs ("Handsome Jack") Myers took the *Charleston's* marines ashore and the amenities of surrender were observed.

Hostilities ceased on 12 August. On 13 August (the apparent extra day was the consequence of a cut cable and the international date line) the American Army came out of the trenches it had thrown around Manila and entered the city. Years later, in testifying before the House Naval Affairs Committee, Admiral Dewey said that if he had had five thousand marines embarked with his squadron at Manila Bay he could have taken Manila on 1 May and the Philippine Insurrection might have been avoided.

Marines in the Spanish-American War: A Brief History
by Lieutenant Colonel David E. Kelly, USMCR

Prelude to the War

On the eve of the Spanish War, the small United States Marine Corps of 3,500 men and officers was involved in efforts to justify its traditional roles in a changing world. The Navy was modernizing its fleet, and many Navy reformers questioned the utility of Marines on board naval vessels. By the end of the war, however, the Marine Corps would enjoy the most public recognition since its founding, with exploits of its heroes emblazoned in newspapers, periodicals, and popular books. The Corps would gain additional officers, enlisted men, and funding to expand to over twice its 1890 size and at the turn of the century would begin to deploy units of regimental size to new colonial outposts in both hemispheres. Professionalism grew, and many young officers who fought in battles against the Spanish, including seven future Commandants, would form the nucleus of a senior officer corps that would lead large combat formations into the battles of World War I and supervise the development of the Fleet Marine Corps and modern amphibious warfare. The War with Spain gave the Marines the opportunity to show the Navy and, more importantly, the nation, the many roles that Marines were in a unique position to fill as the United States became a world power.

Throughout much of the 19th century, the festering Cuban situation, entailing recurrent revolts followed by the inevitable Spanish repression, impinged upon the relations between the United States and Spain. The breakout of a new revolt in 1895, again threatened the Spanish-American relationship. Although neither U.S. President Grover Cleveland nor his successor, William McKinley, wanted war with Spain, events outside of their control disturbed the precarious peace between the two nations. A strident U.S. "Yellow Journalism," fueled by the rivalry between the Hearst and Pulitzer newspaper empires aroused American public opinion against Spain with vivid accounts of Spanish "war crimes" and Concentration Camps.

Despite the discord, by the beginning of 1898, President McKinley believed that his efforts to defuse the situation had borne some fruit. Spain had relieved its notorious General Valeriano Weyler and repudiated his reconcentration policy as well as promising some sort of autonomy for Cuba. The American president was hopeful that diplomacy would end the bloodshed.

Two incidents in early 1898, however, would dash these newborn hopes. On 9 February, William Randolph Hearst's *New York Journal* published on its front page an intercepted letter of the Spanish Minister to the United States, Enrique Dupuy DeLome to a friend. In the letter, DeLome said among other things that McKinley was "weak and a bidder for the admiration of the crowd," and that he, DeLome, still hoped for a Spanish military victory over the rebels to save Cuba for the mother country. A week later, the Spanish government announced De-Lome's resignation and issued a formal letter of apology to the United States, but by that time, an explosion had ripped apart the U.S. second class battleship USS *Maine* in Havana Harbor.

The sinking of the *Maine* provided the spark that ignited the war. The McKinley administration intended the visit of the ship to Cuba as part of an effort to relieve the tension between the two countries. When the *Maine* arrived in early February, 1898, the populace of Havana greeted the ship, sailors of Spain and the U.S. mingled ashore, and the officers attended a bullfight. Then on the evening of 15 February, two distinct blasts roared through the ship at anchor in the harbor. Captain Charles Sigsbee, USN, had been alone in his cabin writing letters when the explosions occurred. His orderly, Marine Private William Anthony, collided with him in the smoke-filled passageway outside his cabin, and informed him that the ship was sinking. When the two got above decks, they saw a tangle of twisted metal, and Sigsbee ordered the survivors into the water. More than 260 sailors and Marines perished with the sinking of the ship.

When word of the disaster reached the United States, the "Yellow Press" went wild with accusations against the treachery of the Spanish. Both the U.S. Navy and the Spanish convened separate boards to investigate the sinking. Despite McKinley's rejection of Spain's offer for a joint investigation, Spanish authorities in Havana allowed U.S. divers and armor experts to examine the ship. The Spanish board eventually concluded that the sinking was due to internal explosions. The U.S. Navy board, however, determined that the blasts had been triggered by an external explosion, but assigned no blame. No evidence of any external explosive device was ever found, but the American public and politicians saw the event as another act of Spanish treachery and clearly blamed Spain for the catastrophe. (A 1976 investigation of the explosion by Admiral H. G. Rickover, USN, concluded that the explosion was actually due to a spontaneous ignition of bituminous coal dust in the coal bunkers on board, located adjacent to the *Maine* forward ammunition magazines.)[1]

With Congressional and public pressure demanding action, McKinley gave the Spanish government until 15 April to take action on general affairs in Cuba. In the interim, Congress appropriated 50 million dollars for the emergency, 30 million of that sum for the Navy including the Marine Corps.

Colonel Charles Heywood, the Marine Corps Commandant immediately took several steps to prepare his Corps for war including the continuing distribution to Marines of the new Winchester-Lee bolt-action, "Straight pull" 6mm, 5-shot, magazine-fed rifles and the necessary ammunition for the weapons. There was also discussion about the formation of Marine expeditionary battalions.

While the mission of any Marine battalion was still not specific, on 13 April, Captain William T. Sampson, USN, commanding the North Atlantic Squadron at Key West, Florida, observed to Navy Secretary John D. Long that if the Navy was to establish a blockade of Cuba, "it will be necessary to hold certain small places" and recommended "a battalion of Marines of 400 men, ready to land,

and hold such places." Sampson wanted this battalion together with its transport and supporting field pieces by 20 April. He also asked for the formation of a second Marine battalion for the same purpose.[2]

After Heywood received verbal orders from Long on 16 April to organize a battalion for expeditionary duty with the North Atlantic Squadron in Caribbean waters, he stripped the East Coast Marine stations and barracks of men to form a Marine battalion at the Brooklyn Navy Yard. Marines from the barracks at Newport, Rhode Island; Washington, D.C.; League Island (Philadelphia); Norfolk, Virginia; Annapolis, Maryland; Portsmouth, New Hampshire; and Boston, Massachusetts; and all receiving ships on the East Coast assembled at the Brooklyn Navy Yard, under the command of Lieutenant Colonel Robert W. Huntington, a Civil War veteran. Originally this "First" Battalion was to have totaled about 400 officers and men, but Commandant Heywood received orders from the Navy Department to add two companies to the battalion to create one battalion of 623 enlisted Marines and 23 officers rather than two 400-man battalions as originally proposed by Sampson. A second battalion was never formed as the manpower required to build the one battalion left only 71 Marine guards on the East Coast.[3]

Lieutenant Colonel Huntington formed his First Battalion of Marines into five infantry companies of approximately 100 men each (A, B, C, D, E) and one artillery company equipped with a battery of four 3-inch rapid fire landing guns. Each company consisted of one first sergeant, four sergeants, four corporals, one drummer, one fifer, and 92 privates, led by one captain and two lieutenants.[4] Not all of the men were seasoned veterans. Many had enlisted in the *Maine*-induced war fervor, and were just beginning to learn the basics of military drill and discipline. Roughly one-third enlisted after the beginning of 1898.[5]

One enlisted new Marine with the battalion, Frank Keeler, recalled that only a few weeks before he had visited the Charleston Navy Yard in Boston Massachusetts, and was impressed with the Marines at drill in their "neat uniforms [and by] their manly appearance." He later asked a Marine sentry "if more Marines were wanted," the guard replied "Why my boy they want all they can get at present. Don't you know they are inlisting (sic) them for the War?" In short order, Keeler had become a Marine. His training consisted of drill and police work, with weekends off for liberty. According to Keeler, a short time later, he and 33 other Marine privates, 4 corporals, and 2 sergeants received orders to move from Boston to the Brooklyn Navy Yard.[6]

For a few days, the battalion remained at Brooklyn going through its initial "shakedown" phases. While many of the Marines were new recruits like Keeler, who himself had only a little over three weeks in uniform, a number of veteran troops provided some leavening for the battalion. On 22 April the battalion loaded stores on board the USS *Panther* and late in the afternoon marched through the streets outside of the Navy Yard to the accompaniment of the Navy Yard band playing the popular tune "The Girl I Left Behind Me" before embarking on board the *Panther*. The *Panther*, formerly the *Venezuela*, had originally been outfitted to transport a battalion of 400 men, and in the two days prior to sailing, hasty arrangements had been made to handle the additional 250 souls.

The *Panther* sailed south, bound for Key West, Florida, with a stopover on 23 April at Hampton Roads, Virginia. The *Panther* left Hampton Roads on 24 April, under convoy of the USS *Montgomery*, and arrived at Key West, Florida, on 29 April.

En route, Lieutenant Colonel Huntington provided Marines to the ship for signal duty, lifeboat crews, and anchor watch once at Key West. He also conducted instruction in loading and firing the Lee rifles while underway at sea, each Marine firing ten rounds. For many recruits this was the first time that they been able to fire a rifle. The four-gun artillery battery also received similar instruction, each of the 3-inch naval landing guns firing one round.

By the time the *Panther* arrived at Key West, the United States was at war with Spain. After no satisfactory reply from Spain, on 11 April, President McKinley finally sent a message to Congress asking for the authority to use military force, perhaps still gambling that the Spanish would finally back away from war. On the 19th, Congress approved a joint resolution that recognized the independence of Cuba, including the Teller Amendment prohibiting the U.S. acquisition of the island, and the authorization for the President to use any means necessary to carry out this policy. Five days later Spain answered with a declaration of war against the U.S. The U.S. Congress then passed its own declaration of war retroactive to 21 April.

By this time, the United States fleet had established its blockade around Havana, and soon became obsessed with discovering the location of the Spanish squadron of Admiral Pascual Cervera y Topete, which left European waters at the end of April and headed west. The uncertainty about the location of Cervera's squadron postponed for the time being any landing of American troops including the Marine battalion.

With Dewey in the Philippines

While the fleet in the Atlantic waited for Cervera, the Asiatic Squadron under Commodore George Dewey had already taken the offensive. As early as 25 February, the then Assistant Secretary of the Navy Theodore Roosevelt had warned Dewey about the possibility of war with Spain and directed him to be prepared to undertake "offensive operations in the Philippine Islands." On 22 March, the USS *Mohican* arrived at Honolulu, Republic of Hawaii, with ammunition for the batteries of the USS *Baltimore* and the ships of Dewey's squadron. Three days later, the *Baltimore*, fully coaled and carrying an extra supply of fuel on deck, with a Marine detachment of 52 on board, under Captain Otway C. Berryman, USMC, and First Lieutenant Dion Williams, USMC, left Hawaii to join up with the bulk of Dewey's squadron at the British protectorate of Hong Kong. Arriving there on 22 April, the ship searched for the U.S. squadron, recognizing it only by the United States flags the ships flew. Dewey's squadron sported the new war color, a dull gray. The *Baltimore* immediately went into dry dock to have its hull scraped and the entire upper works painted war gray, and two additional rapid fire guns mounted to increase its firepower. When the work was complete on Sunday, 24 April, the British Neutrality Proclamation had gone into effect, and Dewey's squadron was requested to leave Hong Kong waters. There was little doubt where Britain's sentiments lay, as Dewey had recently purchased two English ships, the collier *Nanshan* and the supply ship *Zafiro* during his wait in Hong Kong. He would use both ships to help sustain his fleet. On 25 April a tug brought cable messages out to Dewey. The most important read:

> War has commenced between the United States and Spain. Proceed at once to the Philippine Islands. Commence operation at once, particularly against the Spanish fleet. You must capture vessels or destroy. Use utmost endeavors.[7]

Another message advised Dewey to wait for the arrival of the American Consul at Manila, Mr. O. F. Williams, who had recently left that city and would arrive at Hong Kong with an update on the conditions there. Mr. Williams arrived on 27 April, and the squadron left that afternoon for Manila.

Dewey faced a daunting task. He was 7000 miles from home port in San Francisco and none of his ships had sufficient coal to steam there from Hong Kong. A long siege in the Philippines was out of the question, so the challenge would be to meet and defeat the Spanish fleet there. Dewey received valuable military intelligence from Consul Williams, including the size and number of Spanish ships present when he departed Manila, and the disposition of the shore batteries guarding the entrance to Manila Bay. In Lieutenant Dion Williams' notes of the meeting:

> There are batteries on Corregidor Island at the entrance to the bay and on the mainland on both sides of the entrance. There are also batteries on heavy guns at Manila and on Sangley Point near Cavite.[8]

By the evening of 27 April, the squadron had reached the northern end of the island of Luzon, and Captain N. M. Dyer, USN, of the *Baltimore* first read to his crew the inflammatory war proclamation of the Governor General of the Philippines and then addressed them:

> We are going to Manila to capture and destroy the Spanish ships there; we are going to fight under the Stars and Stripes--the flag of the greatest nation the world has ever seen--and we are going to win. Every one of you has his duty to do and must make every shot tell.[9]

Ships prepared for imminent action during these last days in April. The wood paneling of ships' wardroom areas was torn out and thrown overboard to lessen injuries from shattered wood and fire from enemy gunfire. Sailors and Marines wrapped ships boats at the davits in heavy canvas to prevent damage to help protect them from shell fire fragments, and all Navy and Marine gun crews drilled incessantly. On the *Baltimore*, the Marines manned three main battery guns: Number 1, an 8-inch forecastle gun; Number 3, a 6-inch waist gun on main deck; and Number 5, an 8-inch gun on the poop. One large concern was making every round count, for if several engagements with the Spanish became necessary, Dewey's squadron had only the ammunition that it had brought along with it and was thousands of miles away from any resupply.

On 30 April, the *Petrel* and *Boston* reconnoitered the coast north of the island of Luzon while the *Baltimore* sailed to Subic Bay to search for Spanish vessels. Finding none, Dewey met with his captains and told them that they would go directly into Manila that evening, running the forts at the entrance to the bay at night. They would sail in a single column of the six fighting ships spaced 400 yards apart, with running lights extinguished. Despite reports of "torpedoes" (19th century term for underwater mines) in the entrance to the harbor, Dewey determined to get into the harbor as quickly as possible to confront the Spanish fleet. This was not very surprising for a leader like Dewey to come to such a decision. Both he and Captain Dyer of the *Baltimore* had served under Admiral Farragut's command when the admiral steamed past the batteries and "torpedoes" at Mobile Bay during the Civil War.

By 23:30 the fleet had reached the channel south of Corregidor Island at the entrance of the bay and a signal rocket from shore announced that the ships had been spotted. At 00:15 on 1 May, the Spanish battery south of the channel fired a shot, and ceased after firing a few more shots and being fired upon by the U.S. ships. By 02:10 the fleet was well within the bay and Dewey give the order to turn on running lights. As dawn broke, the fleet was west of Manila, searching for Spanish ships. The fleet then turned starboard at around 05:00 to approach the Spanish naval station at Cavite in the southern part of the bay. Spanish ships began firing on the U.S. ships, and the *Olympia* fired the first U.S. shots of the war. Dewey's fleet made three passes to the west across the front of Cavite, and two to the east. Although Spanish fire was generally inaccurate, the *Baltimore* was struck six times and several officers and men wounded, the *Olympia* three times, and the *Boston* once. Within two hours, several Spanish ships were on fire, including the flagship, the *Reina Christina*.

At 07:35, Dewey signaled the fleet to withdraw from action. Later he explained that he had received a report that most of his ships were down to only five rounds of ammunition remaining for each gun on all of his ships, and he wanted to redistribute ammunition and confirm the report. Once the ships had withdrawn north from the vicinity of Cavite, he learned that not even half of the ammunition stores of the ships had been expended. At this point Dewey gave orders to serve breakfast to crew members, who had been at battle quarters throughout the night without rest or food.

At 0900, the Spanish ship *Castilla* exploded from a fire that had been started by a U.S. shell. Many of the remaining Spanish ships had withdrawn behind Bacoor Bay. One hour later, the *Baltimore* was in position to fire at the battery at Sangley Point and received permission to engage it. At a range of 3,000 yards the Baltimore fired on the battery and also at the *Don Antonio de Ulluoa* behind Sangley Point. By noon, most of the Spanish ships were on fire and were being abandoned by their crews. The element of surprise had worked to Dewey's advantage. The Spanish had evidently believed that any American action in the Philippines would begin with a blockade of Manila Bay and other important ports, and that any attack on the fleet or city would be preceded by a reconnaissance. The Spanish also had several ships undergoing repairs and were not able to move them into the harbor proper. They had adopted a defensive posture from the moment Dewey steamed into the harbor. Dewey's aggressive actions gave him the initiative.

After destroying the Spanish fleet, the American fleet kept a close watch during the night of 1 May to insure that no small Spanish torpedo boats approached in the darkness. The following day, two ships went to the entrance of the bay and demanded the surrender of Spanish forces manning the batteries there. The Spanish officers and men surrendered and were transported to Manila, as Dewey did not wish to be burdened with caring for prisoners of war.

On 3 May, Dewey learned that the Spanish had abandoned the Arsenal at Cavite, and First Lieutenant Dion Williams went ashore with a detachment of Marines from the *Baltimore* to take charge of the Arsenal and town and protect property there. After the Marines established order ashore, Sergeant James Grant and Corporal Joseph Poe hoisted the United States colors over the arsenal, the first raising of the U.S. flag on Spanish soil. (This flag was later sent to the U.S. Naval Academy). The Marines found many dead Spanish in the area, and sent for ships' surgeons to help care for wounded Spanish sailors, soldiers, and Marines found in two buildings in the town. Many of the wounded were sent by ferry to Manila where they could be attended to by their own doctors. In his diary Williams noted:

> I went through all the buildings of the navy yard (Arsenal) to inspect the conditions and everywhere could be seen the evidences of the hasty departure of the former garrison. In the offices papers and records are strewn over the floors, and in the houses of the officers everything is in confusion . . . . The powder and shell magazine doors stood open and loose powder from torn bags was strewn over the floors; these doors were closed and sentries put over them to prevent accidental explosions.[10]

The town seemed like an old time "navy-yard town" to the Marines, with plentiful liquor shops and other places of "amusement."

On 4 May, the Marines went into the town of San Roque, on the land end of the causeway that connected Cavite with the mainland. The native Filipinos were celebrating the departure of the Spanish, drinking and noisily firing captured Spanish weapons into the air. That morning several Filipinos claiming to be members of the "Risal Army" approached the Arsenal gate and asked to be armed with captured Spanish weapons so that they could press the fight against the Spanish in Manila. At that time, no weapons exchanged hands, but Dewey would later allow the arming of some of the Filipinos to harass the Spanish. Also that morning Captain W. P. Biddle, USMC, and a Marine detachment from the *Olympia* relieved the *Baltimore*'s Marines, and for the next several weeks guard duty at the Arsenal was performed by the Marine Detachments of the *Olympia, Baltimore, Raleigh* and *Boston*. Dewey's orders had been fairly clear about what to do to the Spanish fleet (to "capture or destroy"), but that having been accomplished in a lightning strike on 1 May, little thought had been given about how to deal with the Spanish land forces remaining in and around Manila. The war had begun over Cuban independence issues, and few in the United States knew that there had been a separate independence movement taking place in the Philippines under the leadership of Jose Risal and later Emilio Aguinaldo. Soon leaders in the United States and Spain would make decisions which would eventually lead to the Philippine Insurrection. On 6 May, Dewey sent a dispatch boat to Hong Kong to cable the news of the naval victory to Washington.

With the Atlantic Squadron and the First Marine Medals of Honor

While the news from Dewey's squadron electrified American public opinion, the Atlantic Squadron continued its blockade of Cuba with still no sign of Cervera's fleet. The U.S. naval vessels also had the task of searching for and destroying the underwater communication cables, which connected Cuba with Spain, and the rest of the world. Cables from Havana, Cuba, all went to Key West, Florida, so it was easy for the U.S. to eliminate service at that terminal junction. The other cables were on the southern regions of Cuba. On 11 May, the Navy sent out a small force to cut the cables, which ran south, out of the harbor of Cienfuegos, a city on the south coast of Cuba. Early that morning, nearly the entire crews of two ships on duty off the harbor, the *Marblehead* and the *Nashville*, volunteered for the adventure. Lieutenant E. A. Anderson of the *Marblehead* told the men, "I want you to understand that you are not ordered to do this work, and do not have to unless you want to."[11] The *Marblehead* took a position about 1,000 yards off the Colorado Point lighthouse, on the east side of the entrance to the harbor of Cienfuegos. Each ship provided one steam cutter (with a five-man crew, three additional men for the one-pound Hotchkiss gun, and six Marines selected for their marksmanship abilities) and one sailing launch (with a 12-man crew, coxswain and chief carpenter's mate and blacksmith armed with rifles and revolvers).

Cable stations along the Cuban coast were usually protected by a series of defensive trenches so that anyone trying to grapple for the cables in shallow water would have to face rifle, machine gun and one-pound Spanish gunfire. Running in close to the shoreline exposed everyone in the open boats to danger. The Navy did have specialized cable cutting ships, but these were in use in the northern part of the island nearer Havana. The *Marblehead* and *Nashville* began a shelling of the shore area near the lighthouse, and Spanish soldiers abandoned the positions hidden by thick grass. The Navy succeeded in destroying a cable house and barracks on the shore. The four small boats approached the shoreline and at about 200 feet from land the steam cutters stopped and the launches continued to row toward shore while sentries looked into the green water to find the cables. As sailors found and grappled the first cable into the launches and began to saw and hack at it with makeshift tools, the Spanish moved back into their positions and opened fire on the open boats.

The crews successfully cut a boat length out of the first cable they found, a six-inch armored cable, and began to grapple for the next despite the increasing enemy fire. As each cable was cut, ranges were taken and measurements made so that the cables could later be made functional if needed. The Spanish began to fire lower in an attempt to damage or sink the cutters, and many shots fell harmlessly short. Some did make their mark, however, and the crews had to begin bailing water that leaked into the launches. Navy oarsmen kept the vessels in position, and the first sailor wounded fainted shortly after being hit by a Spanish bullet. The Marines in the stern of the boats fired carefully at targets ashore. Finally the second six-inch armored cable was cut, and the crews began to work on the third cable. It was at this point that the Spanish fire reached a crescendo. It was estimated that nearly 1,000 Spanish rifles and guns were firing, and more crew members fell.

The crew continued its business in a determined workmanlike manner, and those wounded did not call out in pain:

> The conduct of the men was worthy of all praise. They worked intelligently and cheerfully at the exhausting labor of picking up and cutting the heavy cables, and, when under a heavy fire and one of the crew badly wounded, continued to work, without confusion, until ordered to stop.[12]

The larger supporting Navy ships began to fire shrapnel at the shore area near the lighthouse, and this forced many of the Spanish soldiers to break and move to positions further from the waterline behind the lighthouse. Unfortunately, the small cutters and launches continued to be hit by the Spanish gunfire from shore positions, and even though more and more sailors and Marines were wounded, the crews grimly kept hacking at the last stubborn cable. Finally after a half hour of this intensified fire, Lieutenant Anderson gave the order to move away from shore and this cable was dropped partially intact into the water, but Spanish communication with Cienfuegos had been greatly disrupted by the mission. After an ordeal that lasted a total of two and a half hours, two men lay dead in the launches, six were wounded, two fatally and four others seriously. For this action the Navy crews of the launches all received the Congressional Medal of Honor, as did the seven Marines from the *Nashville* (Private Frank Hall, Private Joseph H. Franklin, Private Joseph F. Scott, Private Pomeroy Parker, Private Oscar W. Field, Private Michael L. Kearney, Sergeant Philip Gaughn) and the five from the *Marblehead* (Private Herman Kuchneister, Private Walter S. West, Private James Meredith, Private Edward Sullivan, Private Daniel Campbell). Private Patrick Regan died of wounds and Private Herman Kuchneister was wounded severely through the jaw.

As an eager nation waited for sightings of the main Spanish fleet, the reports of this heroic action filled the newspapers in the United States. The Navy and the Marine Corps shared in the glory earned by the heroes of this expedition.

Throughout this time, Marine ships detachments drilled on their secondary batteries, and manned lookout positions on ships patrolling to establish the position of Admiral Cervera's squadron. The Navy Department ordered Commodore Winfield Scott Schley's "Flying Squadron" from Hampton Roads to scout southeast, while recently promoted Rear Admiral William T. Sampson and his ships headed to Puerto Rico to search for Cervera. On 15 May, Sampson learned that Cervera's squadron had reached Curacao the previous day. Cervera successfully evaded further detection by the U.S. Navy until he entered the safety of the harbor at Santiago de Cuba on 19 May.

Why Guantanamo

Once the Navy located the Spanish squadron, the War Department decided to land the Army expeditionary corps to capture the city of Santiago, while the Navy would keep the Spanish squadron bottled up in the harbor. Admiral Sampson looked for a place nearby to serve as a base of operations and a place where ships could coal. The harbor of Guantanamo was 40 miles east of Santiago, and offered a harbor large enough and protected from the weather to support the U.S. fleet in the southeastern section of Cuba. The Navy could coal at sea in 1898, but it required calm seas and an area safe from enemy incursion, as the ships involved in a coaling operation would come to a stop and transfer the coal from a collier to the warship in canvas bags. Given the limits on the steaming range of the coal-fired ships engines of the time, the distance to Key West (610 nautical miles) had ruled that Florida town out as a support base for the naval operations off Santiago. Thus, Guantanamo would serve as the "advance naval base" for the Navy to support the larger naval and land operations in and around Santiago.

These factors led to the eventual movement of Huntington's First Marine Battalion from Key West to seize the harbor at Guantanamo, where the Marines would be used to establish the advance base. At Key West, the Marine battalion had remained on board ship until receiving orders to go ashore hastily on 24

May, as the *Panther* was needed to tow the monitor *USS Amphitrite* to blockade duty off Havana. Huntington attempted to offload all supplies and ammunition overnight, but the captain of the *Panther*, Commodore George C. Reiter, ordered Huntington to leave on board the ship half of his 6 millimeter ammunition (225,000 rounds), allegedly to serve as ballast for the *Panther*, and one-half of his 3-inch ammunition (18 boxes) needed for the *Panther*'s three 3-inch guns. The commanding officer of the base at Key West, Commodore George Collier Remey, modified the order so that Huntington was able to take all of his 6 millimeter ammunition ashore with the battalion.

Once ashore in Key West, Huntington established camp, and detailed a guard of 33 men into Key West for the protection of public property and the naval station. He had already expressed concern to Commandant Heywood concerning the health of the men at Key West due to limited supplies of clean water, the swampy and unhealthy conditions at the camp area, and the expense of procuring commissary stores and fuel. While at the camp, brown linen uniforms arrived from the Quartermaster in Philadelphia. The Battalion's quartermaster, Captain Charles McCawley reported that, " . . . the appearance of the men in this comfortable, businesslike uniform excited favorable comments from Army and Navy officers who came in contact with the battalion.[13] The Marines at the camp felt that the training provided by Huntington was better preparing them to fight, and they were anxious to go to Cuba and meet the Spanish "Dons" in combat.[14]

In the meantime, on 6 June, Sampson had bombarded the defensive works at Santiago to unmask their batteries and also sent the cruiser *Marblehead*, captained by Commander Bowman H. McCalla, and the auxiliary cruiser *Yankee* into Guantanamo Bay. These ships drove the Spanish gunboat *Sandoval* back into the 12-mile-long inner harbor. They also drove Spanish defenders from a blockhouse on the hill above Fisherman's Point on the eastern shore of the harbor, known today as McCalla Hill. The auxiliary cruiser *St. Louis* was in the harbor, cutting cables that connected Guantanamo with Mole St. Nicholas in Haiti to the east and with Santiago de Cuba to the west. These cables were Guantanamo's last underwater cable connections with the outside world. On 7 June, Captain Mancil L. Goodrell, USMC, the fleet Marine officer on board Sampson's flagship the *New York*, led a small landing party composed of 20 Marines from the *New York*, another 40 Marines from the USS *Oregon* (under Captain Francis W. Dickens and Lieutenant Austin Rockwell Davis), and 20 Marines from the *Marblehead* (under Sergeant Samuel Mawson) ashore, checking for a suitable landing area on the eastern shore area and destroying the cable station at Playa del Este.

While Sampson kept the Spanish squadron bottled up at Santiago, the Marines performed the first successful armed landing by U.S. forces in Cuba. On 7 June at 22:00, Huntington's battalion had reboarded the *Panther* and left Key West, arriving off Santiago de Cuba early on Friday, 10 June, then sailing to Guantanamo, finally arriving at 13:00. One hour later, the 23 officers and 623 enlisted men of the battalion began moving ashore under the watchful guns of the Navy ships *Marblehead*, *Texas*, *Resolute*, and *Yosemite*. The move was made in whale boats and steam cutters without opposition from the Spanish regulars and Cuban loyalists in the area. Skirmishers landed to protect the unloading operations.[15] The Marine battalion burned huts and shacks at the small fishing village in the area and quickly established a camp and outposts near the top of the hill selected by Captain Goodrell, under the cover of the guns on board the ships. The burning was done partially to avoid the possibility of yellow fever, since medical theory at the time held that the wet, filthy conditions found in tropical areas caused the disease. The fact that mosquitos spread yellow fever and malaria was still unknown. Marines of the battalion brought food and supplies ashore and hastily stacked them. Fifty Marines then went to work with picks and shovels to begin digging trenches while others erected tents in the camp that measured about 150 by 25 yards on top of the hill. Huntington renamed the hillside Camp McCalla, honoring Commander McCalla, commander of the *Marblehead* and of the local naval expedition. Color Sergeant Silvery raised the Stars and Stripes over the camp. (This flag is currently on display at the Museum of the Marine Corps Historical Center in the Washington Navy Yard, Washington, D.C.). Huntington established a picket line along a path about 500 yards from the camp for security. During the first night ashore, one alarm was sounded but no actual attack took place.

Communication between the Marines ashore and the Navy in the harbor depended upon visual sighting by use of "wigwags" with signal flags. During daylight hours there were four Marines ashore who were adept at the "wigwag" according to the dispatch filed by novelist Stephen Crane of *Red Badge of Courage* fame and now a civilian war correspondent working for Pulitzer's *New York World*.[16] After nightfall, the Marines continued to communicate with the ships in the harbor, using two signal lanterns placed at the top of the hill. When the *Marblehead* signaled to shore, the land signal lights had to be exposed to acknowledge and return messages. One lantern remained stationary on top of a cracker box, while one of the signal men had to stand up and expose another light to answer or send a message from shore to ship. The battalion adjutant, Lieutenant H. L. Draper, used the famous author Crane as an assistant to relay messages to the signal men to send to the ship. The Spanish would attempt to use the lights as an aiming point, but remarkably, none of the signal men was wounded during any of the night time fighting. Things had begun quietly with the unopposed daytime landing, but after the first night ashore heated up quickly. At 17:00 on Saturday, 11 June, a fire fight broke out near an outpost, and the two Marines on the post, Privates James McColgan and William Dumphy, were later found dead of rifle wounds.[17] After nightfall, the camp received many attacks from several directions. This became the pattern for the next two nights ashore. According to Stephen Crane, the Spanish forces had learned how to fight like the Cuban *insurrectos* in their years of attempting to put down the revolt by those seeking independence from Spain. Spanish regulars and Cubans loyal to Spain formed the bulk of the opposition forces in the Guantanamo area. Bullets from the Spaniards' Mauser rifles filled the air. At about 01:00 on Sunday, 12 June, the

Spanish made a combined attack from the south, southeast, and southwest. Crane left a vivid account in his dispatches from the fighting:

> It was my good fortune--at that time I considered it my bad fortune, indeed--to be with them on two of the nights when a wild storm of fighting was pealing about the hill; and, of all the actions of the war, none were so hard on the nerves, none strained courage so near the panic point, as those swift nights in Camp McCalla. With a thousand rifles rattling; with the field-guns booming in your ears; with the diabolic Colt automatics clacking; with the roar of the *Marblehead* coming from the bay, and, last, with Mauser bullets sneering always in the air a few inches over one's own head, and with this enduring from dusk to dawn, it is extremely doubtful if any one who was there was able to forget it easily. The noise; the impenetrable darkness; the knowledge from the sound of the bullets that the enemy was on three sides of the camp; the infrequent bloody stumbling and death of some man with whom, perhaps, one had messed two hours previous; the weariness of the body, and the more terrible weariness of the mind, at least some of the men did not come out of it with their nerves hopelessly in shreds.[18]

U.S. Navy surgeon John Gibbs received a fatal shot while standing outside his tent during one of these nighttime engagements on the night of 11-12 June. Sergeant C. H. Smith was also killed, and two more Marines wounded. The *Marblehead* and the *Dolphin* both used searchlights to illuminate the brush and bombarded the surrounding area with their guns, especially on the flanks of the battalion, to attempt to suppress the Spanish rifle fire. Lieutenant Colonel Huntington decided to move the camp off the hill to a more easily defensible area closer to the bay that afternoon (12 June).[19] Another eyewitness account, that of Private John H. Clifford, described the defenses of the camp:

> Four colt machine guns with three-inch field guns and 50 men were on the left of the hill, 75 men were on out-post duty, one company and the Artillery Battery lower base at Fisherman's Point and the remainder of the battalion was scattered in lots of 20 to 30 men at different places on outpost or in the trenches. At times

the cooks of the companies did their share with
the rifle.[20]

Lieutenant Colonel Huntington estimated that about 160 enemy were engaged at the first nighttime fire fight. Huntington received intelligence reports
from recently landed Colonel Alfredo Laborde of the Cuban insurgents that the
Spanish force attacking the Marine Camp had its headquarters in the vicinity of
the well of Cuzco, about two miles southeast of Fisherman's Point. The next
nearest fresh water source was nine miles away, closer to the Spanish garrison in
the Guantanamo City area. This Spanish base at Cuzco therefore posed the most
direct threat to the Marine camp on the bay, as a source of fresh water was essential for the Spanish forces to continue their harassing attacks. Laborde estimated that approximately 400 Spaniards operated out of the valley.

On the morning of 12 June, 50 Cuban insurgents under the command of
Lieutenant Colonel Enrique Tomas reinforced the Marine camp and helped to
clear brush from the front of the Marine positions to deny the enemy conceal-
ment enjoyed for the previous two days. Huntington also had a trench and barricade constructed around the relocated camp for better defensive protection from
attack. Ships guards from both the *Texas* and the *Marblehead*, as well as sailors
from the collier ship *Alhambra* and the transport *Panther* also came ashore to
assist the Marines in the defense of the camp.[21]

The *Marblehead* sailed to bombard the well at Cuzco. Despite these actions,
the Spanish again attacked that night and acting Sergeant Major Henry Good and
Private Charles Smith died in this night of fighting. The Spanish renewed their
assaults at about 0800 on 13 June, and again at about the same time the next
morning. Huntington could not expect relief from any U.S. Army forces, then
being readied in Florida for the invasion of Santiago, nor did he have any more
Marines to replenish his exhausted battalion, which had fought nearly nonstop
for four days by this time. Huntington and some of his older company grade officers were nearing the point of exhaustion from the nightly fighting. Commander
McCalla had also kept his ships' crews at General Quarters each night of the attacks to support the Marines ashore who were there ostensibly to protect the bay
for him.

With the approval of Commander McCalla, Huntington decided to destroy
the Spanish water source at Cuzco Well and relieve the Spanish pressure on
Camp McCalla.[22] Fifty-two year old Captain George F. Elliott was placed in
command of the little expedition. (Elliott rapidly rose in rank after the war, from
major in 1899 to brigadier general commandant in 1903.) Two companies of
Marines totaling 160 men, Company C under First Lieutenant Lewis Clarke Lucas and Company D under Captain William F. Spicer, and 50 Cubans under
Lieutenant Colonel Enrique Tomas, departed Camp McCalla at 09:00 on Tuesday, 14 June to destroy the well at Cuzco and force the Spanish there to withdraw towards the port town of Caimanera. The dispatch boat USS *Dolphin* was
assigned to provide gunfire support for the attack. According to Private Clifford's account, three Colt machine guns also accompanied Captain Spicer's

Company C. Stephen Crane accompanied Elliott and would soon write the dispatch that immortalized Sergeant John Quick for his "Wigwag" signal to the *Dolphin* later in the battle. The Marines and Cubans moved generally southward as the morning quickly grew hotter, on a torturous footpath through the dense cactus and thorny vines. Altogether they traveled about six miles. The Marines were armed with their Lee rifles with firepower much like that of the Spanish Mausers. They reached the horseshoe-shaped valley at Cuzco about 11:00, racing to reach the crest of the ridgeline overlooking the valley before the Spanish in the area could. The plan called for the two companies under Elliott to approach the valley along the cliffs by the sea (to the west of the well), while a smaller platoon-sized force from Company A under Second Lieutenant Louis J. Magill would advance on Elliott's left flank along an inland valley and hold a picket line for the main force to keep open a route back to Camp McCalla.

On the approach of the Cuban guides, the Spanish battalion in the valley opened fire and the fight was on. The Marines and the Cuban insurgents poured fire into the valley. Companies C and D moved into position under heavy fire from the Spanish in the valley.

With the Spanish firing from well-hidden positions in the heavily-vegetated valley at the well, Captain Elliott called for a signal man to communicate with the *Dolphin*, commanded by Commander H. W. Lyon, USN, to begin firing into the valley at the Spanish. This would force the Spanish to move and reveal their positions to the Marines and their Cuban allies. Elliott also wanted the *Dolphin* to shell the blockhouse that had been used as the Spanish headquarters at Cuzco. According to Crane, when Elliott called for a signalman, a redheaded "Mick" named Clancy responded. The Marine attempted to signal the *Dolphin*, without response, due to the heavy vegetation on the hillside that faced the sea. It was necessary for the signalman to climb to the top of the hill where he could be clearly seen by the ship, and also by the Spanish! Crane did not know the Marine's real name, in part because the correspondent had left the area when the battle was over on a newspaper dispatch boat and sailed to Haiti to file his famous newspaper account of the battle, "The Red Badge of Courage Was His Wig-Wag Flag," that appeared in *The New York World* on 23 June 1898. Evidence points to a Private John Fitzgerald as the "red-headed mick" of Crane's tale. Fitzgerald eventually received the Medal of Honor for gallantry at Cuzco Well, but not until 3 December, 1910, when Elliott, his former company commander had become to Commandant.[23] The only other Medal of Honor for actions at Cuzco would go to Sergeant John Quick. The *Dolphin* began firing into the valley with some effect, but around this time it was discovered that Lieutenant Magill's platoon had crested the ridge at the northern end of the valley and was now directly in the line of the Dolphin's 5-inch gunfire!

Hearing the fighting in the valley, Second Lieutenant Magill and his platoon from Company A had moved to the "sound of the guns" to support the engaged forces to his south. His platoon crested the ridge to the left center (northern section) of the horseshoe ridge, and he sent one of his men to report this to Captain Elliott. On the positive side, this move by Magill enabled the Marines and their

Cuban allies to get many of the Spanish in a deadly crossfire and greatly decreased the volume of Spanish return fire. On the negative side, the *Dolphin* and Elliott did not immediately know that there would be a friendly force at this location of the ridge right in the line of fire of the *Dolphin*'s guns. Some of the shells were beginning to overshoot the blockhouse and land near Magill's little force. According to Stephen Crane,

> It was no extraordinary blunder on the part of the *Dolphin*. It was improbable that the ship's commander should know of the presence of Magill's force, and he did know from our line of fire that the enemy was in the valley.[24]

When Elliott realized that the naval gunfire was now firing on the Marine platoon to his left, he called for another signalman to relay a cease-fire message to the *Dolphin*. Sergeant Quick responded and tied a large blue polka dot scarf to his rifle, went to the top of the ridge and turned his back on the Spanish below to begin signaling to the ship off the coast to the south. In Crane's account:

> He was the very embodiment of tranquillity in occupation. He stood there amid the animal-like babble of the Cubans, the crack of rifles, and the whistling snarl of the bullets, and wig-wagged whatever he had to wigwag without heeding anything but his business. There was not a single trace of nervousness or haste . . . I [never] saw Quick betray one sign of emotion. As he swung his clumsy flag to and fro, an end of it once caught on a cactus pillar, and he looked sharply over his shoulder to see what had it. He gave the flag an impatient jerk. He looked annoyed.[25]

The *Dolphin* ceased its firing, but its shells had been effective in moving the Spanish forces from hiding. The Marines and their Cuban allies continued to pour rifle fire on the fleeing Spanish. Elliott estimated that he was opposed by four companies of Spanish regulars and two companies of Cuban loyalists, totaling 500 men.

While the battle raged, Colonel Huntington back at Camp McCalla sent two more strong parties to help Elliott's force and provide protection should a withdrawal from Cuzco be necessary. First Lieutenant James E. Mahoney and First Lieutenant Clarence Ingate with 50 Marines each were dispatched.

The Spanish began a straggling retreat around 14:00, and shortly after 15:00, Lieutenant Lucas and 40 Marines moved down from the crest of the hill into the valley and destroyed the well and house recently occupied by the Spanish. Elliott reported some 60 enemy killed, and 17 Spanish enlisted men and one officer were captured. First Lieutenant James E. Mahoney's Company E arrived around 16:00, too late to participate in any of the battle.

Captain Spicer, commanding officer of Company D was overcome by the heat and was sent to the *Dolphin*, along with 12 Marines in Elliott's account (according to Commander McCalla's report, 23 were taken on board the *Dolphin* due to heat prostration). One Marine was wounded slightly, and two Cubans were killed in the action. Lieutenant Magill also captured a heliograph outfit and destroyed the signal station near Cuzco. Lieutenant Wendell C. Neville fell on the hillside after the fighting was over and injured his hip and leg. The Marines sent their canteens down from the crest to the *Dolphin*, and gratefully received distilled water from the Navy ship. Freshened with the precious water, the force began its return march to Camp McCalla that afternoon and arrived about 19:00. For the first night since arriving in Cuba, Huntington's battalion slept without interruption.

When Admiral Sampson visited the base in his flagship *New York* on 18 June, the Marines were firmly established ashore, while the battleship *Iowa* and the auxiliary cruiser *Yankee* were peacefully coaling in the bay. The *Marblehead, Dolphin, Panther*, the hospital ship *Solace*, the lighthouse tender *Armeria*, and three colliers lay at anchor in the bay. The advance base was operational, now providing the Navy a protected bay for minor shipboard repairs and coaling operations.

The Spanish on the eastern part of the bay withdrew northward to Guantanamo City, via Cayo del Toro and Caimanera. Spanish forces began to add to the earthworks on Cayo del Toro (the peninsula that jutted into the channel that connected the upper and lower portions of the bay), and at a bluff south of Caimanera. The *Marblehead*, joined by the *Texas* and the *Yankee*, bombarded these threatening sites on 16 June, driving Spanish troops from their positions. The Yankee ships had unknowingly sailed through Spanish mine fields, discovered when the *Marblehead* brought up what it thought to be a buoy fouled on a propeller. The buoy turned out to be a Spanish mine that had failed to detonate. In the next few days, the Navy brought up 14 Spanish mines, none of which exploded, due to mechanical faults and fouling caused by barnacles and growths. During the sweeps, the small steam launches and cutters were fired upon by 250 Spanish soldiers on Hicacal Beach, on the western shore of the bay opposite the little Marine camp. These Spanish infantrymen were there to guard the minefield in the harbor. Colonel Huntington and his force now had a new mission: to clear the area near Hicacal Beach of Spanish forces so that the mine clearing could continue and U.S. ships could use the bay without disruption.

On 25 June, Huntington prepared to rout this Spanish force with two companies of Marines and 60 Cuban rebels. He took Companies C (under Captain Elliott) and E (under Lieutenant Mahoney) at 03:00 and left camp for the other side of the bay. In the darkness they crossed the bay in 15 small Navy boats, but on arrival on the western shore discovered that the positions there had been abandoned by the Spanish. Huntington estimated that 100 men had occupied the position the day before. By 07:30 the force reembarked and went back to their camp.[26] The land threat now eliminated on the western entrance to the harbor, Navy mine clearing operations could proceed unhindered in the lower bay.

The 7,000 Spanish troops at Guantanamo City under General Felix Pareja had been directed to hold that city at all costs. After the Navy cut the undersea cables, the only communications with other regions of Cuba would have been by overland messenger. However, General Pareja had no knowledge of events that would soon take place when the U.S. Army made its assault on Santiago in July. Cuban insurgents surrounded Guantanamo City, and not one Spanish messenger successfully made it out of the city. Fifteen messengers who tried were executed as spies.[27]

Huntington's men settled into a routine of continued vigilance, patrols and local pickets in the area surrounding Camp McCalla, but had no more engagements with the Spanish forces. Fifteen Marines served as pickets during daylight hours, and a full company of 100 Marines and its officers went on watch during the nights. The battalion would maintain this vigilance until its departure from Camp McCalla.

Under guidelines set forth by Commander McCalla and stringently enforced by Lieutenant Colonel Huntington, the Marine camp employed field sanitation measures that resulted in a very light sick list. Food was properly prepared, the men drank only distilled water provided by the Navy, and specified areas set aside for "head" facilities. Daily, two companies of Marines would go down to the beach area to wash their clothes and themselves.

In early July the battalion received some "reinforcements" in the form of three newly minted second lieutenants, fresh from a hasty weeks-long indoctrination at Marine Barracks, "Eighth and I," in Washington, D.C. The three were some of the new officers that Commandant Heywood had been able to enlist from civilian life for the duration of the war. One of these earnest young officers was Second Lieutenant Smedley Darlington Butler, not yet 17 years old and son of a Pennsylvania congressman. The other two were Second Lieutenants George Reid and Peter Wynne. Dressed in their hot, heavy, black braided uniforms, Butler and his two compatriots struggled up the hill at Camp McCalla looking for the commanding officer of the Marines. They came upon a group of grizzled, dusty and dirty old timers sitting on some boxes, and demanded that these "old salts" address them with the proper respect due officers. When they asked the unkempt men where Lieutenant Colonel Huntington was, one of the old men responded that Butler was talking to the Colonel at that moment! The young officers were quickly put to work learning how to perform nightly inspections of the picket outposts.

Operations at Santiago

In the meantime, the Army had made an unopposed landing at Daquiri, Cuba, on 22 June, and had launched a ground campaign against Santiago. The Naval forces under Rear Admiral Sampson, USN, and the Army V Corps under

General William R. Shafter, USA, had differing perceptions as to how to attack the Spanish positions at Santiago, and neither officer was in overall command of the operation there. Suffering from the heat, poor sanitation measures, overtaxed and disorganized supply lines, and illness, the Army fought the elements as well as the enemy. On 24 June, an Army division sustained casualties of 16 dead and 52 wounded at Las Guasimas against Spanish regulars. Later, on 1 July, Shafter's V Corps fought battles outside of Santiago at El Caney and San Juan Hill (more properly Kettle Hill), where Theodore Roosevelt's famed "Rough Riders," fought as dismounted cavalry. After these two victories, Shafter paused to consolidate the positions there and move the rest of his force towards Santiago. His force had suffered casualties of about 10 percent killed or wounded. Also, almost half the force was also suffering from malaria, typhoid, and dysentery. The exhausted soldiers lay within sight of Santiago, yet feared a Spanish counterattack. Shafter wrote to Admiral Sampson, "Terrible fight yesterday . . . I urge that you make every effort to force the entrance to avoid future losses among my men, which are already very heavy."[28]

Early on Sunday, 3 July, while Admiral Sampson went ashore 10 miles east of Santiago, near Siboney, to confer with General Shafter over plans to attack the Spanish forces in the city, the Spanish squadron began its daylight dash out of the harbor of Santiago. Commodore Winfield Scott Schley of the *Brooklyn* directed the action of the U.S. squadron in Sampson's absence. Admiral Cervera led the escape attempt in his flagship, the *Maria Teresa*. At 9:29 a.m., Marine Private Joseph O' Shea fired the first American shot from his six-pound gun on board the USS *Oregon*. (The *Oregon* had recently completed its 66 day dash from Bremerton, Washington around the southern tip of South America to join the U.S. squadron at Cuba, and its Marines had participated in the first landings at Guantanamo in June). This shot missed, but was the first of a barrage from the U.S. squadron which resulted in the complete destruction of another Spanish squadron by the U.S. Navy in two months. Captain Francis William Dickens, USMC, of the *Oregon*'s Marine detachment commented:

> Every man on guard had an exposed station,
> and the only reluctance ever shown by any of
> them promptly to obey was when ordered to
> take shelter behind the turrets, while the alacrity
> with which they ever sprang to their posts
> showed that they were all animated by the spirit
> that has given the Marine Corps its reputation
> for bravery and faithfulness for a full century.[29]

During the pursuit of the Spanish ships, the American crews needed to keep the engines stoked and full of coal. Captain Philip, USN, said of the Marines of the *Texas*:

> Besides their work at the secondary battery in all engagements, I desire to call attention to special instances: During the chase on July 3 it was reported to me that the firemen and coal heavers were giving out, and the engineers desired more men from the deck. The main battery having already been drawn upon for this extra work, I directed Lieutenant Radford (USMC) to detail fifteen or twenty men to go in the fire room to shovel coal. Immediately, and with a rush to be first, all the Marines started for the fire room to aid the *Texas* to maintain her speed in the chase.[30]

Marine officers in command of ships detachments on the *Brooklyn* (Captain Paul Murphy, USMC), the flagship *New York* (First Lieutenant Rufus H. Lane, USMC), and the *Indiana* (Captain Littleton W. T. Waller, USMC) gave similar reports. Waller's gun crews reportedly got off 500 rounds from their 6-inch guns in the 61-minute melee.[31] Commandant Heywood later tried to emphasize the effectiveness of the fire of the Marine-manned batteries, but neither the Navy nor Marines had exceptional accuracy with ships' batteries. The sheer volume of fire and speed of pursuit was probably more responsible for sinking Cervera's squadron than Marines manning the secondary batteries. Of the some 8,000 shells fired by Sampson's fleet, examination of four Spanish cruisers showed only 120 hits. At day's end, the *Maria Teresa, Pluton, Furor, Oquendo, Viscaya,* and *Colon* were either aflame or scuttled near the shore. Of Cervera's 2,150 men, 1,782 were captured. The U.S. lost no one to gunfire from the Spanish.

The stunning naval victory did not end the friction between the Navy and the Army, as Admiral Sampson still hesitated to enter Santiago Harbor due to the threat of the land based batteries of the fortress El Morro guarding the entrance and the potential threat posed by other Spanish shore batteries and underwater torpedoes (mines). The channel entering the harbor was also partially obstructed by the USS *Merrimac* that had been purposely sunk by the Navy in an attempt to bottle up the Spanish fleet. General Shafter had wanted the Navy to bombard the city of Santiago from the harbor while his forces would approach from the southeast on land. The feud would have long lasting results since the Navy saw only inherent problems in working with the Army forces without a clear overall commander of an operation. Working with Marine landing forces was much easier for naval officers to coordinate, as exemplified in the landing at Guantanamo. As events turned out in Santiago, the Spanish Army, short on food and without hope of naval resupply now that the fleet was destroyed, negotiated a surrender of forces in the city to General Shafter's forces. U.S. forces entered the city on 17 July.

The Invasion of Puerto Rico

Major General Nelson Appleton Miles, USA, a Civil War veteran and famed Indian fighter, was the highest ranking Army officer in the War Department with the title Major General Commanding the Army and had long recommended the invasion of Puerto Rico. In his position, however, he commanded no forces, although entitled to pass on all Army orders cojointly with the Secretary of War, and claimed independent jurisdiction over the Adjutant General's Office and the Bureau of Inspection.[32] He had disagreed with the Secretary of War, Russell A. Alger, during the initial war planning over a joint operation with the Navy at Havana. He felt that it would take months properly to train and equip a large invasion force, and felt that the unhealthy climate of Cuba during the rainy season would be ruinous to the army. He argued that initial land operations begin in Puerto Rico with its more healthful climate. When Puerto Rico had been subdued, a large invasion force could then move on to Cuba after the rainy season.[33]

With the fall of Santiago in July, and the subsequent diplomatic efforts to end the war, Miles believed that the U.S. should proceed at once against Puerto Rico to establish control before hostilities concluded with the Spanish still in control there. General Miles received permission to assemble his invasion force and, on 21 July, sailed from Guantanamo in a squadron escorted by the battleship *Massachusetts*.

General Miles decided to begin the invasion of Puerto Rico at Ponce, a port city in the south of the island, and then move inland and northward towards San Juan, partly because Ponce was suitable for landing his forces and also because he thought that the Puerto Ricans in the area would welcome the Americans. Miles insured that the haphazard landings and rash movements that characterized Shafter's Santiago campaign would not be repeated, and he carefully planned to move men and materials in a more systematic fashion. An Army brigade landed near Guanaco on 25 July under the watchful batteries of U.S. Navy ships. This landing spot was on the opposite coast of where the reinforcements were to land, but Miles justified it by saying that it surprised the Spanish. Troop transports to Puerto Rico from Tampa and Charleston would be diverted from their original landing areas, and the invasion would continue.

During the night of 26-27 July, the *Dixie, Wasp, Annapolis,* and *Gloucester* entered the harbor at Ponce, and Lieutenant Greenlief A. Merriam, USN, of the *Dixie* went ashore under a flag of truce to demand the immediate surrender of Ponce. The town was surrendered under the condition that the 700 Spanish troops under Colonel San Martin could withdraw unmolested. At 0500 the next morning, Lieutenant Merriam, followed by the *Dixie's* Marine Detachment under First Lieutenant Henry C. Haines, received the surrender of the port. The Marines raised the U.S. flag, posted a guard, and mounted a Colt automatic gun on top of the customs house. Ponce had formally passed into American hands and the next morning General Miles began landing his forces without incident there.[34]

On board the light cruiser *Cincinnati*, First Lieutenant John A. Lejeune's 40-man Marine detachment had grown anxious to participate in fighting while waiting for Cervera to appear in May. However, the ship was sent to Norfolk for needed repairs, and was absent from Cuban waters while Huntington landed at Guantanamo, when General Shafter landed near Santiago, during the battles of San Juan Hill and El Caney, and when Cervera made his unsuccessful dash out of Santiago harbor. The *Cincinnati* arrived at Guantanamo on 15 July where it received word that the Army under General Miles would invade and occupy the island of Puerto Rico and that it would rendezvous with other naval vessels and transports near Cape San Juan, Puerto Rico. At Cape San Juan, the *Cincinnati* discovered that inhabitants of the town of Fajardo friendly to the U.S. had been supplied with arms from the *Columbia*, but had been attacked by a Spanish force of 700 or 800. These American sympathizers had fled to a lighthouse on Cape San Juan. During the night of 8 August, after the *Cincinnati*'s arrival, Spanish forces attacked the lighthouse which was now guarded by a naval detachment from the American cruiser. The ship's secondary batteries fired at the approaches to the lighthouse with the aid of its searchlights. In the morning, Lejeune and his Marine detachment landed, joined with a landing party from the USS *Amphitrite*, and approached the lighthouse through heavy thickets and woods. They found empty cartridge casings, but no Spanish soldiers. The landing party sent the refugees to a tug which took them to the Port of Ponce, then in U.S. possession.[35] The Army continued its approach to San Juan by land that would give the U.S. a military foothold on the island, and the Peace Protocol agreement of 12 August obviated the need for further fighting.

Taking Guam

The taking of Guam is the one exploit of the war which matches the popular conception of a "Splendid Little War," for it was taken without shots fired in anger in an almost comical manner. After the destruction of the Spanish Asian squadron at Manila in May, the island of Guam, lacking cable communications, was out of touch with events in the war. In June, the USS *Charleston* was convoying three troop ships of soldiers towards the Philippines to participate in actions against the Spanish army at Manila. The *Charleston* entered Apra Harbor and approached the little fortifications of Fort Santa Cruz on 20 June 1898. Captain Henry Glass, USN, ordered the ship's three pound guns to open fire on the fortification. Twelve shots were fired on the little fort with no response. What Glass did not know was that the fort had been abandoned years earlier.

Shortly after the shooting ended, a Spanish officer approached the *Charleston* in a small launch and apologized for a delay in returning the "salute" by the American ship. The Spanish were in the process of moving a small field piece and readying it for a return salute. Captain Glass informed the officer that the United States was at war with Spain, and made him a prisoner of war. However, he paroled him at once to take a demand that the Spanish governor of Guam, Juan Marina, meet with Glass on board the *Charleston* for a conference. When

Marina refused to appear, Glass made preparations for a landing party under Marine Lieutenant John Twiggs Myers and 30 of his Marines to join with two companies of *Oregon* infantry to enforce the demand.

While landing preparations were being made, Lieutenant William Braunersreuther, USN, went ashore at Piti and delivered the ultimatum to the governor. Seeing that he was outgunned and resistance was futile, Governor Marina ordered the three Spanish officers on his staff and their soldiers to bring their arms and equipment for surrender. The four leaders were made prisoners of war and brought to the Philippines on board the *Charleston* when it left Guam.

Glass then took formal possession of Guam, and raised the American flag over Fort Santa Cruz. Bands on board U.S. ships in the harbor played the Star Spangled Banner and the *Charleston* fired a salute. At four in the afternoon, Lieutenant Braunersreuther and a landing force of 16 sailors and 30 Marines under Lieutenant Myers went ashore and disarmed the rest of the 102 Spanish soldiers and 2 officers, and then brought them to the ships. A company of native Chamorros was disarmed and left on the island. Glass then sailed for the Philippines, with no provisions made for occupying Guam.

Final Operations in Cuba and Return of the First Battalion

After the Army's landings and operations against Santiago de Cuba resulted in the surrender of the Spanish garrison there, plans began to be formulated to capture the Cuban town of Manzanillo. On 5 August, Lieutenant Colonel Huntington embarked his battalion at Guantanamo on board the *Resolute*, and made plans for going ashore on 13 August to outflank the Spanish entrenchments there. Before the landing could begin, white flags appeared all over Manzanillo, and the Navy received word that a Peace Protocol had been signed between Spain and the United States, ending the hostilities. The Protocol suspended operations in the Caribbean, and the *Resolute* received orders to sail with its embarked Marines of the First Battalion to Portsmouth, New Hampshire.

The ship arrived at Portsmouth on 26 August and the Marines received a heroes welcome from the local citizens. On 16 September the battalion went into the town of Portsmouth to participate in the "Portsmouth's Welcome to the Heroes of 1898" celebration. The battalion marched in a parade through the town with local bands, naval battalions from several ships, state volunteer units, and local government officials. A huge clambake followed, where the marchers were feted with clams, lobster, corn, potatoes, and bread, washed down with 50 cases of beer and 100 gallons of coffee.[36] Somehow, after this strenuous day of celebrations, the battalion was then able to put on a demonstration of military tactics and a charge up the ramparts of Old Fort Washington located there! Celebrations over, the battalion formed into parade ranks and marched back to its camp. This was the last time that the battalion would mass together. On 20 September, the battalion marched through Boston to the train station to be dispatched to home stations.[37] Upon its return to the nation's capital on 22 September, the Washington, D.C. detachment of three officers and 164 men marched through a rainstorm and were reviewed at the White House by President McKinley himself.

Conclusion

The Peace Protocols of August, 1898, signaled an end to the fighting of the War with Spain, but would open a new world of responsibilities for the Marine Corps. Negotiations in Paris led to the Peace Treaty of December 1898, which gave the United States possession of Puerto Rico, Guam, and the Philippines, as well as a role in establishing a new independent government for Cuba. In Puerto Rico and Guam the occupations would be fairly peaceful, but the Philippines would erupt into the Philippine Insurrection. Emilio Aguinaldo and his independence fighters thought that the United States efforts in the island archipelago would result in the independence of the self-proclaimed republic. However, the United States saw that possession of the islands gave it a valuable naval and trading position near Asia that was strategic both militarily and economically. Within a year Marines would have three battalions in the Philippines to assist in quelling the insurrection there.

Possession of new colonies would provide the need for an expanded Marine Corps, and several prominent Marines including Commandant Colonel Heywood and Major Henry Clay Cochrane (a member of Huntington's staff at Guantanamo) believed that a larger Marine Corps should be formed to be sent on short notice to the new possessions without calling on the Army.[38] The result was a bill signed into law by President McKinley on 3 March 1899 that provided for a Marine Corps of 6,000 enlisted Marines and 201 line officers, and raised the rank of commandant to brigadier general. Officer promotions then came quickly, and 35 of the 43 temporary war time lieutenants took the qualifying examination. Thirty received commissions as permanent first lieutenants. Officer accession became more organized under guidelines set up by Heywood.

The bulk of the Marine Corps saw action during the war. This small military force planted the first American flags in the Philippines, in Cuba, in Guam, and in Puerto Rico. It went into the war ready to perform its roles for the Navy Department on board ship and quickly organized an efficient fighting force to seize Guantanamo. The valor of the 1st Marine Battalion at Guantanamo gained nation-wide recognition during its 100 hours under fire, and ships' detachments participated in all major naval engagements. Of the approximately 3,000 Marines who served during the conflict, over 640 fought the Spanish at Guantanamo, and 2,055 enlisted men served on 57 of the fighting ships of the Navy. This contrasted with the performance of the U.S. Army, which had swelled from its peacetime size of 28,000 to a mammoth force of 200,000 men with the attending problems in organizing, supplying, and training such a force. The Army had approximately 450 killed in combat, but another 5,200 died from disease, and less than 20,000 were actually involved in any combat actions before the Peace Protocols went into effect in August. The Marines had six combat deaths (five at Guantanamo and one off Cienfuegos) and a sick list of less than two percent.

Relations with the Navy, which had sometimes grown acrimonious in the 1890's improved greatly. In March, 1899, Admiral Dewey requested 1,000 Marines to man the naval station at Cavite, Philippines, and in October 1900 Dewey signed a memorandum to the secretary of the Navy advocating the formation of a 400-man Marine battalion to serve as a nucleus of a 1,000 man Marine battalion in event of war to defend an advance base in support of a naval campaign in Asiatic waters.[39]

Marine officers and their allies in Congress would have to continue to justify the need for a separate Marine Corps within the Navy Department after the turn of the century. While these budget and control battles ran into the onset of World War I, many of the young officers like Smedley Butler, Wendell C. Neville, and John A. Lejeune who saw action in the War with Spain would be leading battalion and regimental size units in the Philippines and Cuba, participate in the relief expedition during the Boxer Rebellion in China, and learn to work with the Army and allied forces. This growing professionalism would build the foundation for the stellar performance of the Marine Corps in the land battles of World War I, and foster the creative thinkers of the 1920's who would develop the amphibious doctrine used so successfully in World War II.

The War with Spain signaled a watershed for the tiny Marine Corps. It created much greater public awareness of and support for this small force, bettered the relations between it and the officers of the Navy, and created the foundation for the professional, respected force of the twentieth century.

Notes

1. Admiral H. G. Rickover, USN, *How the Battleship Maine Was Sunk* (Annapolis, 1976), passim.

2. Captain W. Sampson, USN, Copy of Letter from Captain W. Sampson to Navy Secretary John Long, dtd 13 April 1898 (Spanish-American War Files, MCHC, Washington, D.C.).

3. Colonel Charles McCawley, USMC, "The Guantanamo Campaign of 1898," *Marine Corps Gazette*, vol. 1, Sep 1916, No. 3, p. 222, hereafter McCawley, "The Guantanamo Campaign."

4. U.S. Marine Corps, *Annual Report of the Commandant to the Secretary of the Navy*, 24 September 1898, hereafter *Report of the Commandant of the Marine Corps, 1898.*

5. John Henry Clifford, *The History of the First Battalion of U. S. Marines*, (Privately published booklet, 1930, MCHC, Washington, D.C.), pp. 34-48, hereafter Clifford, *The History of the First Battalion.*

6. Frank Keeler, *The Journal of Frank Keeler*, (Marine Corps Paper Series, Number One) pp. 3-4.

7. *Appendix to the Report of the Chief of the Bureau of Navigation*, SecNav, *Annual Report, 1898*, II, p. 23. See also William R. Braisted, *The U.S. Navy in the Pacific, 1897-1909*, (Austin, TX, 1958), 21-22, 25; Ronald Spector, *Admiral of the New Empire: The Life and Career of George Dewey* (Baton Rouge, LA, 1974), 32-5, 43; J. A. S. Grenville, "American Naval Preparations for War with Spain, 1896-98," *Journal of American Studies*, Apr 1968, pp. 33-47.

8. BGen Dion Williams, USMC, "Thirty Years Ago," *The Marine Corps Gazette*, Mar 1928, pp. 1-24. hereafter Williams, "Thirty Years Ago.

9. Ibid.

10. Ibid., p. 15.

11. Henry B. Russell, *An Illustrated History of Our War With Spain* (Hartford, A. D. Worthington & Co., 1898), p. 609.

12. Lieutenant E. A. Anderson, USN, "Cutting of Cables off Cienfuegos," USS Marblehead, 12 May 1898, in *Report of the Secretary of the Navy, 1898*, p. 190.

13. Captain Chas. L. McCawley, USMC, Quartermaster First Marine Battalion, in "Report to the Commandant," 27 September 1898.

14. Clifford, *The History of the First Battalion*, p. 12.

15. McCawley, "The Guantanamo Campaign," p. 224.

16. Stephen Crane, "Marines Signaling Under Fire at Guantanamo", *Wounds in the Rain*, (Books for Library Press, Planeview, NY) 1976 reprint of 1900 book.

17. Colonel Robert W. Huntington, USMC, "Report of the Commanding Officer First Marine Battalion," 17 June 1898. In *Report of the Commandant of the Marine Corps, 1898*, pp. 22-23.

18. Crane, op cit., p. 179.

19. Huntington, op. cit., pp. 22-23.

20. John Henry Clifford, op. cit. p. 14.

21. McCawley, op. cit., p. 232.

22. Commander Bowman H. McCalla, USN, "Report of B. H. McCalla, USN, Guantanamo, Cuba, June 16, 1898," in *Report of the Secretary of the Navy, 1898*.

23. Medal of Honor citation for Pvt John Fitzgerald, 3Dec1910.

24. Stephen Crane, "Red Badge of Courage Was His Wig-Wag Flag," *New York World*, 23 June 1898.

25. Stephen Crane, "Marines Signaling Under Fire at Guantanamo," First published in *McClure's Magazine*, February 1899, and reprinted in R. W. Stallman and E. R. Hagemann eds., *The War Dispatches of Stephen Crane*, (New York: New York University Press, 1964).

26. Huntington file, Battalion Order No.5, (Spanish-American War File, MCHC, Washington, D.C.).

27. LCdr Herbert P. McNeal, USN, "How the Navy Won Guantanamo Bay," *U.S. Naval Institute Proceedings*, Jun 53, p. 619.

28. Nathan Miller, *The U.S. Navy, An Illustrated History* (Annapolis, (USNIP and the American Heritage Publishing Co., 1977), p. 217.

29. John Leonard and Fred F. Chitty, USMC. *The Story of the United States' Marines 1740-1919*, (U.S. Marine Corps Publicity Bureau, New York 1919), p. 113.

30. Ibid, p. 113.

31. Heinl, op. cit., p. 118.

32. Margaret Leech, *In the Days of McKinley* (New York, Harper Bros., 1959), p. 200.

33. David F. Trask, *The War With Spain in 1898* (New York, MacMillan, 1981), pp. 149-150.

34. Henry Cabot Lodge, *The War With Spain*, (NY: Harper & Brothers, 1899), pp. 174-176; Bernard C. Nalty, *The United States Marines in the War with Spain*, (MCHC, Washington, D.C., 1959), p. 31.

35. MajGen John A. Lejeune, *Reminiscences of a Marine*, (NY: Arno Press, 1979), pp. 133-134.

36. Frank Keeler, *The Journal of Frank Keeler*, p. 26.

37. U.S. Marine Corps, *Annual Report of the Commandant of the Marine Corps to the Secretary of the Navy, 1898*, p. 9.

38. Jack Shulimson, *The Marine Corps Search For a Mission, 1880-1898* (Lawrence, Kansas, University Press of Kansas, 1993), pp. 196-197.

39. Ibid., p. 210.

Excerpted from *Semper Fidelis: History of the United States Marine Corps*, Chapter 5: The Marine Corps and the New Navy 1889-1909, The Free Press, 1991, and reprinted with permission of the author and publisher.

The Spanish-American War
by Allan R. Millett

From the time the Department of the Navy first considered a war with Spain, it concluded that the new Navy would be the primary instrument with which the United States would end Spanish colonialism in the Caribbean. After the renewal of the Cuban insurrection in 1895, officers of the Navy War College and the Office of Naval Intelligence drew up and then revised a series of war plans for the fleet in case the United States and Spain went to war. All three major parties endorsed freedom for Cuba during the election campaign of 1896, and the Spanish government would not end its pacification campaign or negotiate away its colonies, hence this planning was prudent. While President William McKinley and the State Department attempted to come to terms with Spain, a Navy War Board of five senior officers reviewed and revised the basic plan drafted in 1896. Essentially, the Navy War Board envisioned offensive operations against the Spanish fleet in the Caribbean and in the western Pacific near another Spanish colony, the Philippine Islands. A defeat in the Caribbean would isolate Cuba and blockade the Spanish armies in Cuba and Puerto Rico, while a victory in the Philippines would allow the American government to hold Manila hostage until a peace was negotiated. However sound the strategic concept, it assumed that the Navy could quickly enlarge its auxiliary fleet in order to support its warships with water, coal, stores, ammunition, spare parts, and maintenance work ships. The Navy War Board recognized that without adequate bases near the theaters of operations (which the Navy did not have) the Navy was more endangered by breakdowns and shortages than by the Spanish navy, which the Office of Naval Intelligence knew was not a first-rate force. Although the Navy War Board did not plan any specific operations to seize temporary bases, its plan implied that such actions might be necessary. In any event, by the end of 1897 the Navy Department had a fairly accurate vision of its responsibilities in 1898.[1]

The events that preceded the actual declaration of war on April 21, 1898, worked to the Marine Corps's advantage. When the battleship *Maine* blew up in Havana harbor on the night of February 15, one of the heroes was a Marine orderly, William Anthony, who escorted Captain Charles D. Sigsbee, USN, to safety from his smoke-filled cabin. Twenty-eight other members of the ships guard perished with their Navy shipmates and became martyrs in the pages of the American press. Since the *Maine* had been sent to Havana to protect American lives and property from Spanish anti-American riots, most Americans assumed that Spanish saboteurs had sunk the *Maine* and killed 266 of the crew. Thus the *Maine* became a popular *casus belli* and exceptionally good copy for the bellicose "yellow press."

The subsequent Congressional demand for action centered on the Navy Department, and Colonel Heywood suddenly found he could recruit the Marine Corps up to its full strength of 3,073 enlisted men. Moreover, Secretary Long wanted to know how much of an emergency defense appropriation of $50 million might be spent on the Marine Corps.[2] With the formal outbreak of war, Heywood asked for more officers and men and received almost all he requested in legislation passed on May 4, 1898. True, the Commandant wanted a permanent enlargement of the officer corps by 103 billets but received permission to commission forty-three second lieutenants for the war only. Heywood, however, was allowed to recruit 1,640 more enlisted men for the war, the exact number he had requested from the naval affairs committees. The Commandant was sure he now had enough men to protect Navy yards, man ships guards, and carry out any other missions the Navy Department might assign. The manpower drought was over, ended by war, Congressional funding, and new public interest in the Marine Corps. The Commandant dared hope that the Marine Corps might have as many as four thousand men even after the war ended. And Congress, in martial good feeling, raised the Commandant to the rank of brigadier general.[3]

Whether or not the Marine Corps would eventually profit from its honeymoon with Congress and its rediscovery by the American people rested as much with Heywood's scattered ships guards and barracks detachments as it did with the Commandant in Washington. After three decades of Marine promises that the Corps needed only a war to prove its military efficiency, it would have been awkward if the War with Spain had not provided new glories to be paraded for the benefit of Congress and the Navy Department.

If the Commandant's claims in the ships guards controversy was anything more than anachronistic rhetoric, the Marines of the Asiatic and North Atlantic squadrons would bear the heaviest responsibility in proving their essential value to the battle fleet. In two major and decisive sea engagements--at Manila Bay, May 1, 1898, and off Santiago de Cuba, July 3--the ships guards had no opportunity to prove their superiority as gunners, simply because both engagements were decided by the fire of the American main batteries. Despite the gross inaccuracy of the Navy's gunners, Commodore George Dewey's squadron and Rear Admiral William T. Sampson's combined squadrons pounded nine Spanish ships into flaming junk with their heavy guns. Although the secondary batteries blasted away with enthusiasm in both engagements, not all of the rapid-fire guns came into action and not all of those that did were manned by Marines. Disappointed when the initial reports of both fleet engagements did not mention the Marine guards, Heywood queried the ships captains and Marine officers about what exactly the Marines had contributed to the stunning American victories. The results of the Commandant's investigation and subsequent studies showed that the Marines had behaved with coolness under fire and had carried out all their duties with efficiency. Marines had committed acts of individual heroism, both at the secondary batteries and as messengers and ammunition-passers. As for the effect of the secondary batteries, it was difficult to find many hits on the Spanish hulks, and the investigators had only the word of the Spaniards that the rapid fire guns had disrupted some of their exposed gun crews and messengers. As it turned out, the Marines aboard Sampson's battleships and cruisers were more often posted as riflemen, signalmen, messengers, orderlies, medical aides, and ammunition-passers than as gunners. Although Heywood later claimed that the Marine gunners played a crucial role in destroying the Spanish squadrons, the testimony of his own officers showed that such was not the case.[4]

Yet the ships guards had, after all, been *there* during the debut of the new Navy, and Marines also participated in other naval actions during the summer of 1898. Marine landing parties from American vessels destroyed cable stations and cut cables in Cuba, captured a lighthouse, raised the flag in the Spanish naval yard at Cavite on Manila Bay, and claimed Apra, Guam, and Ponce, Puerto Rico, as conquests of the United States. They fired their guns in the bombardments of San Juan, Puerto Rico, and Santiago, Cuba. In a "splendid" and almost bloodless war for the United States Navy, the ships guards shared the Navy's public acclaim. That they had done anything special is not so clear.

As it developed, however, a single expeditionary battalion of barracks Marines commanded by a bearded ancient of the Civil War, Lieutenant Colonel Robert W. Huntington, made the greatest contribution to the Marine Corps's reputation for combat valor and readiness. No other unit of comparable size (with the possible exception of the "Rough Rider" cavalry regiment) received as much newspaper coverage during the Cuban campaign. And the experience of Huntington's battalion suggested to some Navy and Marine officers that the Corps might indeed have an important role to play in the new Navy.

On April 16, five days before the war formally began, Secretary Long ordered Colonel Heywood to organize one battalion for expeditionary duty with the North Atlantic Squadron in Caribbean waters. What Long had in mind is unclear, but he or the Naval War Board or Admiral Sampson must have contemplated extemporizing a base in Cuba, for Marine quartermasters purchased three months' supplies and wheelbarrows, pushcarts, pickaxes, shovels, wagons (but no mules), and barbed wire cutters for the expedition. Heywood rushed to the Brooklyn Marine Barracks (commanded by Huntington) to supervise the mobilization, the purchasing of supplies, and the outfitting of a newly purchased Navy transport, the *Panther*. Drawing Marines from East Coast barracks, Heywood created a six-company battalion of 24 officers and 633 enlisted men. One of the companies was armed with four 3-inch landing guns, while the others were infantry. Although the battalion's initial drills were a muddle, the troops (about 40 percent new recruits) were enthusiastic and the officers experienced, if more than a trifle superannuated. After a rousing parade, the officers' wives gave the battalion new flags, the troops cheered "Remember the *Maine*," and the battalion marched to the *Panther* on April 22. As the Marines departed, a Navy yard crowd roared with enthusiasm and the New York newspapers hailed the departing heroes. Colonel Heywood himself was pleased with the battalion's prospects, although he knew the *Panther* would be overcrowded. No one had the slightest idea what the battalion was expected to do, but it was ready for action.[5]

The odyssey of Huntington's battalion became progressively less romantic as the *Panther* plowed south for the Caribbean. While Huntington and the ships captain argued whether Navy Regulations for a Marine ships guard applied to an embarked battalion, the troops ate in continuous shifts, sweated in the packed compartments, listened to lectures, and fired ten rounds each from their new Lee rifles. Miffed by the Marines' reluctance to do chores and anxious to change his ship into an auxiliary cruiser, the ships captain persuaded a commodore at Key West to order the battalion ashore. Shoved ashore without all their supplies on May 24, the Marines continued training and fought the bugs in their hot, dusty tent camp.[6]

Finally the battalion received a mission. By May 28 the Navy had located and blockaded the Spanish squadron in Santiago harbor in southeastern Cuba. Looking for a temporary harbor for coaling his vessels, Admiral Sampson asked that the Marine battalion support his naval expedition into Guantanamo Bay east of Santiago. As Huntington's battalion reloaded on the *Panther* on June 7, Sampson sent the cruiser *Marblehead* and two small auxiliary cruisers into Guantanamo Bay, where they shelled and destroyed the Spanish shore positions and chased a gunboat up the bay. This force was then joined by the battleship *Oregon*, worn by a 12,000-mile cruise around South America. Worried by reports of seven thousand Spanish troops in the Guantanamo area, Commander Bowman McCalla, captain of the *Marblehead* and the expedition commander, had the Marines from his cruiser and the *Oregon* conduct a reconnaissance of a hilly point just inside the bay's mouth. The ships guards found the Spanish gone, and McCalla decided the position was defensible.

On June 10 Huntington's battalion started unloading their supplies, screened by one company. For the next twenty-four hours the Marines wrestled their gear ashore in the heavy heat. While they toiled, the *Marblehead* fired occasional shells in the neighboring hills to discourage any lurking Spanish patrols.[7] The position ashore, named Camp McCalla, was not well organized, but McCalla thought that it could be protected by naval gunfire. Essentially the battalion was supposed to prevent the Spanish from harassing the ships in the harbor with rifle or artillery fire, which could be done with active patrolling and by garrisoning the hill. But until they received some Cuban guides and established their base camp, the Marines were chained to their hill and three outposts beyond it in the heavy brush. The basic defensive position atop the hill close to the beach (selected by the Marine captain on the *Oregon*) was not wide enough to accommodate a tent camp for more than six hundred men, but Huntington raised his tents anyway along the hill's crest above the main trenches and the outposts.

In the early evening of June 11 the battalion began what Major Henry Clay Cochrane, Huntington's second in command, called "its one hundred hours of fighting." As the Marines unloaded, Spanish infantry closed about the weary camp, killed an unwary two-man outpost, and opened night-long harassing fire on the camp. Scurrying to their trenches, the Marines replied with a blind barrage of rifle and Colt machine gun fire, supplemented by a thunderous naval bombardment. For the sleepless Marines the next two nights were much the same, a storm of naval shelling, the whiz of Mauser bullets, signal lamps blinking in the darkness, constant alarms, and wild riflery into the heavy brush. Although the Spanish never closed, their fire killed the battalion's Navy surgeon and two sergeants and wounded three others. Much of the battalion, especially Huntington and the older officers, was soon in a state of near collapse.[8]

Obviously the tactical situation had to be reversed, and there was some question as to who was protecting whom from the Spanish, since the *Marblehead* and the auxiliary cruisers had just spent three nights at general quarters. For a start Huntington, at McCalla's suggestion, moved his camp to the beach area in order to protect it from direct fire and ease his resupply problems. A newly arrived Cuban colonel had a better idea: send an expedition to destroy the only nearby drinking water and the Spanish camp at Cuzco Well, some two miles away. On June 14 Captain George F. Elliott led two infantry companies and a detachment of fifty Cuban scouts on a circular six-mile march toward Cuzco Well. Although the Marines did not surprise the Spanish garrison of battalion strength, they won the foot race to the hill that dominated the Spanish camp and caught the enemy in the valley. At ranges up to 1,000 yards the Marines peppered the Spaniards with rifle and machine gun fire. During the fighting another Marine platoon on outpost duty, on its own initiative closed off the head of the valley and caught the enemy in a crossfire, while the dispatch ship *Dolphin* added its shells to the general firing. The *Dolphin's* shells, fired without much direction, also drove the Marine platoon from its position until the shelling was stopped by a wigwag message from Sergeant John H. Quick. After four hours of fighting the Spaniards withdrew from their cul-de-sac, having suffered at least 160 casualties. A Marine platoon went into the valley to count bodies, destroy the well, and burn the camp, and the action was over. By early evening the Marines were back in their jubilant camp. At the cost of four Cubans and three Marines dead and wounded and twenty heat casualties, the expedition had captured eighteen Spaniards, routed the rest, and ended the attacks on their own camp.[9]

Compared with the fighting soon to follow in the Army's campaign against Santiago, the action at Guantanamo Bay was a minor skirmish of no consequence to the course of the war, but it took on incalculable importance for the Marine Corps. As the first serious fighting by American troops on Cuban soil, it drew a squad of newspaper correspondents, whose reports made it sound as if Huntington's battalion had been on the edge of annihilation. The reporters, among them Stephen Crane, reported the Cuzco Well battle as an epic of bravery and professional skill that proved the military superiority of the Marines. When veteran Marine officers treated their situation with aplomb, the reporters waxed rhapsodic. By the time the skirmish ended, American readers of three big New York dailies *(World, Herald,* and *Tribune),* the *Chicago Tribune, Harper's Weekly,* and the papers served by the Associated Press knew who the Marines were and that they had won a magnificent victory against overwhelming odds. If the Commandant had staged the campaign for public effect, it could not have been more successful.[10]

Having languished at Guantanamo Bay through June and July 1898, Huntington's battalion embarked on the Navy transport *Resolute* and sailed for Manzanillo, Cuba, for another landing. But before the battalion could storm ashore, Spain agreed to an armistice, and as quickly as the war had started it was over. By the end of August the battalion was back in Portsmouth, New Hampshire, to be disbanded and sent to its home barracks for duty.

Huntington's battalion was not allowed to fade away, for its conduct at Guantanamo Bay and its light sick list (only 2 percent) at a time when soldiers were dying in droves in both Cuba and the United States made it a national sensation. Secretary of the Navy Long, with Heywood's prompting, announced that 1898 was the centenary of the Marine Corps's founding and that Huntington's battalion had performed admirably as a dramatic reminder of one hundred years of service. The battalion paraded especially for President McKinley on September 22, and Heywood received requests for more parades from Omaha, Boston, Philadelphia, and New York. By the time the battalion disbanded it had spent as much time parading as it had fighting, but it had been enormously successful at both. After the War with Spain the American public and, by implication, Congress would never again have to ask what a Marine did. Instead the word "Marine" now evoked an image of bravery, discipline, competence, and devotion to duty.[11]

Notes

1. John A. S. Grenville and George Berkeley Young, "The Influence of Strategy upon History: The Acquisition of the Philippines," in *Politics, Strategy, and American Diplomacy* (New Haven: Yale University Press, 1966), pp. 267-296. For the naval campaigns against Spain in 1898, see Captain French E. Chadwick, USN, *The Relations of the United States and Spain: The Spanish-American War*, 2 vols. (New York: Scribner's, 1911). The Marine Corps experience is summarized in Bernard C. Nalty, *The United States Marines in the War with Spain*, rev. ed., Marine Corps Historical Reference Pamphlet (Washington: Historical Branch, HQMC, 1967).

2. Col. Cmdt. C. Heywood to J. D. Long, March 12, 1898, HQMC, "LSSN," RG 127. Throughout the war Headquarters Marine Corps kept extensive clippings on the Corps, preserved in HQMC Scrapbooks, 1880-1901, RG 127. The Marine Corps eventually spent $106,529 from the emergency fund.

3. Col. Cmdt. C. Heywood to J. D. Long, April 25, 1898, September 24, 1898, HQMC, "LSSN," RG 127.

4. Heywood's position is stated in Col. Cmdt. C. Heywood to J. D. Long, and September 24, 1898, HQMC, "LSSN," RG 127, and in "Report of the Commandant U.S. Marine Corps," U.S. Navy Department, *Annual Reports of the Navy Department, 1898* (Washington: Government Printing Office, 1898), pp. 854-862. Detailed analyses of Marine duties are in Lt. Col. R. L. Meade (Fleet Marine Officer) to Col. Cmdt. C. Heywood, August 29, 1898; Capt. L. W. T. Waller to Col. Cmdt. C. Heywood,

September 1, 1898; and 1stLt. R. H. Lane to Col. Cmdt. C. Heywood, August 27, 1898, all HD/HQMC, "Letters Received, 1818-1915," RG 127. The effects of American gunfire are assessed in Lieutenant John M. Elliott, USN, *Effect of the Gun Fire of the United States Vessels in the Battle of Manila Bay*, Office of Naval Intelligence War Notes No. 5 (Washington: Government Printing Office, 1899), and Commander "J" (Imperial German Navy), *Sketches from the Spanish-American War*, Part II, Office of Naval Intelligence War Notes No.4 (Washington: Government Printing Office, 1899), pp. 5-15.

5. Entries for April 17-22, 1898, journal of Marine battalion under Lt. Col. R. W. Huntington, 1898, Field Organization Records, RG 127; Col. Cmdt. C. Heywood to J. D. Long, April 23 and September 24, 1898, HQMC, "LSSN," RG 127; Maj. Henry Clay Cochrane diaries, entries for April 19-23, 1898, Henry Clay Cochrane Papers; John H. Clifford, *History of the First Battalion of U.S. Marines* (Portsmouth, N.H.: the author, 1930); and Carolyn A. Tyson, ed., *The Journal of Frank Keeler* (Quantico, Va.: Marine Corps Museum, 1967), pp. 3-4.

6. Lt. Col. R. W. Huntington to Col. Cmdt. C. Heywood, April 30, 1898, and May 25, 1898, and Maj. C. McCawley (battalion QM) to Col. Cmdt. C. Heywood, January 8, 1900, all HD/HQMC, "Letters Received, 1818-1915," RG 127.

7. Lt. Col. R. W. Huntington to Col. Cmdt. C. Heywood, June 17, 1898, and Cmdr. Bowman McCalla, USN, to CINC, Atlantic Fleet, June 19, 1898, both HD/HQMC, "Letters Received, 1818-1915," RG 127, and Maj. Henry Clay Cochrane diaries, entries for June 10-11, 1898, Cochrane Papers.

8. Entries for June 10-14, 1898, journal of Huntington's battalion, RG 127; extracts from the manuscript autobiography of Admiral B. H. McCalla, File OH (Landing Operations), RG 45; Lt. Col. R. W. Huntington to Col. Cmdt. C. Heywood, June 17, 1898, and Cmdr. Bowman McCalla, USN, to CINC, Atlantic Fleet, June 19, 1898, both HD/HQMC, "Letters Received, 1818-1915," RG 127; and Maj. H. C. Cochrane to Mrs. Cochrane, June 14, 1898, Cochrane Papers.

9. Capt. G. F. Elliott to Lt. Col. R. W. Huntington, June 15, 1898, and Cmdr. H. W. Lyons (CO, *Dolphin*) to Secretary of the Navy, August 15, 1898, both HD/HQMC, "Letters Received, 1818-1915," RG 127; Maj. Henry Clay Cochrane diaries entries for June 14 and 15, 1898, Cochrane Papers; and Tyson, *The Journal of Frank Keeler*, pp. 16-18.

10. Charles H. Brown, *The Correspondents' War* (New York: Charles Scribner's Sons, 1967), pp. 279-289; New York *Herald*, June 16, 1898; *ANJ*, July 2, 1898; R. W. Stallman and E. R. Hagemann, eds., *The War Dispatches of Stephen Crane* (New York: New York University Press, 1964), pp. 140-154, 171-172, 267-274; and Maj. Henry Clay Cochrane diaries, entries for June 12-15, 1898, Cochrane Papers.

11. Col. Cmdt. C. Heywood to J. D. Long, September 24, 1898, HD/HQMC, "LSSN," RG 127, and *ANJ*, August 13, 1898; September 24, 1898; October 22, 1898; November 12, 1898; and May 23, 1903.

THE FIRST MONTHS OF THE WAR

Photo courtesy of National Archives 11 I-SC-94543

The American battleship USS Maine is *seen entering Havana harbor in a good-will public relations mission in January 1898. The sinking of the* Maine *on the 15th of February was one of the primary causes of the Spanish-American War.*

Portrait of Marine Private William Anthony who served as orderly to the captain of the Maine, *Charles Sigsbee. On 15 February, Private Anthony led the captain to safety as the ship began to sink.*

Department of Defense (Marine) Photo   521452

Photo courtesy of Naval Historical Center NH95654

Photograph shows Marine recruits being mustered into the Corps at the Charleston Navy Yard, Massachusetts. This photograph originally appeared in Photographic History of the Spanish-American War, *published by the Pearson Publishing Company of New York in 1898.*

Commodore George Dewey is seen on the deck of his flagship, the cruiser USS Olympia, in Manila Bay. In the ensuing battle, Dewey's Asiatic Squadron destroyed the defending Spanish fleet.

Photo courtesy of Naval Historical Center 100318

Marine 1stLt Dion Williams is shown with his detachment of Marines on Cavite Island in the Philippines. Lieutenant Williams' detachment at Cavite in Manila Bay established an advance base for Commodore Dewey's Squadron.

A contemporary illustration shows small boats carrying sailor and Marine volunteers from the U.S. Navy cruisers Nashville and Marblehead *(seen in the background) in attempt to cut the cables south of Cienfuegos. Cuba.*

Photo courtesy of Naval Historical Center NH79952

Marine and sailor volunteers pose in a small boat off the cruiser USS Nashville *at the end of the war, recreating their cable-cutting mission off Cienfuegos.*

Marine and sailor volunteers who participated in the cable-cutting attempt off Cienfuegos, Cuba, are seen back on board the Navy cruiser Nashville. *These volunteers were all awarded the Medal of Honor for their efforts.*

Marines from the 1st Battalion are seen just before landing from the Navy transport Panther *at Key West, Florida. Over the protests of LtCol Robert W. Huntington, the Marine commander,* the Panther's *captain insisted that the Marines go ashore.*

Excerpted from *Crucible of Empire*, edited by James Bradford, Naval Institute Press, 1992 and reprinted with permission of the editor and publisher.

Marines in the Spanish-American War
by Jack Shulimson

I

THE U.S. DECLARED WAR ON SPAIN AT A TIME WHEN THE MARINE CORPS and its officers were uncertain about their role in the American defense establishment. The war, brief as it was, and its aftermath served to delineate the nature of the Marine Corps' mission in the rapidly expanding navy and in the defense of America's colonial possessions.

The publication in the *New York Journal* of the letter in which Spanish minister Dupuy de Lome referred to President McKinley as "weak and a bidder for the admiration of the crowd" and the sinking of the U.S. battleship *Maine* in Havana harbor in February 1898 galvanized American popular opinion against the Spanish. President McKinley attempted to defuse the situation by appointing a board of naval experts to determine the cause of the explosion on the American warship. Headed by Capt. William T. Sampson, the Navy court of inquiry reported on 21 March 1898 that a submarine mine, exterior to the hull, set off the forward magazines of the *Maine*. A Spanish investigating team, on the other hand, blamed an internal explosion in the forward magazines for the disaster. McKinley forwarded the Sampson board's findings to Congress without comment. Even as moderate a figure as Secretary of the Navy John D. Long, however, later observed that the sinking of the *Maine* "would inevitably lead to war, even if it were shown that Spain was innocent of her destruction."[1]

While the war fever spread through the country, the Navy Department reexamined its strategy in the event of a conflict with Spain. In March 1898 Secretary Long appointed an advisory war board consisting of Assistant Secretary Theodore Roosevelt as chairman and three naval officers, including the heads of the Bureau of Navigation and the Office of Naval Intelligence (ONI). The board had the benefit of the extensive ad hoc planning effort that had continued through both the Cleveland and McKinley administrations. Since 1895, the ONI, the War College, and the temporary strategy boards had developed several contingency plans for a war with Spain. Despite the different formulations of the various American planning documents, certain features appeared frequently: a blockade of Puerto Rico and Cuba, a possible land campaign against Havana, a blockade or assault against Manila in the Philippines, and a possible naval attack in Spanish home waters.[2]

Once the war board was formally established, it recommended to the secretary that the Navy take the offensive and not be relegated to a passive coastal defense role. Based on the consensus of the earlier war planning effort, the board suggested the close blockade of Cuba and extension of the blockade to Puerto Rico. The Navy was also to concentrate on the poorly defended outposts of Spain's insular empire, including the Philippines. As Secretary Long later explained, Spain's "undoing lay in her possessions in the East and West Indies"; there Spain was the most vulnerable and would be forced to send scarce men and ships to shore up its defenses. The board rejected any immediate operations aimed at the Spanish homeland in favor of a strategy of American sea dominance in the Caribbean and Pacific.[3]

As the naval plans took on more seriousness, the military prepared for what now appeared inevitable. Congress passed on 9 March 1898 a $50 million emergency appropriation to be shared between the War and Navy departments. The Army received $20 million, which mostly went into the coastal fortification program. War Department planners visualized only a limited mobilization. They expected the National Guard to staff the coastal defenses while the Regular Army expanded from its 28,000-man peacetime strength to form an expeditionary corps of 75,000 to 100,000 men. This corps would land in Cuba only after the Navy had established its mastery over the Spanish fleet. War Department officials failed to stock supplies for a large army because they simply "did not expect to raise one" in a war against Spain.[4]

The Navy, on the other hand, used a good portion of its approximately $30 million of the emergency appropriation to augment the fleet. It purchased cruisers in Europe, acquired several merchant auxiliary ships, and converted several private yachts into gunboats. The department concentrated the preponderance of its warships in the North Atlantic Squadron at Key West, Florida.[5]

The naval buildup also involved the Marine Corps. On 10 March 1898 Secretary Long provided Col. Charles Heywood, the Marine commandant, with guidelines on the use of the Navy's share of the emergency appropriation. The commandant was to incur expenses under the appropriation only after making an estimate of the amounts involved and receiving written approval from Secretary Long and the president. All told, the Marine Corps would eventually receive $106,529.64 under the emergency appropriation. The expenditures included the purchase of one million rounds of ammunition for the newly issued Lee rifles.[6]

Although both Secretary Long and Colonel Heywood wanted to expand the Marine Corps to meet anticipated demands, its role in any pending conflict was still vague. In a March communication to the chairman of the House Committee on Naval Affairs, Long explained the need for more marines in terms of their traditional missions. The usually authoritative *Army and Navy Journal*, nevertheless, carried a story on 12 March 1898 indicating that the Navy secretary had ordered Colonel Heywood to form two battalions ready to deploy at short notice. According to the account, "Two battalions have been made up on paper, and all the available officers of the Corps assigned to places in different companies." About the same time, the *Naval Institute Proceedings* published as one of its prize articles a piece by Lt. Comdr. Richard Wainwright. Although not specifically mentioning marines, Wainwright referred to advanced bases as the first line of defense in conjunction with the fleet. He advocated that such bases "should require such protection as is necessary to render the base safe against cruiser raids, or such light attacks as might be attempted during the temporary absence of the guarding fleet." The only obvious readily available source to establish and provide such protection for an advanced base would be the Marine Corps.[7]

The correspondence of Lt. Col. Robert Huntington, commander of the New York barracks and the most likely commanding officer of any Marine expeditionary force, reflected the uncertainties of the Marine role and the questionable readiness of its aging officer corps. Coincidentally, on the same day as the sinking of the *Maine*, Huntington wrote to Colonel Heywood expressing his concerns about the officer corps, especially in the field grade ranks and among the senior captains. Most had entered the Marine Corps during the Civil War or shortly afterward and had over thirty years of service.[8]

On 30 March 1898, when the possibility of war was much closer, Huntington speculated in a letter to his son about the mission of the Marines. He thought that Heywood planned to send him "to Key West to guard a coal pile." Huntington allowed, however, that "there is of course a possibility that we might go to Cuba. I cannot say I enjoy the prospect very much, but as my view of the war is, that it is one of humanity, I am willing to take the personal risk." Huntington proved right on both counts; he and his marines later went both to Key West and to Cuba.[9]

II

By early April the Navy had completed its initial preparations for operations against the Spanish. At Key West, the North Atlantic Squadron, now under the command of Captain Sampson, consisted of three armored battleships, several cruisers and torpedo boats, and support vessels. On 6 April 1898 Secretary Long ordered Sampson on the outbreak of hostilities to capture all Spanish warships in the West Indies and establish a blockade of Cuba. Sampson would have preferred to attack Havana but admitted "the force of . . . [Long's] reasoning that we would have no troops to occupy the city if it did surrender."[10]

Perhaps to rectify this situation, Sampson asked Secretary Long for the deployment of two battalions of marines to serve with the fleet at Key West. On 16 April Colonel Heywood received verbal orders to make the necessary arrangements. The following day, a Sunday, he met with the headquarters staff and sent out telegrams to Marine Corps commanding officers at East Coast navy yards. Planning to mount the first battalion out of New York within the week, the commandant on 18 April departed Washington to supervise the preparations personally. Back at Marine Corps headquarters, Maj. George C. Reid, the adjutant and inspector and now acting commandant, asked for and received $20,000 out of the emergency appropriation to transport and equip the expedition. By Wednesday, 20 April, the Marines had assembled 450 men from various East Coast navy yards at the New York barracks. At that point the department decided against the formation of a second battalion. Instead, the Marines increased the one battalion by 200 men. When it embarked two days later, the First Marine Battalion, under the command of Lieutenant Colonel Huntington, consisted of 631 enlisted men, twenty-one officers, and one surgeon; and it was organized into six companies, five infantry and one artillery.[11]

On Friday, 22 April, the newly purchased Navy transport, the *Panther* (formerly the *Venezuela),* docked at the Brooklyn Navy Yard. At the battalion's morning formation, Lieutenant Colonel Huntington told the men that they would embark and depart that night for Hampton Roads, Virginia. The troops greeted the news with loud cheers and song and then formed working parties to assist sailors in loading the ship. About 5:00 P.M., "the 'assembly' was sounded and the battalion formed in line in heavy marching order, headed by the Navy Yard band." An hour later, the marines marched out of the navy yard, down Flushing Avenue, and then wheeled into the yard through the east gate. By 8:00 P.M., to the refrains of "The Girl I Left Behind Me," the *Panther* set sail to join the fleet.[12]

On board the *Panther,* conditions were crowded and uncomfortable. The Navy had purchased the ship to carry a battalion of about four hundred men, not six hundred fifty. Furthermore, the troops carried on board the equipment and supplies necessary to sustain them in the field. This included mosquito netting, woolen and linen clothing, heavy and lightweight underwear, three-months' worth of provisions, wheelbarrows, push carts, pick axes, shovels, barbed-wire cutters, tents, and medical supplies. In addition, the artillery company took four 3-inch rapid fire guns. Colonel Heywood observed that the hatches for loading freight and two small ventilators in the aft section provided the only ventilation for the ship. Still, morale among the men and officers was high.[13]

The specific mission of the Marine battalion remained unclear. At the time of the unit's formation, Major Reid wrote that the Marines "are to have no connection whatever with the army, and are to report, and be at the disposal of the Commander-in-Chief of the North Atlantic Fleet." In a message to Sampson on 21 April Secretary Long referred to the Navy Department studying the possibility of "occupying the [northern Cuban] port of Matanzas by a military force large enough to hold it." He later declared that the Marine "battalion was organized especially for service in Cuba." Among the officers and men of the battalion, however, speculation abounded as to their final destination. According to Maj. Henry Clay Cochrane, a senior officer in the battalion, "Porto [*sic*] Rico is rumored," but he believed that "some port near Havana is more likely."[14]

By the time the battalion departed New York, the uncertainties and confusion of the general U.S. mobilization forced both the Army and the Navy to reconsider many of their initial assumptions. Acting on the president's message of 11 April, Congress on 19 April passed a joint resolution that recognized the independence of Cuba, demanded the withdrawal of the Spanish military forces, disclaimed any intention of the United States to annex the island, and authorized the president to use the U.S. armed forces to carry out the policy. McKinley signed the resolution the following day and sent the Spanish an ultimatum. In the meantime, after Congress rejected a War Department measure that would have increased only the Regular Army, the administration agreed with congressional leaders to support the establishment of a Volunteer Army as well as to expand the regular forces. As war approached, however, the Army, unlike the Navy, was not ready.[15]

On 20 April President McKinley held his first council of war. At the meeting, Maj. Gen. Nelson A. Miles, the commanding general of the Army, reported that the Army would not be ready for any large expeditionary campaign for at least two months. Like many other veterans of the Civil War, Miles opposed frontal assaults against well-entrenched positions. He advocated a blockade by the Navy, small raids by the Army along the Cuban coast in support of the Cuban rebels, and the seizure of Puerto Rico. The Army's position surprised Secretary Long and the other naval officers. While rejecting Sampson's initial assault plans against Havana, Secretary Long and his Navy planners had expected the Army--in conjunction with the Navy--to prepare for an offensive against the Cuban capital before the rainy season began. In fact, a joint Army-Navy board had earlier in the month proposed the landing of a small Army force at Mariel, a port town about twenty-five miles west of Havana, to establish a base of operations against the larger city. At this point, President McKinley, who had served in the Civil War as a major, overruled Long and the Navy and supported Miles's position.[16]

The conference enunciated a rather cautious military strategy in the Caribbean. McKinley approved the imposition of a blockade of Cuba, the resupply and other logistic support of Cuban insurgents, and limited U.S. land operations in Cuba. The Navy was to assume the main burden of the war. On 21 April 1898 Secretary Long promoted Captain Sampson to rear admiral and ordered him to "blockade coast of Cuba immediately from Cardenas to Bahia Honda" in the north and the southern city of Cienfuegos, "if it is considered advisable."[17]

On 22 April Sampson's squadron left Key West for Cuban waters. That same evening the *Panther,* with the First Marine Battalion embarked, pulled out of New York Harbor for Hampton Roads off Fortress Monroe. Arriving there the following evening, Lieutenant Colonel Huntington reported to Capt. Winfield Scott Schley, the commander of the Navy's Flying Squadron. Huntington received orders that the battalion would stay on board the *Panther* and await a warship that would escort the transport to Key West. Two more Marine officers, Maj. Percival C. Pope and First Lt. James E. Mahoney, joined the battalion at Fortress Monroe, bringing the number of officers to the full complement of twenty-three. Because of his seniority, Pope became second in command. Major Cochrane was assigned to the battalion staff and, in somewhat of a huff, wrote in his diary that he and Pope were unsure of their positions in the battalion.[18]

Huntington took advantage of the short interlude at Fortress Monroe to drill the troops and hold firing exercises. On the afternoons of 24 and 25 April the infantry companies practiced "volley and mass firing" while all four guns of the artillery company fired at least one round. Although morale remained high, two of the enlisted men came down with high fevers that developed into pneumonia. Another man fell off a rope ladder and was evacuated to the Army hospital ashore with a fractured limb.[19]

The men remained in good spirits when the cruiser *Montgomery* arrived to accompany the *Panther* to Key West. At 8:05 A.M. on Tuesday, 26 April, the transport steamed out of port and passed the battleships *Texas* and *Massachusetts* and the cruiser *Brooklyn* of the Flying Squadron, still at anchor. As the *Panther* went by the ships, the crews crowded the decks and "sent up cheer after cheer." The Marines returned the cheers, but several of the older officers who had served in the Civil War had their reservations. Major Cochrane observed, "some of us felt anything but jolly at leaving behind the beauties of spring to be replaced by the perils of the sea and the hardships of war." On 29 April, after a three-day voyage, including a somewhat stormy passage around Cape Hatteras, the two ships arrived at Key West.[20]

On the same day, a seven-ship Spanish squadron under Adm. Pascual Cervera consisting of three cruisers, one battleship, and three destroyers set out from the Portuguese-owned Cape Verde Islands and headed west. This departure caused the Army to postpone indefinitely a planned six-thousand-man "reconnaissance in force" on the southern coast of Cuba. The Navy simply did not have enough ships both to escort the Army transports and to watch for the Spanish squadron, which could appear at any time. The departure of the Spanish squadron may also have caused the postponement of a Marine landing in Cuba. In letters to his sons and wife, Major Cochrane observed that the Marines had expected to "land in Cuba last Saturday [30 April], but now we must lie here [at Key West] for a week."[21]

III

While the U.S. fleet in the Caribbean waited for Cervera's squadron to make its appearance, the Asiatic Squadron under Commodore George Dewey had already taken the offensive. Having forewarned Dewey in late February to attack the Spanish in the Philippines in the event of hostilities, the Navy Department on 24 April 1898 informed the commodore that war had begun and that he "was to proceed . . . to the Philippines" to "commence operations at once." Acting on these orders, Dewey and his squadron slipped into Manila Bay under the cover of darkness shortly after midnight on Sunday, 1 May 1898. Although challenged by a few rounds from Spanish shore batteries on El Fraile Island near the entrance of the bay, the American naval squadron successfully eluded the Spanish defenses. Lying at anchor outside the protection of the land batteries at Manila, the older Spanish vessels were no match for Dewey's relatively modern cruisers. In the ensuing battle, which lasted a little more than seven hours, the American squadron sank or left as burning hulks all the enemy warships. At a cost of nine crewmen slightly wounded, the Americans had inflicted more than 370 casualties on the Spaniards, including 161 killed.[22]

Despite his overwhelming victory in the Philippines, Dewey's options to exploit his success were limited. As he informed Washington, "I can take city [Manila] at any time, but not sufficient men to hold." He estimated, "To retain possession and thus control Philippine Islands would require . . . [a] well-equipped force of 5,000 men." In the meantime, Marine 1st Lt. Dion Williams and a detachment of marines from the cruiser *Baltimore* occupied the

Spanish naval station at Cavite, which served as a base of operations for the fleet, until reinforcements from the United States could arrive.[23]

News of Dewey's victory electrified American public opinion and reinforced the demand for a similar initiative in the Caribbean. Even before he officially heard the news from Manila, President McKinley had reversed his earlier decision to refrain from a major land campaign against Havana. In a conference on 2 May the president approved an expedition against Mariel that he had rejected at the April meeting. The vanguard of these forces were to be the troops encamped at Tampa under Maj. Gen. William Shafter, idle since the canceled "reconnaissance in force" mission. The plans for this operation went through several reiterations because there were major differences among many of the principals, including Secretary of War Russell A. Alger and Major General Miles, as well as between the Army and Navy. Although overruled by the president, Miles still opposed any major land campaign until after the rainy season. Admiral Cervera's squadron also remained a wild card. As Secretary Long informed Rear Admiral Sampson on 3 May, "No large army movement can take place for a fortnight and no small one will until after we know the whereabouts of the Spanish armored cruisers and destroyers."[24]

While the Army and Navy planners examined the feasibility of a Cuban campaign, the Marine battalion remained on board ship at Key West. On 30 April Lieutenant Colonel Huntington reported to Sampson on board the latter's flagship. The Navy commander at this time had no orders for the Marine commander, "as the plan of campaign had not yet been completed." Huntington's adjutant, 1st Lt. Herbert L. Draper, told Major Cochrane that Sampson stated "he did not want the Marines to go away to the Army. [He] had use for them." On 3 May Sampson departed Key West with a small task force in the hopes of intercepting Cervera's squadron off Puerto Rico, leaving the Marine battalion to fend for itself. [25]

At Key West, the Marine battalion settled into a routine of drills, almost daily disputes with the Navy commander of the *Panther,* and rumormongering. Every morning the ship's small boats took the companies of the Marine battalion ashore for the drills. Although most of the officers had several years of service, the enlisted men of the battalion were largely raw recruits and required both discipline and training. Major Cochrane overheard another Marine officer describe a battalion parade as "a little Army, little Navy, and some Marine Corps." Even Huntington mentioned to his son that the men "have little idea of obeying orders" and that some were prone to stealing.[26]

On 23 May the *Panther* received orders to tow the monitor *Amphitrite,* which had been in Key West for repair, back out to the American blockading fleet. Forced to disembark in the early hours the following morning, the Marine battalion established a campsite on the beach, in effect becoming marooned at Key West without its transport.[27]

While Huntington futilely protested against his forced "grounding," his subordinate officers speculated about their mission and about their futures and the future of the Marine Corps. In typical fashion, Major Cochrane reflected much of this sentiment. Writing to his wife in early May, Cochrane observed that the Marines "are not hurrying very much to get to Cuba--unless we can have the prestige of being first. Every forward plan is suspended until the Spanish fleet is encountered." Most of his correspondence with his wife reflected the Marines' hopes for new legislation that would increase the Corps and permit promotions for the officers. Cochrane's wife noted that the war "should be an immense advantage to the Marine Corps." By late May and early June, however, Cochrane's optimism for favorable legislation had diminished: "When I think that war was declared on the 25th of April . . . , and that we embarked on the 22d, organized, equipped, and ready for duty, it annoys me that so little benefit comes from it."[28]

IV

As Huntington and his officers vented their frustrations against the Navy and against their forced inactivity at Key West, Colonel Heywood and his staff in Washington busied themselves in placing the Marine Corps on a wartime footing and lobbying for permanent legislation to benefit the Corps. They were more successful in the former activity than the latter.

At the beginning of the crisis, Heywood and his staff hoped to obtain from Congress a significant increase in personnel and a restructuring of the officer corps. The commandant was forced to settle for much less than he wanted. This was due, in part, to the legislative strategy of the McKinley administration. Congress had been considering reform of the naval officer corps for some time; the administration was supporting its own reform program, and did not want half-measures attached to the appropriation bill.[29]

On 28 March 1898 Colonel Heywood submitted a formal request for proposed legislation to Secretary Long for the restructuring of the Marine officer corps. The recommended bill contained many of the same provisions that the Corps had pushed through the years: the rank of brigadier general for the commandant, promotion for most other senior officers, an increase in the total number of officers, the temporary increase of rank for the Fleet Marine Officer, and the presidential appointment of all new staff officers in accordance with seniority in the staff and then from the list of senior Marine captains of the line. This bill contained one new wrinkle, however, in that it provided for the appointment of one-quarter of the new second lieutenants from the ranks of meritorious noncommissioned officers who passed the required examinations. Secretary Long forwarded the bill to the House Naval Affairs Committee. In its report, the committee incorporated Heywood's bill with the reform measures suggested by the Roosevelt personnel board.[30]

The incorporation of the Marine bill with the broader Navy personnel legislation, however, had its disadvantages. Because of the administration's admonition to the House Naval Affairs Committee, Congress would not consider the restructuring of the officer corps in the Naval appropriation bill. Because of the war, the Marine Corps realized through the appropriation legislation some expansion in its enlisted ranks and in the number of temporary officers. Congress authorized the inclusion of the 473 enlistments tentatively approved in

March into the permanent organization and permitted the Marine Corps to recruit another 1,640 men for the emergency. The final appropriation measure, signed on 4 May 1898, contained a stipulation that allowed the president to appoint--"if an exigency may exist"--such officers to the Marine Corps as may be necessary from civilian life or from the ranks of meritorious noncommissioned officers of the Corps. These officers could serve only through the emergency and could not be appointed above the rank of captain .[31]

If Major Cochrane's reaction was typical, officers of the Marine battalion considered the measure to be grossly inadequate. Cochrane wrote to his wife in disgust that "the bill has caused great indignation among the lieutenants in our party," who probably had expected to be promoted to captain. He observed that the new second lieutenants from civilian life would all probably be the "sons of post traders." Cochrane also disapproved making officers of noncommissioned officers, writing that their temporary appointments would make them "unfit for their duties after the war." He reserved his greatest criticism, however, for what was not in the legislation. He believed that, in the same situation, the "Army would have gotten three colonels and so on with them, and thirty-six captains." All the Marines received, according to Cochrane, were some additional men and "acting second lieutenants to officer them." In agreement, Cochrane's wife replied, "I cannot see that the condition of the officers in the Corps has been improved one bit and it was such a chance to have gotten a really good organization."[32]

Colonel Heywood miscalculated in his legislative stratagem. He went along with the Navy Department policy to divorce the wartime mobilization from the permanent reform of the Navy and Marine officer corps. The commandant apparently believed that Congress would pass the Navy Department-sponsored personnel bill that would amalgamate the line and engineers. This bill now included the changes that Heywood had forwarded relating to the Marine Corps officers. Despite assurances from Heywood that the legislation was "sure to go through," many Marine officers, including Major Cochrane, remained skeptical. The skeptics proved correct. Congress was not about to touch the controversial amalgamation and "plucking" issues in the midst of the war when more pressing matters were at hand. Last-minute efforts by Heywood and his staff to separate the Marine legislation from the overall naval personnel bill failed, and there was no major wartime reformation of the Marine officer corps.[33]

Temporary officer appointments were permitted by the appropriation act, however, so the Marine officer corps did gain a wartime infusion of new blood. A jaundiced Major Cochrane provided his wife with advice for a young relative who wanted to obtain one of the new Marine commissions from civilian life. According to Cochrane, "the usual plan should be pursued." The candidate should first "make written application supported by testimonials . . . from well known men as to his character, ability, and general meritoriousness, and then to follow that up with any political, naval or social influence that he or his father or friends may have." Observing that Secretary Long was from Boston, Cochrane suggested that the young man should try to find someone from Massachusetts who could "in political parlance 'reach' him [Long]." If the candidate could not obtain someone who knew Long, "perhaps he can 'reach' Senator Lodge, Senator Hoar, or a Boston M. C. [member of Congress]." Cochrane concluded rather sardonically, "Permission to be examined once secured and the rest is easy."[34]

The system was not quite as simple as Cochrane described it. Although influence certainly helped in obtaining a commission, it was not enough to ensure one. Being from Massachusetts and knowing Secretary Long more often worked against an aspirant than for him. After recommending two young Massachusetts men for commissions, Secretary Long directed that no further appointments be made from that state. Even after receiving an endorsement of both the secretary of the Navy and the commandant of the Marine Corps, the candidates had to appear before an examining board. The Navy Department and Marine Corps were inundated with young and not-so-young applicants who wanted to go to war as Marine second lieutenants. To weed out the unfit, the board tested the applicants for physical, mental, moral, and military attributes and ranked each candidate by merit. On 21 May Colonel Heywood wrote Secretary Long that "the number of candidates already authorized to appear before the board for examination is more than sufficient to fill all the places created by the Act of May 4, 1898."[35]

By early June the examining boards had selected twenty-four men from civilian life to serve as Marine second lieutenants. Of this number, two were either the son or nephew of a member of Congress and at least seven were the sons or close relatives of military officers, while the remainder usually had some military education or experience. Although the law actually left the number of temporary commissions open-ended, Secretary Long and Colonel Heywood had decided on twenty-eight new officers for the time being. With the completion of the selection of the officers from civilian life, the remaining four officers were to come from the ranks of meritorious noncommissioned officers. Eventually the Navy Department raised the quotas so that forty-three officers served as temporary Marine second lieutenants until the end of the war. Of this total, forty were from civilian life and three were former noncommissioned officers.[36]

The selection of the new lieutenants from the enlisted ranks was somewhat different from that of the officers from civilian life. A noncommissioned officer who wanted an appointment had to submit an application through official channels to the commandant. He needed the strong endorsement of his commanding officer. Heywood would then recommend whether or not the man should be permitted to take the officer examination.[37]

Even here, however, political influence played its role. Sgt. Frank A. Kinne, hardly representative of the Marine enlisted ranks, was one of the selectees. He came from a comfortable, middle-class family. His father, G. Mason Kinne, was the assistant secretary of the Pacific coast division of a prominent international insurance company. The elder Kinne had enlisted in the Volunteers during the Civil War and risen to the rank of colonel. He was a past master of the Grand Army of the Republic and knew Secretary of War Alger. The father imposed on Alger to recommend his son for one of the second lieutenant openings. The son was a high school graduate and had received an appointment to the U.S. Military

Academy at West Point but had been unable to attend because of illness. He then joined the Marine Corps and had five years of service; at the time of his application, he was an acting lieutenant on board the cruiser *New York*. Secretary Alger penned a short note to Secretary Long, describing the elder Kinne as "an old personal friend and his statements are entitled to every consideration." Sergeant Kinne received a commission.[38]

The remaining two noncommissioned officers, Sgt. Robert E. Devlin and Charles G. Andresen, were both with the deployed First Battalion before receiving their commissions. In his letter of recommendation, in which he stated that he knew each "to be a worthy and capable noncommissioned officer," Colonel Heywood asked that both men be examined at the First Battalion headquarters rather than called back to Washington. Andresen came from a much more typical enlisted background than Sergeant Kinne. Born in Norway, Andresen had immigrated to the United States as a young man and enlisted in the Marine Corps. Showing an aptitude as a soldier, he rose quickly through the ranks. At Fisher's Island in Long Island Sound, apparently during a fleet landing exercise, he served as first sergeant to Capt. Littleton W. T. Waller, who was so impressed that he highly recommended Andresen for a commission. Thanking Waller for his efforts, Andresen wrote: "Without your kindly assistance and advice it would have been impossible for me to have reached the place, where I now find myself."[39]

Although the process for selecting the new officers was subject to the vagaries of political influence, it still provided objective criteria to determine qualifications. This system rejected more than one candidate with an impeccable social and personal background because of physical or mental failings. With the possible exception of the noncommissioned officers, however, most of the candidates came from middle-class or upper-middle-class families and almost all had completed high school. Given the large number of candidates seeking commissions, the examining boards had the luxury of selecting only those who showed the most promise for a military career.

The training of the new officers was quick and pragmatic. With the outbreak of the war, the Marine Corps School of Application graduated its class in April 1898 at the Washington barracks and temporarily suspended operations. The Marine Corps then used the barracks and school's facilities to indoctrinate the new officers. As Colonel Heywood observed, "The newly appointed officers were hurriedly drilled and otherwise prepared for duty as rapidly as possible, and distributed among the auxiliary cruisers, the various posts, and the First Marine Battalion."[40]

V

By June 1898, the Marine Corps battalion's days at Key West were numbered. On 18 May 1898, having eluded both Sampson's North Atlantic Squadron and Commodore William S. Schley's Flying Squadron, Admiral Cervera and his small fleet had entered the harbor of Santiago on the southern coast of Cuba. For several days the whereabouts of the Spanish fleet remained unknown to the Americans. On 27 May Commodore Schley, whose ships had just missed sighting the Spanish flotilla earlier, asked permission to abandon the quest for Cervera temporarily and return to Key West for recoaling. Following the advice of his Navy War Board, Secretary Long denied the request. The secretary observed that the Navy needed to know if Cervera was in Santiago and that Schley must surmount the difficulties of refueling. Long suggested that Schley might want to use the Guantanamo Bay area, about forty miles to the east of Santiago, for a coaling station. On 29 May, two days after first requesting relief, Schley, off Santiago, reported the enemy in port.[41]

At the same time that he had cabled Schley, apparently concerned that the latter would not be able to stay off Santiago, Secretary Long also sent a message to Sampson at Key West asking him if he could blockade Santiago and also "occupy [Guantanamo] as a coaling station." Sampson responded affirmatively and ordered Schley to maintain the blockade at all costs.[42]

On 31 May Capt. Charles D. Sigsbee, the captain of the cruiser *St. Paul*, departing Santiago with dispatches from Schley, recommended to Secretary Long that Guantanamo "be seized, and the shores garrisoned by United States troops." He believed it "a fine base for operating against Santiago." The occupation of Guantanamo also would prevent the Spanish from placing "plunging fire" on ships attempting to use the bay for recoaling. Sigsbee reported that Sampson agreed with his appraisal. According to Sampson, after "the establishment of the blockade [of Santiago], my first thought was to find a harbor which could serve as a coaling station and as a base for the operations of the fleet pending a decisive action." In any event, whether at the urging of the department or on his own initiative, the admiral ordered the reembarkation of the Marine battalion still at Key West and directed the cruiser *Marblehead* under Comdr. Bowman H. McCalla to reconnoiter Guantanamo.[43]

The Marines were more than ready to depart. The forced inactivity was causing some discord among the officers and some bad press. On 2 June Major Cochrane stated at the officers' mess that Marine Capt. George Elliott was so loud in his clamor for war as to be disquieting." Lieutenant Colonel Huntington retorted that the *New York Herald* contained a statement that "Marines would rather eat than fight." Two days later a telegram ordering the battalion to prepare for reembarkation broke the tedium of the camp routine. By 6 June the battalion was back on board the *Panther,* except for a small guard detachment left behind and Major Pope, who was ill. The *Panther* sailed to join the fleet off Santiago the following day to "great cheering" from the crews of the ships still in port.[44]

Although their spirits were revived, the Marines still had no idea of their mission. Major Cochrane speculated that they were to reinforce Army transports in an attack on Santiago. On the morning of 10 June, when the *Panther* joined the fleet off Santiago, Sampson informed Huntington that the Marine battalion was to seize Guantanamo and hold it as a base for the fleet. Commander McCalla would serve as the overall commander of the expedition. Earlier the *Marblehead* had bombarded Spanish positions and landed a small reconnaissance detachment under the command of Marine Capt. M. D. Goodrell. Goodrell selected a campsite for the Marine battalion on a hill near an abandoned Spanish blockhouse and then returned to the ship. The *Panther* rendezvoused with the *Marblehead* on the afternoon of the tenth. McCalla sent Goodrell on board the *Panther* to brief Huntington on the situation ashore. As the Marine battalion landed, the first company formed a skirmish line and ascended the hill. According to Huntington, "we went ashore like innocents and made a peaceful camp and slept well on the tenth."[45]

Although Marine pickets heard strange noises and saw some lights during the night, there was no sign of the Spanish except for abandoned equipment, some personal belongings, and two old muzzle-loading field artillery pieces. The next morning, fearing the spread of disease, the Marines destroyed most of this material and the blockhouse. They also continued to unload their heavy equipment and move it to their campsite. Huntington and his officers were not too happy with the selection of their base camp. They were in a clearing on top of a hill, surrounded by thickets and dense underbrush, but overlooking the water. Capt. Charles McCawley, the battalion quartermaster, called the site a "faulty one" from a "military point of view." About eleven hundred yards to the front was a larger ridgeline that dominated the Marine held hill. According to McCawley, "had the enemy been at all energetic or possessed of an ordinary amount of military knowledge they could have, in occupying this hill with sharpshooters, rendered our positions untenable."[46]

On 11 June, although not occupying the hill, Spanish troops made their presence known. At about 5:00 P.M. Spanish snipers killed two marines on an outpost. Huntington sent out a patrol, but it failed to locate the Spanish. The Marine commander, however, still felt secure. As he later wrote his son, "I do not know why I did not expect a night attack for we had a flurry in the P.M., but I did not." The enemy, however, returned on five occasions during the night. Major Cochrane, who had been directing the movement of supplies across the beach, came up to the Marine camp--now called Camp McCalla in honor of the Navy commander--with reinforcements from the working parties during one of the lulls. First limiting themselves to minor probes, the Spaniards attacked in force after midnight. Cochrane called it "the beginning of 100 hours of fighting."[47]

Despite the heavy intensity of firing in the darkness, Marine casualties were relatively low. The Navy surgeon with the battalion received a mortal wound in the first major attack. About daybreak, the enemy struck in force again, killing a Marine sergeant and wounding three others. The fighting continued sporadically on the twelfth, but the Marines suffered no further casualties during the day. Cochrane wrote his wife: "We have been having no end of racket and excitement . . . . We are all worn out with the tension of fighting the scoundrels all night and all day and have another night coming on. Bullets went over my head and cannonading and fusilading all around but never close enough to hurt."[48]

With the continuing attacks on the afternoon of the twelfth, several of the Marine officers thought that the Spanish would overrun their camp if they remained. The Marines entrenched the top of the hill and moved their base camp to a lower site. Believing the enemy was bringing up more reinforcements, some of the company commanders even proposed that the battalion reembark on board the *Panther*. Major Cochrane argued forcibly against any such move, but Lieutenant Colonel Huntington remained noncommittal. Huntington reported back to Commander McCalla and referred to the possible evacuation of the battalion. Reputedly, the commander replied, "You were put there to hold that hill and you'll stay there. If you're killed I'll come and get your dead body." The matter of withdrawal soon became moot as about sixty Cuban insurrectionists, familiar with the terrain and area, reinforced the Marines.[49]

The Spaniards continued to harass the American outposts and lines through the night and next day. According to the battalion's journal, "during the night many persistent and trifling attacks were made on the camp in reply to which we used a good deal of ammunition." Major Cochrane was more direct, stating there "was a vast deal of panicky, uncontrolled, and unnecessary fire." Again casualties were low, but the Marines lost their sergeant major, Henry Good, to a sniper's bullet.[50]

At this point, Lieutenant Colonel Huntington was ready to take the offensive. The Cubans informed him that the enemy numbered some four to five hundred troops and made their headquarters six miles to the south in the village of Cuzco, whose well contained the only source of water for the Spaniards. On the fourteenth, Huntington sent two companies under the command of Captain Elliott to destroy the well. Although moving through dense underbrush and rugged terrain and encountering stiff opposition along the way, the Marines accomplished their mission. In the fighting they sustained three wounded and lost several men to heat prostration; their Cuban allies lost one man and suffered several wounded. Supported by ship's batteries from below, the Marines took a heavy toll of the enemy, including the capture of one Spanish lieutenant and seventeen enlisted men.[51]

Deprived of their water supply, the Spanish troops withdrew from the immediate environs of the Marine Corps camp. The Marines' nearest enemy was now the Spanish garrison at the city of Guantanamo, twelve miles to the north, which was estimated to contain three thousand to seven thousand men. With Cuban insurrectionists in control of the countryside, the Americans had little to fear from the garrison. There soon developed an unspoken modus vivendi. As Lieutenant Colonel Huntington observed to his son, "The Spaniards do not trouble us and [we] only talk of troubling them."[52]

Following the action of 14 June, the Marine Corps battalion spent the rest of its time at Guantanamo improving its fortifications and camp. The marines also began to bask in the first publicity of their exploits. On the second day, several news correspondents, including novelist Stephen Crane, arrived at Guantanamo and began to file their dispatches. A few articles were critical. For example, the reporter for the *New York Times* observed "that given a free rein with repeating rifles, 500 nervous troops can waste 10,000 rounds of ammunition, killing shadows, in a single night, and not think even then that they have done much shooting."[53]

But the *Times* article was very much the exception. More often the headlines spoke of "First in the Fight" and "The Gallant Marines." Crane, who represented the *New York World,* was particularly friendly to the men of the First Battalion.

In an article entitled "The Red Badge of Courage Was His Wig Wag Flag," Crane stated that Captain Elliott's attack on the Cuzco well "was the first serious engagement of our troops on Cuban soil." The novelist told about the heroics of Sgt. John Quick, who exposed himself to enemy fire in order to signal an American ship to cease a bombardment that threatened the Marine advance. Crane also had high praise for Huntington, referring to him as the "grey old veteran . . . and the fine old colonel" who provided the brave example to his men. Captain Elliott in his report declared that Crane accompanied him on the expedition to Cuzco and "was of material aid during the action, carrying messages to fire volleys, etc. to the different company commanders." Not lost on the public was the fact that the Marine Corps had landed and fought the Spanish while the Army, under Major General Shafter, still remained at Tampa.[54]

VI

The question of the launching of the Army expedition preoccupied the military commanders and government policymakers throughout most of May. Finally, on 26 May, the Naval War Board, the secretaries of War and the Navy, and Maj. Gen. Nelson Miles, in a meeting with President McKinley, agreed to an Army campaign against Santiago. They based their decision on the assumption that Cervera's fleet had taken refuge there.[55]

When the Navy had determined that, indeed, Cervera's entire fleet was in port, the War Department, on 31 May, ordered Maj. Gen. William Shafter to embark his troops on Army transports and steam with Navy protection to Santiago, but various problems delayed the departure of the Army for two weeks.[56] This delay hardly made for harmony in the relations between the Army and Navy off Cuba. Although Sampson and Shafter's first meeting on 20 June went well, the two leaders were soon at loggerheads. Sampson's main purpose was the destruction of Cervera's fleet, while Shafter's was the capture of the city of Santiago and its defending garrison. Each wanted the other to act first.

In order to reach an agreement, Sampson asked Shafter for a conference. On 3 July Sampson steamed westward from Santiago on board his flagship, the *New York*, to meet with Shafter at the latter's headquarters. About half an hour after setting out, Sampson, spotting smoke near the entrance of Santiago harbor, realized that Cervera had decided to try to head out and reversed course to attack the Spanish. By the time he reached the scene the battle was virtually over and the Spanish fleet destroyed.

The victory did nothing to solve the dispute between Shafter and Sampson. Although Cervera's fleet was no longer a factor, the Army had not yet taken Santiago. President McKinley directed that Shafter and Sampson meet and determine how they would cooperate to force the city to surrender. Sampson agreed to meet Shafter at Siboney, but fell ill and sent Capt. French E. Chadwick to represent him.[57]

At the conference with Shafter on 6 July, Captain Chadwick again presented Sampson's proposal that the Marines and Army capture the Socapa and Morro fortified heights to permit the Navy to clear the mines. Eventually Sampson and Shafter reached an agreement of sorts. The Navy would first shell the city of Santiago at long range with its large guns. If at the end of the bombardment the Spanish had not surrendered, Marines from the fleet, with the assistance of Cuban troops, would attack the Socapa heights. At the same time, Sampson would attempt to force the entrance with some of his smaller ships. It was unclear whether Shafter would provide troops to assist in the taking of the Morro.[58]

The commanders implemented only part of the agreement. Although on 10 and 11 July Sampson's ships fired on the city from outside the harbor entrance, the admiral and Shafter soon reverted to their original positions. Shafter still wanted Sampson to force the entrance of the harbor, but Sampson refused to do so until the ground troops had reduced the artillery batteries on the heights. At the heart of the question was the feasibility of an assault on the Morro. The Army said such an attack was not possible and the Navy said it was. For his part, Marine Maj. Robert L. Meade, who was the fleet marine officer and who would have commanded the Marine assault force on the Morro, agreed with Sampson, with some qualifications. After examining the terrain following the surrender of Santiago, he later wrote: "The most difficult part . . . would be in reaching the crest from the beach through almost impassable maniqua plants. Nothing but a narrow trail reached the crest . . . . Under such circumstances an inferior force could conduct a defense with success if properly handled but as the army in the near vicinity had successfully assaulted positions similarly defended I was certain that my assault would have been successful also, if undertaken."[59]

Events, however, overtook the dispute. With continuing Army reinforcements from the United States, including 1,500 troops under Major General Miles, Shafter squeezed the vise around the city. Finally, on 15 July, after extended negotiations and in the face of overwhelming odds, the Spanish commander of the Santiago garrison agreed to surrender.

VII

With the aborting of the campaign against the heights, the First Marine Battalion, even after the destruction of Cervera's fleet and the surrender of the city of Santiago, remained at Guantanamo Bay until the beginning of August. There had been some discussion about the battalion joining Major General Miles and his planned expedition against Puerto Rico. The War Department, however, vetoed Marine participation.[60]

At Guantanamo, the Marines established a garrison routine. Three of the temporary lieutenants joined the battalion, together with enlisted replacements. The Marines maintained their vigil and manned their outposts, but at the same time entered into a more relaxed regimen. They nevertheless held to a high standard of health discipline, using only distilled water from the ships, burning their garbage, and changing their clothes whenever they could. One of the first battalion orders related to basic toilet habits: "Men are forbidden to ease themselves except at the latrine, and will not urinate inside the Fort or near the ramparts." On 23 July Major Cochrane observed that "our camp continues healthy, and we are trying to keep it so." In contrast to the Army, the Marines did not suffer one case of yellow fever and sustained only a 2 percent sickness rate.[61]

By the end of July, the Marine battalion was prepared to depart Guantanamo. In order to place further pressure on the Spanish in Cuba, the Naval War Board wanted to extend the naval blockade to western Cuba, where the Spanish still used ports on the southern coast that were connected by rail to Havana. The board directed that the Marine battalion seize the Isle of Pines off the southwestern coast as a "secure base for coal and against hurricanes, for the small vessels which alone could operate in the surrounding shoal water." Lieutenant Colonel Huntington at this point had some private doubts about the capability of the older officers to continue. He believed that another campaign "would clear Huntington, Harrington, Elliott, and Spicer off the roles of this battalion." Huntington stated, however, that "Cochrane . . . takes such selfish care of himself that he might last, unless somebody killed him."[62]

Fortunately for Huntington and his officers and men, they did not have to endure the hardships of further strenuous ground combat in a tropical climate. On 9 August, escorted by the cruiser *Newark*, the battalion departed Guantanamo on board the Navy transport *Resolute* for the Isle of Pines. Joined the following day by two other ships off Cape Cruz, Comdr. Caspar F. Goodrich, the captain of the *Newark* and task force commander, decided on a small digression. Acting on a suggestion from one of the ship captains, he ordered, en route to the Isle of Pines, the capture of the city of Manzanillo, west of Santiago. Although the Navy ships bombarded the city on 12 August, the news of the signing of the peace protocol calling for an armistice made the proposed landing of the Marine battalion unnecessary.[63]

Although Commander Goodrich and Lieutenant Colonel Huntington expressed disappointment about not attaining additional glory for American arms, other Marine officers were much less enthusiastic. Captain McCawley, the battalion quartermaster, later observed that the Americans badly underestimated the size of the Spanish garrison. According to McCawley, the Spanish troops numbered nearly 4,500, not the 800 that Goodrich and his commanders had thought. Although reinforced by Cuban forces to the north of the city and by naval gunfire, the Marine battalion might have faced an almost impossible task.[64]

Upon the return of the Marine battalion from Cuba, Colonel Heywood exploited the Marine record in the war to enhance the Corps' status within the naval and military establishment. Rather than immediately dissolving the First Battalion, he kept the unit together at Portsmouth, New Hampshire, for over three weeks, ostensibly to permit the men "to rest and get the malaria" out of their system. On 10 September Colonel Heywood visited the Marine encampment and reported to Secretary Long that "the men are looking very well, none of them being sick, and there has not been a death by disease since the battalion left for Cuba." The Navy Department and the press were not slow to compare the 2 percent sickness rate of the Marine battalion with the ravages that malaria and yellow fever caused among Shafter's troops at Santiago.[65]

Finally, before disbanding in mid-September, the First Battalion paraded before the president and other dignitaries in Washington. In a heavy rain, but before a large, cheering crowd, the Marines, dressed in their campaign uniforms, passed in review to the strains of "Hot Time in the Old Town Tonight" played by the Marine Corps Band. President McKinley complimented the men on their appearance and declared, "They have performed magnificent duty and to you, Colonel Heywood, I wish to personally extend my congratulations for the fine condition your men are in."[66]

Although the Marine leadership accepted with great satisfaction the public acclaim received by the Marine battalion, they still believed that the primary role of Marines in the future would be manning the secondary batteries on battleships. Even before the end of the war on 9 August 1898, Colonel Heywood sent out letters to selected ship commanders and to ship detachment Marine officers to determine the effectiveness of Marine gunnery in the sea battles of Santiago and Manila Bay. In his annual report, the commandant claimed that the secondary batteries caused the greatest damage to the Spanish ships at Santiago and that their raking fire forced the enemy to abandon their guns. He observed that a large percentage of the guns were manned by Marines.[67]

The accounts by both Marines and naval officers were less conclusive than Heywood professed for them. On the *Indiana,* for example, Marine Capt. Littleton W. T. Waller reported that only about a third of the Marine detachment actually manned the guns. As Capt. H. C. Taylor, the ship commander, pointed out, the Marines on the secondary battery fired about half as many as the seamen because the Marines manned the "port battery of 6-pounders, while the starboard battery was the one engaged." Another ship's commander, Capt. Robley D. Evans of the *Iowa,* agreed with Taylor: "I do not think it desirable to single out an individual division of this ship's company for special report. All the ship's company, of which the Marine Guard forms a division, have done their work in a manner creditable to themselves and their ship." Even more to the point, however, was the fact that naval gunnery during the battles of Santiago and Manila Bay was notoriously poor. American naval guns of all calibers averaged between 1 to 5 percent hits for ammunition expended.[68]

Still, neither the public nor Congress was overly concerned with the technicalities of naval gunfire. In fact, the inadequacies of the aimed firing during the two sea battles did not come out until several months later, and then appeared only in professional journals and official reports. Heywood's report containing lists of marines breveted for gallantry in action and accounts of marines in battle both on land and at sea served to satiate the nation's appetite for heroes. As the *New York Times* shrewdly noted, "This is the sort of stuff that members of Congress will read when they receive the request of [the] Colonel Commandant . . . to have an increased allowance of men and money to the Marine Corps in the next naval appropriation bill."[69]

For the Marine Corps and the nation at large, the war was over. The protocol of 12 August between the two countries ended hostilities and called for a peace treaty to be negotiated in Paris. Spain agreed to relinquish Cuba, give Puerto Rico to the United States, and permit the United States to occupy Manila until the conclusion of the formal treaty determined the fate of the Philippines. Ironically, on 13 August, the day after the protocol was signed, American forces captured Manila after token resistance by Spanish defenders. In the final Treaty of Paris, signed on 10 December 1898 and ratified in February 1899, the Spanish ceded the Philippines to the United States. Almost completely unnoticed during the war, the United States had also formally annexed the Hawaiian Islands. Thus, the immediate result of the Spanish-American War was to make the United States an imperial power in both the Caribbean and the Pacific.

The Spanish-American War also had a lasting effect on the Marine Corps. Although nearly 75 percent of Marine strength was on board ship, it was Huntington's battalion that caught the public eye and signaled portents for the future. As Colonel Heywood quickly remarked, the Marine battalion with the fleet "showed how important and useful it is to have a body of troops which can be quickly mobilized and sent on board transports, fully equipped for service ashore and afloat, to be used at the discretion of the commanding admiral." Heywood also pointedly observed that the Marine force stood "always under the direction of the senior naval officer," and thus posed no "conflict of authority" inherent in Army-Navy relations.[70]

The Spanish-American War proved to be the crucible for the Marine Corps. While not fully knowing how they would use it, naval authorities immediately ordered the establishment of a Marine battalion with its own transport. Although numbering less than a quarter of the active Marine Corps, this battalion's activities not only received public approbation but also had implications for the future relationship of the Marine Corps with the Navy. Despite a somewhat rocky start at Guantanamo, the First Marine Battalion proved itself in combat. By seizing the heights on Guantanamo, it provided a safe anchorage for Navy ships. In effect, the Marines seized and protected an advance base for the fleet blockading Santiago.

Navy strategists and planners also learned another lesson from the war. They quickly realized that Army and Navy officers may have very different and even possibly conflicting goals in a military campaign. The dispute between the Army and Navy at Santiago reflected the separate approaches of professional Army and Navy officers. For Major General Shafter and his staff, the vital objective was the capture of the Spanish garrison and the city of Santiago. On the other hand, Rear Admiral Sampson's and the Navy's aim was the destruction of Cervera's fleet. For his part, Shafter designed an overland campaign to capture the city and was unwilling to sacrifice men to take the Morro and Socapa heights overlooking the narrow channel into Santiago Bay. At the same time, Sampson refused to chance the loss of any of his ships by running the channel. Although both commanders attained their desired ends, their basic conflict remained unresolved. For the Navy, the message was that it could not depend upon the Army to secure land-based sites for naval purposes. The Navy required its own land force, and it had this in the Marine Corps.

Notes

1. David F. Trask, *The War with Spain in 1898* (New York, 1981), xii-xiv, 35; John D. Long, *The New American Navy,* 2 vols. (New York, 1903), 1:141.

2. Trask, *War with Spain,* 72-78, 88-90; J.A.S. Grenville, "American Naval Preparations for War with Spain, 1896-98," *Journal of American Studies* (Apr. 1968), 33-47. For copies of some of the original plans see Lt. William Kimball, "War with Spain," 1 June 1896; Plan of Operations Against Spain, 17 Dec. 1896; Plans of Campaign Against Spain and Japan, 30 June 1897; all in War Planning Portfolio 11, OAB, Naval Historical Division, Washington, D.C.

3. Trask, *War with Spain,* 83-90; Long, *New American Navy* 1:165:66.

4. Graham A. Cosmas, *An Army for Empire: The United States Army in the Spanish-American War* (Columbia, Mo., 1971), 87-89. See also Trask, *War with Spain,* 145-49; and Russell F. Weigley, *History of the U.S. Army* (New York, 1967), 299.

5. Trask, *War with Spain,* 82-88; Margaret Leech, *In the Days of McKinley* (New York, 1959), 195-96.

6. Secretary of the Navy [SecNav] letters [ltrs] to Commandant of the Marine Corps [CMC], 10 Mar., 6 and 11 Apr. 1898, Letters Received, "N," RG 127; CMC ltrs to SecNav, 13 and 15 Mar., 6 and 9 Apr. 1898, Letters Sent to the Secretary of the Navy [LSSN] 7:187, 194-95, 245-46, 252, RG 127, National Archives [NA], Washington, D.C.; CMC, *Annual Report, 1898,* 6.

7. SecNav ltr to CMC and copy of ltr to C. A. Boutelle, 10 Mar. 1898, Letters Received, "N," RG 127, NA; *Army and Navy Journal* (12 Mar. 1898), 515; Lt. Comdr. Richard Wainwright, "Our Naval Power," *United States Naval Institute Proceedings* (Mar. 1898), 39-87, 48.

8. Lt. Col. R. W. Huntington ltr to CMC, 15 Feb. 1898, Letters Received, "N," RG 127, NA.

9. Huntington ltr to Bobby, 30 Mar. 1898, Col. R. W. Huntington Papers, Marine Corps Historical Center [MCHC], Washington, D.C.

10. Long ltr to CinC, U.S. Naval Force, NA, 6 Apr. 1898, and Sampson ltr to SecNav, 9 Apr. 1898, reprinted in *Appendix to the Report of the Chief of the Bureau of Navigation,* 171-73.

11. CMC ltrs to SecNav, 18 and 23 Apr. 1898, LSSN 7:250-52, 266, RG 127; Acting CMC ltr to SecNav, 19 Apr. 1898, Letters Received, "N," RG 127; entries for 17-22 Apr. 1898, and Battalion Orders 1-3, 19-20 Apr. 1898, in Journal of the Marine Battalion under Lt. Col. Robert W. Huntington, Apr.-Sept. 1898, RG 127, NA [hereafter Journal of the Marine Battalion]; CMC, *Annual Report, 1898,* 7, 10; Charles L. McCawley, "The Marines at Guantanamo," n.d., MS, 2-4, Maj. Gen. Charles L. McCawley Papers, MCHC; "Marine Battalion at Guantanamo," reprinted in *Appendix to the Report of the Chief of the Bureau of Navigation, 440-41.* Graham A. Cosmas observed that the "Marine mobilization coincides in time with the order for concentration of most of the Regular Army at Chickamauga Park, New Orleans, Mobile, and Tampa, which went out on 15 April [1898]" (Cosmas, comments on author's draft chapter, Mar. 1990).

12. "Marines to Start Tonight," clipping from *Brooklyn Eagle,* 22 Apr. 1898, General Clipping File, Maj. Henry Clay Cochrane Papers, MCHC; *New York Times,* 23 Apr. 1898, 4; McCawley, "Marines at Guantanamo," 2-4; "Marine Battalion at Guantanamo," 440-41; CMC, *Annual Report, 1898,* 6.

13. "Marine Battalion at Guantanamo," 440-41; CMC ltr to SecNav, 23 Apr. 1898, LSSN 7:250-52, RG 127, NARA; Cochrane ltr to Betsy, 22 Apr. 1898, Cochrane Papers.

14. Maj. George C. Reid ltr to Pendleton, 12 Apr. 1898, in Maj. Gen. Joseph H. Pendleton Papers, MCHC; Long message to Sampson, 21 Apr. 1898, reprinted in *Appendix to the Report of the Chief of the Bureau of Navigation*, 174-75; Cochrane ltr to Betsy, 23 Apr. 1898, Cochrane Papers; Long, *New American Navy* 2:5.

15. Trask, *War with Spain*, 54, 150-52; Cosmas, *Army for Empire*, 93-102.

16. Leech, *Days of McKinley*, 198-99; Trask, *War with Spain*, 153-54; Cosmas, *Army for Empire*, 102-7; Long, *New American Navy* 2:9.

17. Trask, *War with Spain*, 108, 153-54; Cosmas, *Army for Empire*, 107; Long ltr to Sampson, 21 Apr. 1898, reprinted in *Appendix to the Report of the Chief of the Bureau of Navigation*, 174.

18. Entries for 23-26 Apr. 1898 in Journal of the Marine Battalion; entries for 23-28 Apr. 1898, diary, Cochrane Papers; Lt. Col. R. W. Huntington report to CMC, 30 Apr. 1898, Letters Received, Historical Section, RG 127, NA; McCawley, "Marines at Guantanamo," 8-10; CMC, *Annual Report, 1898,* 6.

19. Entries for 23-26 Apr. 1898 in Journal of the Marine Battalion; entries for 23-28 Apr. 1898, diary, Cochrane Papers, MCHC; Lt. Col. R. W. Huntington report to CMC, 30 Apr. 1898. Modifications continued to be made on the Lee rifles. See Chief, Bureau of Ordnance ltr to CMC, 22 July 1898, Letters Received, "N," RG 127, NA.

20. Entries for 26-29 Apr. 1898 in Journal of the Marine Battalion; Cochrane ltr to Betsy, 26 Apr. 1898, folder 51, Cochrane Papers; McCawley, "Marines at Guantanamo," 8.

21. Trask, *War with Spain*, 162-63; Cosmas, *Army for Empire*, 111-12; Leech, *Days of McKinley*, 198-99; Cochrane ltr to Betsy and boys, 4 May 1898, Cochrane Papers.

22. Long ltr to Dewey, 24 Apr. 1898, and Dewey report to SecNav, 4 May 1898, reprinted in *Appendix to the Report of the Chief of the Bureau of Navigation*, 67, 69-72.

23. Dewey to Long, 4 and 13 May 1898, reprinted in *Appendix to the Report of the Chief of the Bureau of Navigation*, 68, 97-98; Trask, *War with Spain*, 105; Bernard C. Nalty, *The United States Marines in the War with Spain*, rev. ed. (Washington, 1967), 6.

24. Cosmas, *Army for Empire*, 121-30; Leech, *Days of McKinley*, 214-16; Trask, *War with Spain*, 163-67; Long ltr to Sampson, 3 May 1898, reprinted in *Appendix to the Report of the Chief of the Bureau of Navigation*, 366. Cosmas observed it was his understanding that "McKinley had unofficial reports of Dewey's victory at the time he began to revise strategy on 2 May" (Cosmas comments to the author, Mar. 1990).

25. Entry for 30 Apr. 1898 in Journal of the Marine Battalion; McCawley, "Marines at Guantanamo," 10; entry for 3 May 1898, diary, Cochrane Papers; Trask, *War with Spain*, 114.

26. Entries for 1-24 May 1898 in Journal of the Marine Battalion; entry for 31 May 1898, diary, Cochrane Papers, MCHC; Huntington ltr to Bobby, 27 May 1898, Huntington Papers, MCHC.

27. Huntington ltrs to CMC, 25 May and 3 Nov. 1899; McCawley ltr to CMC, 8 Jan. 1900, and Commodore George C. Remey endorsement to CMC, 25 May 1898, Letters Received, Historical Section, RG 127, NA; Huntington ltr to Bobby, 27 May 1898, Huntington Papers.

28. For examples of this correspondence, see Cochrane ltrs to Betsy, 6, 9, 12, 28 May and 1 June 1898, and Betsy ltrs to Cochrane, 24 and 25 Apr. 1898, folder 51, Cochrane Papers.

29. *New York Times*, 25 March 1898, 3.

30. CMC ltr to SecNav, 28 Mar. 1898 with enclosures, LSSN 7:210-77, RG 127, NA; U.S. Congress, House, *Reorganization of Naval Personnel, HR 10403, with Accompanying Report*, HR 1375, 55th Cong·, 2d sess., 1898, 12-13.

31. U.S. Congress, Senate, 55th Cong., 2d sess., 29 Apr. 1898, *Congressional Record* 31: 4422; CMC, *Annual Report, 1898,* 11.

32. For the Cochrane correspondence, see Cochrane ltrs to Betsy, 6, 9, 12-13 May 1898, and Betsy ltr to Cochrane, 12 May 1898, folder 51, Cochrane Papers.

33. U.S. Congress, House, 55th Cong., 2d sess., 19 May 1898, *Congressional Record* 31:5058-59; CMC, *Annual Report, 1898,* 16-17; SecNav, *Annual Report, 1898,* 54-57; Cochrane ltrs to Betsy, 12 and 28 May 1898, folder 51, and entry, diary, 4 June 1898, Cochrane Papers.

34. Cochrane ltr to Betsy, 1 June 1898, folder 51, Cochrane Papers.

35. CMC ltr to SecNav, 5, 9, 13-18, 20-21, 25 May and 6 June 1898, LSSN 7:305, 308-14, 329-45, 353, 370-74; Asst. SecNav ltr to CMC, 3-4 May 1898, Letters Received, "N," RG 127, NA.

36. Asst. SecNav ltr to CMC, 3-4 May 1898, Letters Received, "N," RG 127, NA; CMC, *Annual Report, 1898,* 11. The records do not indicate why a fourth NCO was not commissioned. Sergeant Henry Good, the sergeant major of the Marine battalion under Huntington, was nominated. One can surmise that his untimely death at Guantanamo prevented his appointment and that the war ended before another choice could be made.

37. CMC ltr to SecNav, 18 June 1898, LSSN 7:415, RG 127, NA.

38. C. Mason Kinne ltr to Secretary of War, Gen. R. A. Alger, and attached ltrs and endorsements, 24 June 1898, Letters Received, Historical Section, RG 127, NA.

39. CMC ltr to SecNav, 6 June 1898, LSSN 7:372-74, RG 127, NA; Lt. Charles G. Andresen ltr to Waller, 5 May 1899, L.W.T. Waller Papers, 1896-1902, MCHC.

40. Capt. F. H. Harrington, School of Application ltr to CMC, 18 Apr. 1898, Letters Received, Historical Section, RG 127, NA; CMC, *Annual Report, 1898, 11,* 15. See also Hans Schmidt, *Maverick Marine, General Smedley D. Butler and the Contradictions of American Military History* (Lexington, Ky., 1987), 7.

41. Exchange of messages between Long and Schley, 27-29 May 1898, reprinted in *Appendix to the Report of the Chief of the Bureau of Navigation,* 397-400.

42. Exchange of messages, 28-30 May 1898, reprinted in ibid., 398-400.

43. Sigsbee ltr to SecNav, 31 May 1898, reprinted in ibid., 412-14; Rear Adm. William T. Sampson, "The Atlantic Fleet in the Spanish War," *Century Magazine,* n.d., 886-913, 903, in Printed Material Folder, H. C. Taylor Papers, Library of Congress [LC], Washington, D.C.

44. Entries for 1-7 June 1898, in Journal of the Marine Battalion; entries for 1-7 June 1898, diary, Cochrane Papers, MCHC.

45. Entry for 4 June 1898, diary, Cochrane Papers; McCalla ltr to Sampson, 19 July 1898, reprinted in Maj. Richard S. Collum, *History of the United States Marine Corps* (New York, 1903), 348-49; McCawley, "Marines at Guantanamo," 9; Nalty, *The United States Marines in the War with Spain,* 9; Huntington ltr to Bobby, 19 June 1898, Huntington Papers.

46. McCawley, "Marines at Guantanamo," 15-17.

47. Ibid.; entries for 11-12 June 1898 in Journal of the Marine Battalion; Huntington ltr to Bobby, 19 June 1898, Huntington Papers; entries for 11-12 June 1898, diary, Cochrane Papers.

48. Entries for 11-12 June 1898, diary; and Cochrane ltr to Betsy, 12 June 1898, folder 51, both in Cochrane Papers.

49. Entries for 11-12 June 1898 in Journal of the Marine Battalion. The discussion about the proposed evacuation is contained in Cochrane's diary (entries for 11-12 June, 25 Aug. 1898, and in flysheet in back of diary for 1898, Cochrane Papers) referring to interviews with several other witnesses. He also mentions the incident in a letter to his wife (Cochrane ltr to Betsy, 14 June 1898, folder 51, Cochrane Papers). Cochrane was not a

witness to McCalla's refusal and gives conflicting accounts. In a separate report Commander McCalla only stated: "The mistake of locating the camp between the main position and the outpost was corrected . . . at my suggestion" (McCalla ltr to Sampson, 19 July 1898, reprinted in Collum, *History of the United States Marine Corps*, 348-49).

50. Entries for 12-13 June 1898, Journal of the Marine Battalion; entry for 13 June 1898, diary, Cochrane Papers.

51. Entries for 14 and 19 June 1898, Journal of the Marine Battalion.

52. Huntington ltr to Bobby, 4 July 1898, Huntington Papers.

53. Journal of the Marine Battalion; McCawley, "Marines at Guantanamo," 28, 31-40; entries for 13-15 June 1898, diary, Cochrane Papers; *New York Times*, 17 June 1898.

54. Clippings "First to Fight" and "The Gallant Marines," n.d., n.p., General Clipping File, Cochrane Papers; R. W. Stallman and E. R. Hagemann, eds., *The War Dispatches of Stephen Crane* (New York, 1964), 140-54, 171-72, 267-74; Capt. G. F. Elliott ltr to Huntington, 18 June 1898, reprinted in CMC, *Annual Report, 1898*, 29.

55. Trask, *War with Spain*, 172-73; Cosmas, *Army for Empire*, 179-80.

56. Long ltr to Schley, 27 May 1898, reprinted in *Appendix to the Report of the Chief* of the Bureau of Navigation, 397; Long message to Sampson, 31 May 1898, quoted in Sampson, Report of Operations of North Atlantic Fleet, 3 Aug. 1898, reprinted in ibid., 480.

57. Trask, *War with Spain*, 291- 93; Rear Adm. W. T. Sampson, Report of Operations of Blockading Squadron off Santiago, 15 July 1898, reprinted *in Appendix to the Report of the Chief of the Bureau of Navigation*, 609-10; SecNav, *Annual Report, 1898*, 14.

58. "Minutes of a conversation between Captain Chadwick of the Navy, representing Admiral Sampson, and General Shafter," 6 July 1898, reproduced in Sampson, Report of Operations, 15 July 1898, 610. Chadwick in his history, however, states that Shafter had agreed to attack the Morro (French Ensor Chadwick, *The Relations of the United States and Spain, The Spanish American War*, 2 vols. [New York, 1911, reissued in 1968], 2:208). Trask agrees with Chadwick that Shafter agreed to attack the Morro, "although for unexplained reasons this aspect of the plan was not made explicit in the minutes of the meeting" (Trask, *War with Spain*, 293). Cosmas comments that from "3 July on, Shafter was engaged in his own negotiations with the Spanish commander, General Toral, looking to the surrender of the garrison. I'm not sure how thoroughly, or even whether, he kept Sampson filled in on this" (Cosmas comments to author, Mar. 1990).

59. Lt. Col. Robert L. Meade ltr to Maj. Charles L. McCawley, 18 Mar. 1899, McCawley Papers.

60. Entries for 17-21 July 1898, diary, Cochrane Papers; Trask, *War with Spain*, 350, 353.

61. First Marine Battalion Order no. 3, 21 June 1898, Journal of the Marine Battalion; McCawley, "Marines at Guantanamo," 45-48; Cochrane ltr to Betsy, 23 June 1898, Cochrane Papers.

62. A. T. Mahan, "The War on the Sea and Its Lessons," *McClures*, n.d., 527-34, 532, in Printed Material Folder, Taylor Papers; Huntington ltr to Bobby, 29 July 1898, Huntington Papers.

63. G. F. Goodrich ltr to CinC North Atlantic Fleet, 13 Aug. 1898, reprinted in *Appendix to the Report of the Chief of the Bureau of Navigation*, 301-3.

64. Ibid.; McCawley, "Marines at Guantanamo," 43-45.

65. Cochrane ltr to Betsy, 22 Aug. 1898, Cochrane Papers; Chief, Bureau of Navigation ltr to CMC, 8 Aug. 1898, Letters Received, Historical Section, and CMC ltr to SecNav, 10 Sept. 1898, LSSN 7:567-68, RG 127, NA; Ira Nelson Hollis, "The Navy in the War

with Spain," *Atlantic* (Nov. 1898): 605-16, Printed Matter Folder, Taylor Papers, LC; *Army and Navy Journal,* 17 Sept. 1898, 68. Malaria and yellow fever played havoc with the U.S. Army's Fifth Corps before Santiago. On 27 July 1898, more than 4,000 soldiers in the corps were in the hospital and a few days later the death rate reached fifteen per day (Cosmas, *Army for Empire,* 251-52). Although Marine Corps sanitary practices in part accounted for their low sickness rate, the Marines were fortunate that the Guantanamo sector remained dry and bred few of the mosquitos that spread the yellow fever and malaria among the Army troops.

66. *Army and Navy Journal,* 24 Sept. 1898, 95.

67. CMC, *Annual Report, 1898,*14; Army and Navy Journal, 27 Aug. 1898, 1,088.

68. Capt. Littleton W. T. Waller ltr to Colonel Commandant, USMC, 1 Sept. 1898, in CMC, *Annual Report, 1898,* 44-45; H. C. Taylor ltr to SecNav, 18 Sept. 1898, Correspondence Folder, July-Sept. 1898, Taylor Papers, LC; Capt. R. D. Evans ltr to Lt. Col. R. L. Meade, 31 Aug. 1898, Letters Received, Historical Section, RG 127, NA; Lt. John Ellicott, USN, *Effect of the Gun Fire of the United States Vessels in the Battle of Manila Bay* (1 May 1898), Office of Naval Intelligence, War Note No. 5, Information from Abroad (Washington, 1899).

69. CMC, *Annual Report, 1898;* "Record of the Marines," *New York Times,* 23 Oct. 1898,13.

70. CMC to SecNav, 12 Dec. 1898, LSSN 7:84-85, RG 127, NA.

Published and condensed with the permission of the author from his unpublished biography of Henry Clay Cochrane.

Crucible of the Corps
by James Holden-Rhodes

Land the Landing Force

To Bowman Hendry McCalla, Commander, USN, commanding the third rate cruiser *Marblehead* went the duty of reconnoitering Guantanamo Bay. Upon receipt of his orders, McCalla asked Admiral [William T.] Sampson "to send for the Battalion of Marines."[1] Accompanied by the auxiliaries *St. Louis* and *Yankee*, the three ships arrived on the 7th of June off Guantanamo with the mission of cutting the cables which linked Cuba with the outside world. At Key West, the First Battalion of Marines [under Lieutenant Colonel Robert W. Huntington] had re-boarded the *Panther*. As McCalla finished his reconnaissance of the harbor in the early morning hours, the *Panther* was approaching the north coast of Cuba. The Spanish gunboat, *Sandoval*, that had driven the *St. Louis* from the harbor, several days earlier, now appeared on the scene. After observing the profile of the large guns of the *Marblehead*, the *Sandoval* wisely put about and ran back up the channel towards Caimanera, while the field guns on Cayo del Toro attempted to take the *Marblehead* under fire without effect . . . .

Following the action in the bay, a small boat approached the *Marblehead* carrying two Cuban insurgents. They had been sent by General Calixto Garcia (the same Garcia who figured with U.S. Lieutenant Rowan in the "Message to Garcia") to report the position of Cuban forces, whose outposts occupied positions on the coast from the mouth of the Yateras to a point fifteen miles west of Santiago. Leaving the *St. Louis* in the harbor, McCalla steamed to Sampson's flagship, *New York*, which was in blockade position off Santiago. The admiral was briefed by the Cubans and the *Marblehead* was then ordered to return to Guantanamo to await the arrival of the Marines . . . .

Admiral Sampson confirmed the rumor that had been making the rounds aboard the *Panther* and ordered the battalion to proceed directly to Guantanamo Bay. The USS *Oregon*, "McKinley's Bulldog," which had raced to cover fifteen thousand miles in sixty-six days, arrived at Guantanamo early on the morning of the 9th to take on coal from colliers tied up in the bay. On board was Captain M. C. Goodrell, USMC. Goodrell, the Fleet Marine Officer, had instructions to find a position ashore for the battalion. Going ashore with the Marine detachments from the *Oregon* and the *Marblehead*, Goodrell reconnoitered the leeward side of the bay and selected a site on a hill above the beach at Fisherman's Point. Returning to the *Marblehead*, Goodrell discussed the site with Commander McCalla and several of the Cuban insurgents. They agreed with Goodrell's recommendation and McCalla formally approved the location.

Entering the harbor on the morning of the 10th of June, the *Panther* and the monitor *Yosemite* found everything in order for the landing. Goodrell went ashore with the combined detachments from the *Marblehead* and *Oregon* and moved up to the high ground above the beach to screen the landing. Steam launches from all ships formed up to tow the pulling boats, loaded with Marines, ashore. Bounding through the surf singing "There'll Be A Hot Time In The Old Town Tonight," four companies were landed in heavy marching order and moved quickly to the high ground where one company replaced Goodrell's force, while Color Sergeant Richard Silvey raised the flag above the still smoldering logs of the fort.[2]

In accordance with strict instructions from Commander McCalla, the huts and the remains of the blockhouse on the crest of the hill were to be burned in order to avoid the possibility of yellow fever . . . .

Around 9 p.m., noises were heard to the front of the lines. "Assembly" was sounded and [Captain George F.] Elliott's C Company swept around the perimeter and through the thick brush as best they could. Nothing was found. Shortly after midnight, Huntington sent his adjutant to the *Marblehead* with a message that stated that an attack was expected at dawn.

[Major Henry Clay] Cochrane, who had remained on the *Panther* with two companies, supervised the off-loading of men and supplies. Concurrently, three outposts were established near or along avenues of approach to what was now called McCalla's Hill.[3]

The question of how much intelligence was available to the battalion is a subject of much speculation. While it is clear that Commander McCalla, Lieutenant Colonel Huntington, and Major Cochrane were well versed on the strategic aspects of the Cuban campaign, it is less clear to what degree, tactical intelligence was available.

Executive officer by default Cochrane felt that the battalion could have engaged in signals interception by reading the heliograph message traffic that was passed between the garrison at Cuzco and General Pareja's headquarters in Guantanamo City. Cochrane's daily journal reveals that Huntington was still suffering from malarial fever and was frequently flat on his back. The strained relationship between the two men appears to have precluded any interchange--to include any intelligence matters. Cochrane's diary reveals nothing that would lead one to believe that the battalion had any solid tactical intelligence prior to the battle.

Thus, the 600-man battalion, located seventeen miles from an enemy force of seven thousand men, remained blind. During mid-afternoon, Lieutenant Colonel Huntington was joined by the self styled "Colonel" Laborde of the Cuban insurgents . . . . While conversing with Huntington in the Marine camp, firing broke out to the south--the area assigned to Lieutenant [Wendell C.] Neville . . . .

Several volleys were fired by the Spanish forces, who had been able to sneak up and surprise the outpost held by Sergeant Smith and Privates Dumphy and McColgan. "Hold on boys, don't fire until you get the command," yelled Neville. He had his glasses watching the hills. Word was given to open fire and for half an hour a steady firing was kept up, driving the Spaniards back . . . . Privates William Dumphy and James McColgan became the first Marine casualties at Guantanamo.[4]

"In Many a Fight We've Fought for Life and Never Lost Our Nerve"

The battalion was formed into an elongated square that was anchored on the rubble of the Spanish blockhouse on what was called Crest Ridge . . . . Company F, under Captain F. H. Harrington, with the 3-inch guns, was held in reserve in the center of the camp. Companies C and E, under the command of Captain Elliott and Lieutenant Mahoney, formed the eastern flank. Captain B. R. Russell's B Company held the short but critical southern lines. The western flank was held by Captain W. F. Spicer's D Company. Captain Allan C. Kelton's A Company held the foot of the ridge on the beach to protect the battalion stores.

Under the command of Lieutenant Cyrus S. Radford, the Marine detachment of the USS *Texas* had come ashore to join the battalion. Their first duty was to form a burial detail. Under sporadic Spanish fire, the last shovels of dirt were thrown over the two graves . . . .

Going into the second night on Crest Ridge, the thick chaparral had not been cleared from in front of the Marine positions, and fields of fire were nonexistent. At 9 p.m. the rising moon silhouetted the white tents atop the hill. A steam launch from the *Marblehead* with a machine gun mounted forward, was launched and moved slowly up the bay searching for the enemy. The night sky which had been heavily clouded, now built up with storm clouds and heavy winds obscured noise and movement. Searchlights from the ships in the harbor played upon the shore. Correspondents in the harbor thought it "resembled a transformation scene at the theater." To add to the tense situation a steady rain began to fall, turning the reddish soil to sticky clay.

Cochrane spent the early part of the night "patrolling the camp." To his great dismay, he noted that many of the company commanders had gone to ground. Captain B. R. Russell "stuck to his gun like a leach."[5] Shortly before midnight, Cochrane discovered that the west side of the perimeter had no outposts. Armed with his service revolver, he led out a squad of Marines and set them into position. No sooner had this been accomplished then the enemy, who had isolated the outposts and kept them under heavy fire, launched an attack against the southwest corner of the perimeter, where Company B and Company C were linked. Cochrane watched part of the B Company line waver and drop back as the assault hit and then, without command the men stiffened and held. Assaulting in force up the moderate incline, the attack was slowed and finally broken by several Marine volleys. Nonetheless, Spanish elements were able to reach the lines and in at least one case break through. So close was the fighting, that the officers used their pistols . . . .

For correspondent Stephen Crane, who five years earlier at age 22 had become the celebrated author of *The Red Badge of Courage*, a book which "set a model for succeeding writers on the emotions of battle," this night became his baptism of fire. Just at the moment of the Spanish assault, Crane was:

> In search of [Surgeon John Blair] Gibbs, but I soon gave over an active search for the more congenial occupation of lying flat and feeling the hot hiss of the bullets trying to cut my hair. For the moment I was no longer a cynic. I was a child who, in a fit of ignorance had jumped into a vat of war. I heard somebody dying near me. He was dying hard. Hard. It took him a long time to die. He breathed as all noble machinery breathes when it is making its gallant strife against breaking, breaking. But he was going to break. He was going to break. The darkness was impenetrable. The man was lying in a depression within seven feet of me . . .[6]

Responding to a report that the southwest parameter had been breached, Huntington, accompanied by Adjutant Draper, was moving towards the hospital tent when Gibbs was hit. "'Where's the doctor?' yelled Draper. 'There's some wounded men over there. Where's the doctor?' A man answered briskly: 'Just died this minute, sir'".[7] . . . during a short lull in the fighting, a signal was sent to the *Marblehead* requesting that her surgeon be sent ashore. Climbing the hill alone and under fire, Dr. A. M. P. McCormack joined the battalion. So narrow was the crest of the ridge that Gibbs body was left were he had fallen.

The intensity and confusion of the battle is borne out by the fact that Major Cochrane thought that Gibbs had been killed by a wild shot from the pistol of Colonel Laborde who walked the line, firing his pistol throughout the fight. Crane, on the other hand, wrote that, ". . . Three Spaniards had sneaked to the edge of camp, shot Gibbs, and then ran helter-skelter down the hills when our Cuban guide--Colonel Jose Campina--fired upon them."[8] Evidence lends credence to Crane, although two days later at Cuzco, Laborde apparently shot one of his own men, with the same pistol.

The Spanish had broken through the gap between the two companies on the southwest corner, where, by chance, the hospital tent had been erected . . . .

A series of probing attacks continued against the ridge and the outposts until 4 a.m. when simultaneous attacks were launched against the Crest and the outposts: "It was dark and the great growth of bushes prevented us from seeing them getting between us and the main camp. Laying where we were, hungry and suffering from want of sleep, we fought until daybreak. Sergeant Smith was [shot] through the head and died instantly."[9] Sergeant Smith had been in charge of the outpost at which Privates McColgan and Dumphy had been ambushed, and had barely escaped with his own life. Now, his luck had run out . . . .

Newsmen who had spent the night aboard ships in the harbor, began to climb the hill. At the ruins of the blockhouse, Cochrane conferred with Huntington and recommended that the main body of the battalion be repositioned. He suggested leaving a strong outpost on the crest and moving the remainder of the battalion towards Playa del Este, one hundred yards to the west. Such a move he argued would enable the Marines to make better use of the terrain. In addition he requested that more Hotchkiss field pieces be brought ashore. Cochrane understood Huntington to agree with him, and took his leave to talk to the correspondents. Huntington turned to talk to several of the company commanders who were waiting nearby. After discussing the events of the night with them, Cochrane wished them well and ". . . a dispatch boat was rushed to cable" the story.[10]

Huntington indicated to Cochrane that he was going to the *Marblehead* to confer with Commander McCalla, but did not mention anything specific. As the battalion commander made his way down the hill, Captains Russell and Spicer took Cochrane aside . . . . Arguing that the battalions' position on the hill was untenable, and, that the men were exhausted, they asked Cochrane to "give up and reembark on the *Panther*." Aghast, Cochrane, . . . " refused positively and advised against the thought of such a thing . . . ." Glancing towards the beach, Cochrane saw Lieutenant Colonel Huntington and Adjutant Draper boarding a gig from the *Texas*. Huntington's intent was now clear . . . .[11]

Visiting . . . on board the *Texas*, Bowman McCalla heard the haggard Huntington argue that the Marines' position on the hill was untenable. He requested that the battalion be reembarked at once. McCalla, affectionately known in the service as "Billy Hell" thanks to an incident in which he had applied the flat of his sword to a recalcitrant sailor, flew into a rage: "Leave this camp? No sir, that camp is named for me. Never, my family would suffer. You were put there to hold the hill and you'll stay there! If you are killed, I'll come out and get your dead body."[12] . . .

As the chastised Huntington was returning to the beach, the Marine detachment of the *Texas* was forming the honor guard for the burial of Dr. Gibbs. At the moment that Gibbs was laid alongside Marines Dumphy and McColgan, the Spanish opened fire on the hill, but no one was hit. The tents which had been riddled with bullets were struck and trenches were dug, something, noted Adjutant Draper, that, ". . . should have been done on landing" all canvas was torn down. The tents which had been badly shot up were piled up in front of the trenches as breastworks. Picks, spades, and shovels had been brought ashore and were now put to use. Half a dozen newsmen were pressed into service when additional field pieces and machine guns were brought ashore. Along with the Marines, they slipped into harness and pulled the field guns up the steep path.

As if to further make his point, Bowman McCalla sent a flag ashore. "At 1:15 o'clock . . . the American flag was raised . . . the first flag that was raised to stay. Three cheers went up from the battalion, and from all the ships in the harbor came back an answering echo. Several of the ships fired a salute and blew their steam whistles . . . ."[13]

The three new field guns were used during the afternoon to shell the enemy who appeared from time to time in groups. The only artillery piece on the hill the night before had not been used for fear of hitting the outposts. The Marine detachment from the *Marblehead* was sent ashore and joined Company D on the right flank. Bluejacket volunteers from the *Panther* and the collier *Abarendas* also came ashore. All indications pointed to the Spanish building up for another major attack.

Venturing forth from the critical northeast outpost, Lieutenant "Buck" Neville led his men against a small stone fort near the eastern edge of the bay. Under heavy Spanish fire, Neville moved his men into position and then assaulted the fort. The defenders broke and ran, leaving fifteen dead. At almost the same time in the harbor, the gunboat *Dolphin* took a Spanish [blockhouse] under fire from 2000 yards off the beach. The site was quickly destroyed and the occupants scurried inland.

During mid-afternoon the men on the ridge were allowed to go to the beach to wash. The Spanish waited until a large group had disrobed and gone into the surf before they opened fire. Naked Marines scrambled ashore under a hail of bullets, and clothed only in hats and cartridge belts, ran for cover with rifles in hand . . . .

The question to be considered prior to following the battle into the third night, is why Lieutenant Colonel Robert W. Huntington had taken counsel of his fear. To those around him during the battle he appeared to be "calm and watchful . . . going the rounds as though night attacks were merely a matter of ordinary detail. Surely soldiers never had better examples afforded."[14] A veteran of the Corps since winning a commission in 1861, he had served as a platoon leader in Reynold's Battalion during the retreat at the ill-fated First Battle of Bull Run--an event reported as "the first instance in Marine Corps history where any portion of its members turned their backs to the enemy."[15] As a Captain he commanded a company during the Panama Expedition of 1885. He was a staunch member of the Marine reformers. The fact that he had shown personal bravery throughout the night unlike several of his subordinate officers who had gone to ground, further clouds the question. Why he faltered when the firing had almost stopped, may be found in his age and health. The youngest captain in the battalion was George Elliott at 51 years of age. Major Henry Clay Cochrane was 56. Huntington was of the same generation--old men fighting a young man's war against an enemy force at least three times larger in numbers in temperatures that reached above the hundred degree mark throughout their time in Cuba. He had been sick since Key West, and remained in poor health throughout the campaign. Reflecting to his son, he wrote that, " . . . I am sure six months of active campaign would clear Huntington, Harrington and Elliott and Spicer off the rolls of this battalion. I am not sure about Cochrane because he takes such selfish care of himself that he might last . . . ."[16]

From a tactical standpoint, the disposition of the battalion followed the doctrine and teaching of the day. The issue of the location of the camp and the lack of entrenchments spark immediate controversy--then and today. From first viewing, Huntington was not happy with the location selected for the Marine camp. In a letter to Commandant Heywood he wrote that: "The hill occupied by us is a faulty position but the best to be had at this point. The ridge slopes downward and to the rear to the bay; the space at the top is very small, and all the surrounding country is covered with almost impenetrable brush. The position is commanded by a mountain, the ridge of which is about 1,200 yards to the rear."[17]

Two days after Huntington had written the letter, Bowman McCalla wrote an endorsement in which he also addressed the issue of location and stated that: ". . . Referring to paragraph 4, page 2, the position occupied by the Marines has been pronounced by Major General Perez, of the Cuban army, on the 17th instant, (curiously the same day that Huntington had registered his complaint) to be the only tenable position on the bay which could be successfully held by a small force. He also stated that 5,000 Spaniards could not take it. If the marine position is commanded by a mountain ridge, that mountain ridge is commanded in turn by the ten 5-inch rapid fire guns of the *Marblehead*, and of other ships as may be here. The mistake of locating the camp between the main position and the outpost was corrected on the 11th instant, at my suggestion . . . ."[18] Reading the endorsement, it appears that McCalla had suddenly decided to place great stock in the Cubans, something that he failed to do prior to the battles. For whatever the reason, both men had seized upon the matter as soon as the fighting had ended, causing one to wonder if both did not anticipate some type of trouble from higher headquarters.

While Huntington appears to have been firmly based in the concept of tactics, the application appears to have been somewhat naive or con-fused . . . . in a letter to his son, Huntington wrote: "We went ashore like innocents . . . The night of the 11th we were attacked . . . from seven different positions . . . I can tell you I was bothered how to stand, but more by good luck than good management, and by firing at every flash or any noise, we got through."[19]

Trying to piece the together the situation on the night of 12-13 June, it, is clear that no consolidated operations order had been issued. The outposts were still located at such a distance from the main camp that they could not be reinforced quickly. Again, they operated as islands in the night. The *Marblehead* was not informed of the location of the outposts . . . . If there was a strategy within the battalion, then it was one built around creating a wall of bullets. Huntington thought that ". . . no other course was open to us."[20] The official after action report addressed that situation, stating that it appeared as:

if ammunition was being wasted for it was

impossible to see anyone to fire at, so great was
the darkness. But we all became satisfied
afterwards that the cartridges were well
expended for it convinced the enemy that we
were well provided with ammunition and
prevented him from attempting to get anywhere
near us or in fact to show himself in the small
open space to our front . . . .We had no
information as to the strength of the force
opposed to us but did know that the Spaniards
had 7000 men at Guantanamo, only twelve
miles distant. Furthermore we knew that we had
no chance of reinforcements, as the Army had
not even left the United States. Admiral
Sampson could spare no ships from the
blockade to assist us by landing an armed force,
so that we knew our salvation was in our own
hands . . . .[21]

Cuzco Well

The day proved quiet. Attempts at repairing the Colt machine guns, which
had broken during the night were completed. The cable ship *Adria*, the Glomar
Explorer of her day, was successful in retrieving and splicing the submarine
cable that the *Marblehead* had cut two weeks earlier. Direct contact with
Washington would be possible the next day. Colonel Tomas of the Cuban
insurgents arrived in camp and brought with him an additional 80 men. He
suggested to Col Huntington ". . . the advisibility of sending out an attacking
force in the morning to surprise the Spaniards and if possible to destroy their
well, which project if successful would force them to retreat to Guantanamo
their nearest water supply. Col. Huntington seeing that something desperate
must be done to relieve the terrible strain under which his command was
suffering, no one having had any rest or sleep for 100 hours, readily consented to
the plan . . . ."[22]

Captain George F. Elliott, soon to become the Brigadier General
Commandant five years hence, was selected to lead the force to take the well at
Cuzco . . . .

The hill ahead was almost vertical. At twelve noon the thermometer stood at
105 degrees. Although Elliott was not familiar with the terrain, it was clear that
whoever could reach the top of the hill first--and hold it--would dominate the
valley around Cuzco Well. Moving at a quickened pace, Stephen Crane heard
George Elliott yell, "Now men, straight up this hill. The men charged up against
the cactus, and, because I cared for the opinion of others, I found myself tagging
along close at Elliotts heels."[23]

The fight was now in the hands of the junior officers and sergeants. Cresting the hill, they discovered that the ridge was no more than fifteen feet wide . . . . Horseshoe in shape it opened to the sea and commanded the encircled valley below. The *commandancia* of the Spanish garrison was in plain view, three hundred yards below, as was the well. Nearby was a thicket of shrubbery with large leaves which covered almost an acre. Going to ground on the razor back ridge, the Marines and Cubans lay in the noonday sun and poured a stream of fire into the enemy below.

Lieutenant Magill with 40 Marines had moved up on the ridge to the left of Elliotts' position and had begun to pour a flanking fire into the enemy below. Meanwhile, the *Dolphin* had moved towards the beach and again opened fire. Unbeknowest to her, Magill's men were now on the gun-target line. The shells went over the Spanish and crashed into Magill's position. Cursing Marines went to ground. At this point . . . it became necessary to stop the *Dolphin* at once. Captain Elliott . . . called hurriedly for another signalman. Sergeant Quick arose and announced that he was a signalman. He produced from somewhere a blue polka dot neckerchief as large as a quilt. He tied it on a long crooked stick. Then he went to the top of the ridge, and turning his back to the Spanish fire, began to signal the *Dolphin* . . . Suddenly someone shouted:

> There they go! See 'em! See 'em! Forty rifles rang out. A number of figures and been seen to break from the other side of the thicket. The Spaniards were running. Now began one of the most extraordinary games ever played in war. The skirmish suddenly turned into something that was like a grim and frightful field sport. It did not appear so then for many reasons but when one reflects, it was trap-shooting . . . There were two open spaces which in their terror they did not attempt to avoid. One was 400 yards away, the other was 800. You could see the little figures, like pieces of white paper . . . Soon it was arranged on a system . . . a line of Marines was formed into a firing squad. Sometimes we could see a whole covey vanish miraculously after the volley . . .[24]

Lieutenant Francisco Batista, one corporal, and sixteen privates made up the captured Spanish. One hundred and sixty bodies of their comrades littered the area. When interrogated, Batista revealed that the Spanish force was made up of six companies of the *Siminca* and *Principe Regiments* with two companies of *Practicos*. This force had been brought together from Guantanamo City and Caimanera the day previous, apparently with the intent of launching an assault against McCalla Hill . . . .

As the sun began its descent into the west, the march back to Camp McCalla began . . . . The night was quiet. Cochrane wrote that there:

> . . . was no attack today. The Spanish seem to have been driven off. Precautions continue. All rest in shoes and clothes and men carry rifles to meals . . . Most of the men are worn out and sleeping. Some so tired they could not eat. After breakfast half the command went to the beach for a bath. We were red with dirt, black streaks from smoke from our guns and our faces and hands covered with sores from the poisonous weeds we had been laying on. The red dirt wouldn't start with salt water and we had no soap or brushes, but the bath made us feel better any way.[25]

In Retrospect

In the space of four days, the battles for Guantanamo Bay marked the end of one era and the beginning of another. The battles were the crucible in which a new Corps of Marines was shaped. Forged in the fire of combat, using the weapons of modern warfare employed with tactics that reflected the best thinking of the day, a new generation of Marines was blooded.

In the Marine Corps classic, *Soldiers of the Sea,* Robert Debs Heinl, Jr. wrote that: "The operations of Huntington's battalion highlight important developments of the new Marine Corps of 1898. Like Reynold's battalion in 1861, the battalion was part of the Atlantic Fleet: an embryonic Fleet Marine Force if anybody in those days had thought of the term. Its organization was not that of the casual ship's landing party of the 19th century, but that of a self-contained unit built around the combined arms team. Its mobile base of operations was an 1898 attack transport, for the *Panther,* specifically fitted for expeditionary operations, was referred to repeatedly at the time as the Marine transport. The mission of Huntington's battalion was to land on hostile shores to seize an advanced base for the fleet . . . In other words, by action and not by theory, Colonel Huntington's fleet landing force had set a pattern for employment of U.S. Marines which would still stand more than half a century and three wars later."[26]

Writing in *Semper Fidelis,* Alan R. Millett noted that "Compared with the fighting soon to follow in the Army's campaign against Santiago, the action at Guantanamo was a minor skirmish of no consequence to the course of the war . . . ."[27]

In fact, Guantanamo Bay was the linch-pin to the entire invasion of Cuba and the ultimate capitulation of the Spanish government. Had the Marines retreated or been driven off by the Spanish, the Army landing at Santiago de Cuba would most certainly have been postponed. Simply put, it was a near thing.

Without a coaling station for the fleet, naval vessels would have had to journey to Key West to replenish their bunkers. Certainly the loss of Guantanamo Bay would have given the President and the War Department reason to pause. One can safely postulate that the invasion would have been postponed until the end of the malaria season in the fall, something that was part of the original war plan. Given the confusion of the Army at Tampa and the lack of planning and preparation for war, an assault against an enemy that had just driven American forces off a tactical landing in Cuba would have been relooked.

The strategic diversion that the seizure of Guantanamo Bay gave the United States, and with it the fixing in place of Spanish troops, would have been lost. Spanish morale, inspired by a victory, might well have caused the Spanish high command to awaken from its lethargy. A Marine withdrawal or defeat--politically one and the same--in spite of the loss of the Spanish fleet, would have stiffened their resolve after beating the American "mercenaries." The Spanish government, repeatedly blind to the honest estimate of the situation by men of the caliber of Admiral Cervera would have further locked their shields together, thus further blinding themselves to the facts.

A retreat in the face of the enemy would have meant the end of the Marine Corps. The Navy would have never tolerated a shipmate who turned tail. Interestingly, all who had knowledge of the attempt to withdraw remained silent. Bowman McCalla wrote of the affair in his autobiography in later life, but never called attention to the implications of such an event.

Henry Clay Cochrane interviewed all Marines who had knowledge of the near debacle and recorded their comments in his journal. Even when he could have used the information in a bid for the commandant's office, he remained silent. For those who question the impact of the near breaking of the First Battalion of Marines, it is instructive to note that in the 43 year span of his daily journal entries, the "100 hours of fighting" was the only time that he did not record in depth the events of the day. The intensity of the fighting was such that there simply was not time to place pen to paper. It was not until August, 1898 that he was able to catch up on his diary entries.

It would be another thirty-five years before the Marine Corps would finally seize upon and develop the amphibious mission that eluded it for so long. In 1945, a picture was taken of Marines raising the stars and Stripes on the Island of Iwo Jima. It was said that that the picture of that flag raising ensured that there would be a Corps for another five hundred years. If that was the case, then the flag raised by the First Battalion of Marines on McCalla Hill on the 12th of June 1898 ensured that there would be a Marine Corps.

Notes

---

1. McCalla to Sampson, 1Jun1898 (McCalla File, Naval Historical Center).
2. *New York Herald*, 12Jun1898.
3. Journal of the 1st Marine Battalion, Apr-Sep 1898.
4. Ibid.
5. Henry Clay Cochrane, diary entry, 12Jun1898, Cochrane Papers, Marine Corps Historical Center.

6. R. W. Stallman and E. R. Hagemann, eds., *The War Dispatches of Stephen Crane*, (New York, NY, 1964), p. 363, hereafter *The War Dispatches of Stephen Crane*.

7. Ibid.

8. Henry Clay Cochrane ltr to Stephen Crane, 18May1899, Cochrane Papers.

9. Frank Keeler, *The Journal of Frank Keeler*, (Quantico, VA, 1967, Marine Corps Paper Series, Number One), p. 12.

10. Cochrane, diary entry, 12Jun1898.

11. Ibid.

12. Bowman H. McCalla, "Autobiography," MS, pt III (copy in Navy Library, Naval Historical Center).

13. *New York Herald*, 14Jun1898.

14. Ibid.

15. Col Cmdt to SecNav, 26July1861 as quoted in David M. Sullivan, *The United States Marine Corps in the Civil War--The First Year* (Shippensburg, PA, 1997) p. 145.

16. Huntington ltr to son, 19Jun1898, Col R. W. Huntington Papers, Marine Corps Historical Center.

17. Huntington ltr to Col Cmdt, 17Jun1898.

18. McCalla ltr to Sampson, 19Jun1898 (McCalla File, Naval Historical Center).

19. Huntington ltr to son, 18Jun1898.

20. Ibid., 19Jun1898.

21. Journal of the 1st Marine Battalion, pp. 30-31.

22. Ibid.

23. *The War Dispatches of Stephen Crane*, p. 364.

24. Ibid, p. 365.

25. Cochrane, diary entry, 14Jun1898.

26. Robert D. Heinl *Soldiers of the Sea: The U.S. Marines Corps, 1775-1962* (Annapolis, MD, 1962), p. 117.

27. Allan R. Millett, *Semper Fidelis: The History of the U.S. Marine Corps* (New York, NY, 1980), p.133.

Article reprinted with permission from the author of this article that appeared in
Prologue, Quarterly of the National Archives and Records Administration,
Spring 1998.

"New Glory to Its Already Gallant Record";
The First Marine Battalion in the Spanish-American War
by Trevor K. Plante

On April 16, 1898, five days before war began between the United States
and Spain, in preparation for what he believed was an inevitable conflict, Secretary of the Navy John D. Long ordered the commandant of the Marine Corps,
Charles Heywood, to organize one battalion of marines for expeditionary duty
with the North Atlantic Squadron. By war's end, the First Marine Battalion
could boast they had fought in the first land battle in Cuba and had been the first
to raise the American flag on the island. They could also claim that of the six
marines killed in action in the Spanish-American War, five were from their unit.
The battalion yielded one Medal of Honor recipient, and two of the unit's officers would later serve as commandants of the Marine Corps.[1] The First Marine
Battalion's action in the Caribbean and its favorable press coverage gave the
American public and the U.S. Navy a glimpse of the Marine Corps of the future.

At approximately 9:40 P.M. on the evening of February 15, 1898, an explosion sank the USS *Maine* in Havana Harbor, Cuba. The ship was manned by 290
sailors, 39 marines, and 26 officers. Of these officers and men, 253 were killed
either by the explosion or drowning; seven more died later of wounds. Included
in this number of killed were twenty-eight enlisted men from the *Maine*'s marine
detachment.[2]

The cause of the explosion was a source of contention between the United
States and Spain. On March 21 a U.S. naval court of inquiry called to investigate
the *Maine* incident concluded that a mine in the harbor had caused the explosion.
A Spanish naval court of inquiry reported the next day that the explosion had
been due to internal causes.[3] Although the cause was never established to either
side's satisfaction, the event eventually led Congress to declare on April 25 that
a state of war existed starting April 21, 1898.

The job of organizing the First Marine Battalion was assigned to Lt. Col.
Robert W. Huntington, who had just recently taken command of the Marine Barracks in Brooklyn, New York. Huntington was approaching almost forty years of
service in the Marine Corps, having been commissioned soon after the start of
the Civil War.[4]

On April 17, Lt. Colonel Huntington began organizing the battalion, initially
formed into four companies. A proposed second battalion was never formed because a number of marines were still needed to protect navy yards and installa-
tions in the United States. Instead, the First Marine Battalion was enlarged to six
companies—five companies of infantry and one artillery. Each company had a

complement of 103 men: 1 first sergeant, 4 sergeants, 4 corporals, 1 drummer, 1 fifer, and 92 privates. The battalion was also accorded a quartermaster, adjutant, and surgeon. The color guard comprised 1 sergeant and 2 corporals.[5]

Commandant Charles Heywood made mobilizing the battalion his highest priority. For this reason, both he and the Marine Corps quartermaster made sure that Charles McCawley, the battalion's quartermaster, had the supplies he needed or the funds to get them. On April 18 the commandant went to New York to personally observe preparations, staying until the twenty-third.[6] The battalion quartermaster supplied the unit with ammunition, camp equipment, mosquito netting, woolen and linen clothing, wheelbarrows, pushcarts, pickaxes, shelter tents, and medical stores.[7]

On April 22 the marines were ready to sail. The men marched down the main street of the navy yard to the dock and at 5 P.M. boarded the recently purchased USS *Panther*. Lt. Colonel Huntington noted the "intense excitement manifested by people along the line of march, Navy Yard, docks, harbor front and shipping.[8] At eight o'clock, as the ship pulled away from the dock, the naval band played "The Girl I Left Behind Me" to send off the marines.[9]

The men were overcrowded on the *Panther* because the vessel was too small to hold such a large unit. The ship's dining room accommodated only two hundred men, requiring three mess calls per meal.[10] The ship, originally the *Venezuela*, had been recently purchased and converted to carry about 400 men, but after the additional companies were added, the battalion numbered close to 650 officers and men. The marines expected these crowded conditions to be temporary. At Key West, Florida, they were supposed to transfer to the *Resolute*, which was capable of carrying one thousand men and officers.[11] Unfortunately, the marine battalion would not see the *Resolute* until after it arrived in Cuba in June. The battalion reached Fort Monroe off Hampton Roads, Virginia, on the evening of April 23 and waited for their convoy vessel to arrive. An escort was necessary, for the *Panther* was ill-equipped to defend itself should it encounter an enemy vessel. While at Hampton Roads, Maj. Percival C. Pope and 1st Lt. James E. Mahoney joined the battalion.[12] On April 26 the *Panther* left Virginia accompanied by the cruiser *Montgomery*.

It was not long before tension developed on the *Panther* between the officers of the navy and the Marine Corps. Much of this strain was due to overcrowding, but some stemmed from questions regarding the men's required duty and who was responsible for discipline.[13] Despite these problems, Huntington made the most of precious time. On the twenty-sixth the battalion began its first drills on board ship. The marine infantry companies were armed with Lee straight-pull 6mm rifles. The artillery company was equipped with four three-inch rapid-fire guns. From 2 P.M. to 4 P.M., Companies A, B, C, D, and E (the infantry companies) drilled in volley and mass firing; each man using ten rounds each. Next, the artillery company fired one round from each of the four artillery pieces and then, like the infantry companies, drilled in volley and mass firing of the Lee rifles using ten rounds each.[14]

The *Panther* arrived at Key West, on April 29.[15] On May 24 Comdr. George C. Reiter, of the *Panther* ordered the battalion to disembark and set up camp. This action prompted the commandant of the Marine Corps to telegraph Key West inquiring why the battalion was unloaded when the *Panther* was the sole transport of the marine battalion and had no other duties.[16] While the battalion remained in camp for two weeks, monotony was eased by the arrival of supplies that were more suited for tropical weather. The marines exchanged their heavier blue uniforms for new brown linen campaign suits. With the lighter, cooler uniforms came new-style shoes and lightweight underwear, all very popular items with the officers and men. Huntington continued drilling while at Key West, and the battalion received daily instruction and target practice with their rifles.[17]

The officers were watching the men's health very closely. Huntington was keenly aware of health dangers caused by bad water and exposure to disease. Orders outlined procedures pertaining to water, cooking, and clothing. Water was prepared on board ship and brought to the marines on shore. No one was to drink unboiled water. Cooks were told how to prepare food and water for cooking, and any marine struck by diarrhea was to report it immediately to the medical officer. The men were also ordered to change their clothing whenever it got wet.[18]

While in Key West the battalion sent small detachments to participate in several funeral services held for navy personnel. Colonel Huntington also detailed men to patrol the streets of Key West to guard against men causing trouble while on liberty. The unit received a number of Colt machine guns, and navy Assistant Surgeon John Blair Gibbs also joined the battalion.[19]

On June 7 the naval base at Key West received a telegram from the acting secretary of the navy stressing, "Send the Marine Battalion at once to Sampson without waiting for the Army send Yosemite as convoy."[20] The long wait was over, and that day the battalion finally sailed for Cuba, leaving behind Major Pope sick in the hospital.

On the voyage south, during the night of the ninth, the marines' transport collided with the *Scorpion*, causing damage to the converted yacht's stern rail.[21] The *Panther* arrived off Santiago, Cuba, at 7 A.M. on June 10. Huntington reported to Adm. William T. Sampson, the commander in chief of the North Atlantic Fleet, on board the flagship *New York* and received orders to report to Comdr. Bowman H. McCalla of the *Marblehead*, commanding at Guantanamo Bay.[22]

Shortly after the war began, Admiral Sampson established a blockade of major Cuban ports. Guantanamo Bay was chosen as a good site for coaling navy vessels. Guantanamo has both an inner and outer bay, and the outer bay offered a good anchorage site for ships because of its depth. Sampson sent the marine battalion to protect any ships in the bay from being harassed from Spanish troops ashore.

McCalla had entered Guantanamo Bay on June 7 to clear the outer harbor. A battery near the telegraph station at Cayo del Toro on the western side of the bay fired on the U.S. vessels *Marblehead* and *Yankee*. The Spanish gunboat *Sandoval* soon came down the channel from Caimanera. The two U.S. Navy ships opened fire, silencing the gun battery and forcing the *Sandoval* to return back up the channel. On the morning of June 10, McCalla ordered marines from the *Marblehead* and *Oregon* to conduct a reconnaissance of an area just inside Guantanamo Bay. Capt. M. D. Goodrell led forty marines from the *Oregon* and twenty marines from the *Marblehead*. Goodrell selected a site for the marine battalion to establish their camp, and McCalla then sent him to brief Huntington on his intended position.[23]

The scene outside Guantanamo Bay was an awesome sight on June 10, for the outer bay was dominated by ships. The U.S. Navy vessels present were the cruisers *Marblehead, Yankee,* and *Yosemite;* the battleship *Oregon;* the torpedo boat *Porter;* the gunboat *Dolphin;* the collier *Abarenda;* the *Vixen* and *Panther;* and several private vessels carrying newspaper reporters. The battalion began landing at two o'clock. Four companies disembarked while the other two remained on board to help unload supplies.[24] The marines were ordered to stack their rifles and begin unloading supplies from the *Panther*. Men from Company C, the first company ashore, were deployed up the top of the hill as skirmishers to protect the landing against enemy attack.[25] Sgt. Richard Silvey, Company C, First Marine Battalion, planted the American flag for the first time on Cuban soil. One hundred and fifty feet below the hill where the American flag now flew, houses and huts were in flames, and smoke rose from the small fishing village. McCalla had ordered the marines to burn the village on Fisherman's Point for health reasons, and no one was allowed to enter into any buildings. The remaining two companies disembarked on June 11.[26]

Huntington believed the hill chosen for his camp to be a "faulty position." He did not want his men on top of a hill where "the ridge slopes downward and to the rear from the bay" and was "commanded by a mountain, the ridge of which is about 1,200 yards to the rear."[27] The battalion's position was partially protected by the navy vessels in the bay. Several times the battalion commander requested McCalla's permission to move the marines from this site to a more defensible position, but these requests were repeatedly denied.[28] Despite this difference, Huntington named the marines' position Camp McCalla. Lt. Herbert Draper raised the American flag on a flagpole for the first time in Cuba at Camp McCalla.[29] Eleven days later, Huntington sent this same flag to the commandant of the Marine Corps:

Guantanamo Bay
June 22', 1898

My Dear Colonel:

I sent you by this mail in a starch box the
first U.S. flag hoisted in Cuba. This flag was
hoisted on the 11th June and during the various
attacks on our camp floated serene above us. At

times, during the darkness, for a moment, it has
been illumined by the search light from the
ships. When bullets were flying, and the sight of
the flag upon the midnight sky has thrilled our
hearts.

I trust you may consider it worthy of preservation, with suitable inscription, at Headquarters. It was first lowered at sunset last evening.

I am very respectfully
R.W. Huntington
Lt Col Commd'g Bat'n

In an attack on the marine outposts, Privates Dumphy and McColgan of
Company D were both killed.[30] The bodies were first mistakenly reported mutilated. It was hard to tell the two apart, for both men had received a number of
bullet wounds to the face; McColgan suffered twenty-one shots to the head and
Dumphy fifteen.[31] Soon the enemy made five small separate attacks on the marines' camp. All of these were repulsed. At about 1 A.M. a superior number of
Spanish forces made a more combined attack. In this assault Assistant Surgeon
Gibbs was killed by a bullet to the head.[32] Sporadic firing back and forth continued throughout the night. Using a lesson learned from the Cubans, the enemy
was making good use of camouflage by covering their bodies with leaves and fo-
liage from the jungle.[33] The smokeless powder of the Spanish Mauser rifles also
made the enemy harder to detect.

On the morning of the twelfth, Sgt. Charles H. Smith was killed. Colonel
Huntington moved much of the camp down the hill closer to the beach to a place
known as Playa del Este. Huntington had the marines entrench their positions on
the crest of the hill. Eventually earthworks were constructed in the shape of a
square, with the blockhouse in its center. The artillery pieces were placed in the
corners of the square, and the Colt machine guns were along the sides. Several
newspaper reporters came ashore at the lower camp and offered assistance. They
helped the marines bring the artillery pieces and Colt machine guns up the hill.
The earthworks were constructed about chest high. On the outside of the dirt
walls, trenches were dug measuring about five feet deep and ten feet wide. Later
on June 12, Pvt. Goode Taurman died during an engagement.[34]

Harry Jones, the chaplain from the USS *Texas*, conducted a funeral service
for the slain marines. He had heard about the marine deaths, and after receiving
permission from his ship's captain, offered his services to the battalion commander. A lieutenant and marine guards from the *Texas* provided the funeral escort. Colonel Huntington, the battalion's surgeon, and as many officers and men

who could be spared from the trenches attended the ceremony. The camp was still being harassed by the enemy, and at one point Jones dove into a trench to escape enemy fire. When he got back to his feet, the chaplain found that the marines were still standing at parade rest awaiting the ceremony. The service was conducted almost entirely under enemy fire. The marines' Lee rifles and Colt machine guns returned fire. The chaplain was still being fired on when he returned to his launch with two reporters.[35]

McCalla ordered the captain of the *Panther* to unload fifty thousand rounds of 6mm ammunition. McCalla also cleared up some of the confusion regarding duties by stating in the same order, "In the future do not require Col. Huntington to break out and land his stores or ammo. Use your own officers and crew."[36]

On the night of the twelfth, Sgt. Maj. Henry Good was killed. Another attack was made on the camp the next morning. After almost three days of constant harassment from the enemy either by attack or sniper fire, Huntington decided to take action. He issued an order to destroy a well used by Spanish troops. On the fourteenth, Capt. George F. Elliott set out with Companies C and D and approximately fifty Cubans to destroy the well at Cuzco, which was the only water supply for the enemy within twelve miles. The well, about six miles from the camp, was close to shore, and the USS *Dolphin* was sent to support the mission from sea.[37]

Upon leaving camp, Huntington asked Elliott if he would like to take an officer to act as adjutant. The captain declined, citing the shortage of officers present for duty as the reason. Instead, upon learning that a reporter was accompanying his force, Elliott requested Stephen Crane to act as an aide if needed. Crane's *Red Badge of Courage* had been published in 1895. The marine officer later reported that Crane carried messages to the company commanders while on this mission.[38]

The marines soon engaged in a terrific fight. Near the well they encountered great resistance from superior enemy forces. Lt. Louis Magill was sent with fifty marines and ten Cubans to reinforce Elliott. He was to cut off the enemy's line of retreat but was blocked by the *Dolphin*'s gunfire. To help direct the naval gunfire, Sgt. John Quick volunteered to signal the ship. Using a blue flag obtained from the Cubans, the sergeant began to signal the ship with his back to the enemy and bullets flying all around him.

Later, two lieutenants with fifty men each were also sent to help Elliott, but neither participated in the fight. The Spanish escaped, but not before the marines inflicted a crippling blow. Elliott's force had a remarkably low casualty rate. Only two Cubans had been killed, and two Cubans and three marine privates had been wounded. Lt. Wendell C. Neville had also been injured descending a mountainside during the engagement. Twenty-three marines suffered from heat exhaustion and had to be brought back on the *Dolphin*.[39] McCalla offered his opinion stating, "I need hardly call attention to the fact that the marines would have suffered much less had their campaign hats not been on the *Resolute*" (the ship had not yet arrived at Guantanamo Bay).[40] Overall, the mission was considered a success because the well had been destroyed. McCalla stated, "the expedition was most successful; and I can not say too much in praise of the officers and men who took part in it."[41] In fact, after the action, enemy attacks and sniper fire on the marine camp became almost nonexistent.

The following day, naval gunfire from the *Texas*, *Marblehead*, and *Suwanee* destroyed the Spanish fort at Caimanera on the eastern side of the bay. The three ships were accompanied by two press boats.[42] Three days later, Huntington received orders that no reporters or civilians were to be allowed to land near his camp or enter his lines without a pass from McCalla. Those who disobeyed this order were to be arrested and taken on board the *Marblehead* as prisoners.[43]

At 4:30 P.M. on June 20 the USS *Resolute* arrived and unloaded stores for the battalion. The next day the captain of the *Panther* received orders from Admiral Sampson to transfer all stores including ammunition and quartermaster stores to the *Resolute*.[44] The marines had finally received their larger transport. On June 24 the battalion placed headstones over the graves of Gibbs, Good, McColgan, Dumphy, and Taurman. A detail was sent out to place a headstone over the remains of Sergeant Smith, whose body could not be brought back to camp.[45]

McCalla ordered a reconnaissance to determine if Spanish forces still occupied the extremities of Punta del Jicacal on the eastern side of Guantanamo Bay. The enemy had been firing on American vessels from this point. At about 3 A.M. on the twenty-fifth, Huntington led a detail of 240 men encompassing Companies C and E of the First Marine Battalion and 60 Cubans under Colonel Thomas. The force used fifteen boats from the *Helena*, *Annapolis*, and *Bancroft* to travel to the other side of the bay. The landing was supported by the *Marblehead* and *Helena*, which took positions close to the beach south and west of the point. The landing force went ashore but made no contact with the enemy. They did, however, find signs that approximately one hundred men had been in the area and had left the previous day. The landing party withdrew at about 7:30 A.M.[46]

On July 3 the Spanish fleet was virtually annihilated during the naval battle of Santiago de Cuba, and the U.S. Navy became responsible for a very large number of Spanish prisoners. It was decided to send the prisoners north to Portsmouth, New Hampshire, along with marines to guard them. On July 4 and 5, McCalla detached sixty marines from the battalion, including Capt. Allen Kelton and 1st Lt. Franklin Moses to join the *Harvard*. Prisoners on the *St. Louis* would be guarded by Capt. Benjamin Russell commanding twenty-one marines from the *Marblehead* and twenty-nine marines and a lieutenant from the *Brooklyn*.[47] On July 10 the *Harvard* sailed north for New Hampshire, arriving with the Spanish prisoners at Camp Long just outside Portsmouth.

On the twelfth, McCalla ordered the harbor at Guantanamo under quarantine, with Huntington in charge of enforcing this order. On July 23 a letter from the commandant was read at parade acknowledging receipt of the first flag raised over Camp McCalla and praising the officers and men of the battalion for their conduct. Three days later, a large force of about eighty Cubans left camp. These men had fought and patrolled with the marines since June 12.[48]

The inactivity of the battalion soon led some marines to create their own diversions. On June 29, two privates from Company E left camp without permission and boarded a schooner in the harbor. They remained on board for several hours and later were reported displaying "improper conduct." Both were disciplined with ten days at double irons. Another private was caught buying liquor using a Spanish dollar.[49]

Pvt. Robert Burns supplied some of the men with a good story to tell. One night while on guard duty, the private heard something moving in the bushes approximately one hundred yards ahead. Having orders to shoot anything that moved, the private gave three verbal warnings to halt. There being no response, and still hearing movement in the bushes, Burns fired his weapon into the bushes. In the morning, a sergeant took six men to investigate the situation and found that Burns had not fired on the enemy but rather had downed a very large black pig.[50]

On August 5 the battalion broke camp and embarked on the *Resolute*. The transport left Guantanamo Bay four days later for Manzanillo under convoy of USS *Newark* to assist in the capture of the town.[51] The *Resolute, Suwanee, Hist, Osceola, Alvarado,* and *Newark* all approached Manzanillo and anchored three miles outside town on the twelfth. The *Alvarado* was sent under a flag of truce to demand a surrender from the military commander. The commander replied that Spanish military code would not allow him to surrender without being forced by a siege or military operation. Captain Goodrich allowed time for noncombatants to vacate the town before beginning the naval bombardment. Naval gunfire started at 3:40 and lasted until 4:15, when it appeared that flags of truce were flying over some of the town's buildings. Goodrich ordered a cease-fire, and the navy vessels flying flags of truce approached. The vessels were soon fired upon, and the *Newark* returned fire. The action was soon broken off, and all ships anchored for the night at 5:30 P.M. Naval gunfire resumed at 5:20 A.M. the next morning, and when daylight came, white flags were flying over many buildings in town. A small boat from Manzanillo approached the navy ships and brought word to Captain Goodrich that an armistice had been proclaimed: the war was over. The captain of the *Newark*, observing the disappointment of the battalion commander, reported, "As part of the contemplated plan of operations was the landing of some or all of the marines of Colonel Huntington's command. This officer's regret at the loss of an opportunity to win additional distinction for his corps and himself was only equaled by his careful study of the necessities of the case and his zealous entrance into the spirit of the enterprise."[52]

On the eighteenth, the *Resolute* took on board 275 men from four U.S. Army light artillery battery detachments for transport to Montauk Point, Long Island. The next day, the ship encountered rough seas, and most of the army detachment and marines were sick.[53] After leaving Long Island, *Resolute* headed for New Hampshire, arriving at Portsmouth on August 26. The commandant had personally chosen this location for the battalion to recover from the tropical heat of the Caribbean. Huntington named their new site Camp Heywood in honor of the commandant of the Marine Corps. Six of the battalion's officers received promotions for gallantry, and the commandant commended all the battalion's officers and men and noted the favorable press coverage of the battalion's first few days in Cuba. On September 19, Huntington received orders to disband the battalion.[54]

On reporting that he had dispatched marines to their new duty stations, Huntington concluded his report by stating, "I believe this encampment has been of great benefit to the health of the battalion."[55] The adjutant and inspector of the Marine Corps also found the men at Camp Heywood in good health. In his inspection report the adjutant concluded, "It is worthy of note that during the entire service of this battalion of 25 commissioned officers and 623 enlisted men, from April 22, when they embarked on board their transport at New York to the present time, there has not been a single case of yellow fever nor death from disease of any kind and but few cases of serious illness; a remarkable fact, when it is considered that these men were the first United States troops to land in Cuba, and during their entire service they were subject to the same climatic influences as other troops, among whom fever, diarrhea, dysentery, etc., caused so many casualties."[56]

The quartermaster of the battalion reported to the commandant that because of the use of distilled water for drinking and cooking and the sanitary conditions aided by sufficient food and clothing, 98 percent of the battalion was brought home fit for duty, and "not a single man of the command died from disease."[57] The men had used only distilled water obtained daily from the *Panther, Resolute,* or *Vulcan.* McCawley also had had the foresight to purchase empty wine casks in Key West for use as water containers, increasing the amount of water that could be kept on hand at camp. The excellent health of the battalion can be attributed to this careful preparation of water.

On September 18 a parade was held in the streets of Portsmouth.[58] After the battalion was disbanded, detachments headed for New York, Philadelphia, Norfolk, Washington, and Annapolis left Portsmouth together and passed through the city of Boston. The Washington detachment consisted of 3 officers and 164 men who arrived in Washington on September 22. That morning President McKinley informed the commandant of the Marine Corps that he wanted to review the detachment. Remnants of the battalion were led by the U.S. Marine Band from the Marine Barracks in Washington, D.C. The parade proceeded despite heavy rains while President McKinley and several officers reviewed the troops.[59]

Individual honors were bestowed upon Sergeant Quick and Assistant Surgeon Gibbs. Sgt. John Quick was awarded the Medal of Honor for "cool and gallant conduct" in signaling the *Dolphin* on June 14, 1898, at Cuzco, Cuba.[60] The secretary of war honored John Gibbs, the assistant surgeon killed at Guantanamo, four months after his death by naming an army hospital in Lexington, Kentucky, after him.[61]

Although the majority of marines during the Spanish-American War served aboard ship fulfilling various duties from ship guards to gunners mates, the First Marine Battalion received such wide newspaper attention that it dominated the public view of the marines' role in the war. They received favorable press coverage not only because they were among the first to see action, but because they always encountered an enemy that had superior numbers. The battalion enhanced the reputation of the Marine Corps and showed the American public their usefulness as an American fighting force. Newspapers also reported on the low rate of disease and sickness in the battalion as opposed to the high rate found in army units.

The Spanish-American War showed the navy that the Marine Corps had a role in their future war plans. With the postwar acquisitions of the Philippines and Guam, the navy was now responsible for actively operating in the Pacific Ocean. The navy would need advanced bases and coaling stations if their ships were to successfully operate in this area. The marines would play a vital role, for these bases and coaling stations would need to be captured and held if necessary.[62]

During the Spanish-American War, the First Marine Battalion demonstrated the fast mobilization of the Marine Corps. The battalion was prepared and displayed something future marines would take pride in—the ability to be called and respond at a moment's notice. Marine Corps historian Alan Millett observed that for this era the First Marine Battalion "made the greatest contribution to the Marine Corps's reputation for combat valor and readiness."[63] The battalion could be proud of its accomplishments. The unit dominated what was seen as the Marine Corps role in the war. In his general order acknowledging the one-hundredth anniversary of the Marine Corps in 1898, the secretary of the navy proclaimed that in the war with Spain the Marine Corps added "new glory to its already gallant record."[64]

Notes

---

1. Sgt. John Henry Quick received the Medal of Honor on June 14, 1898. Capt. George F. Elliott rose quickly through the ranks and went on to become the tenth commandant of the Marine Corps serving from October 3, 1903, to November 30, 1910. First Lt. Wendell C. Neville went on to serve as commandant of the Marine Corps from March 5, 1929, to July 8, 1930.

2. "Casualties Occurring on the USS Maine," Statistical Report, Special Appendix, Bureau of Medicine and Surgery, *Annual Reports of the Navy Department for the Year 1898: Report of the Secretary of the Navy. Miscellaneous Reports* (1898), p. 793 (hereinafter cited as Navy Dept. Annual Report, 1898).

3. *Appendix to Report of Chief of Bureau of Navigation, 1898* (1898), pp. 17–18.

4. Huntington served under Maj. John G. Reynolds as a platoon leader at First Bull Run on July 21, 1861. See entry 196, Records of the Bureau of Naval Personnel, Record Group 24, National Archives and Records Administration, Washington, DC (hereinafter, records in the National Archives will be cited as RG ___, NARA); Bernard C. Nalty, *The United States Marines in the War with Spain* (rev. 1967), p. 7.

5. "Report of the Commandant of United States Marine Corps," Charles Heywood, colonel commandant, to the secretary of the navy, Sept. 24, 1898, Navy Dept. Annual Report, 1898, p. 822 (hereinafter cited as Commandant's Report).

6. Commandant of the Marine Corps to the secretary of the navy, April 23, 1898, letter #73, book 7, box 2, entry 6, Press Copies of Letters, Endorsements, and Annual Reports to the Secretary of the Navy, Feb. 1884–Jan. 1904, Records of the U.S. Marine Corps, RG 127, NARA.

7. Commandant's Report, p. 823, and Charles L. McCawley to the quartermaster, U.S. Marine Corps, Sept. 27, 1898, Navy Dept. Annual Report, 1898, p. 884.

8. Entry for April 22, "Journal of the Marine Battalion Under LtCol Robert W. Huntington, Apr.–Sept. 1898," p. 2, entry 153, RG 127, NARA (hereinafter cited as Huntington Journal).

9. John H. Clifford, *History of The First Battalion of U.S. Marines* (1930), pp. 9–10, box 15, Cochrane Collection (PC# 1), Marine Corps Historical Center (MCHC), Washington, DC. *Note:* The *Panther* was purchased as the *Venezuela* on April 19, 1898, from Red D. Line S.S. Co. See Vessels Purchased, Bureau of Construction and Repair, Navy Dept. Annual Report, 1898, p. 516. McCawley to quartermaster, Sept. 27, 1898, Navy Dept. Annual Report, 1898, p. 885.

10. Battalion Order No. 8, USS *Panther,* entry for Apr. 24, Huntington Journal, p. 53; Clifford, *History of the First Battalion,* p. 11.

11. Chief of Bureau of Navigation to colonel commandant, Apr. 22, 1898, April 1898 folder, box 46, Historical Division Letters Received, 1818–1915, entry 42, RG 127, NARA.

12. Commandant's Report, Navy Dept. Annual Report, 1898, p. 824.

13. McCawley to commandant, Jan. 8, 1900, Jan.–June 1900 file, and Huntington to commandant, Nov. 3, 1899, July–Dec. File, box 48, entry 42, RG 127, NARA.

14. Commandant's Report, Navy Dept. Annual Report, 1898, p. 824; entry for Apr. 26, Huntington Journal, p. 2.

15. Pvt. Edward A. Donahue, Company E, was sent to the U.S. Army Hospital in Key West after fracturing his arm from falling off of a Jacob's ladder, hitting the boat, and falling overboard. See entry for Apr. 29, Huntington Journal, p. 3.

16. Telegram #33, box 1, North Atlantic Station—Naval Base, Key West, Telegrams Recvd May 7–Aug. 15, 1898, Records of Naval Operating Forces, RG 313, NARA.

17. McCawley to the quartermaster, Sept. 27, 1898, Navy Dept. Annual Report, 1898, pp. 885–887.

18. Battalion Order No. 13, USS *Panther,* entry for Apr. 28, Huntington Journal, p. 58.

19. Entries for May 12, 13, and 15, Huntington Journal, pp. 5–6; Clifford, *History of the First Battalion,* p. 12.

20. Telegram #107, box 1, North Atlantic Station—Naval Base, Key West, Telegrams Recvd May 7–Aug 15, 1898, RG 313, NARA.

21. Charles L. McCawley, "The Marines at Guantanamo," (ms., n.d.), p. 11, Folder 2, McCawley Papers (PC #360), MCHC.

22. Entry for June 10, Journal, p. 8.

23. "Extracts from the Autobiography of Admiral B. H. McCalla," pp. 1–2, box 381, OH (Shore Operations), Subject File, Naval Records Collection of the Office of Naval Records and Library, RG 45, NARA; First Indorsement by B. H. McCalla, June 19, 1898, of Colonel Huntington's report of June 17, 1898, Navy Dept. Annual Report, 1898, p. 839.

24. Entry for June 10, Huntington Journal, p. 8; McCawley, "Marines at Guantanamo," pp. 12–13; McCalla Report No. 85, June 11, 1898, June 11–12 folder, box 29, Area 8 File, RG 45, NARA.

25. Clifford, *History of the First Battalion,* p. 12; Huntington to Heywood, June 17, 1898, Navy Dept. Annual Report, 1898, p. 838; McCawley, "Marines at Guantanamo," p. 13.

26. Chief signal officer, War Department, to the secretary of the navy, June 11, 1898, and McCalla Report No. 86, June 12, 1898, June 11–12 folder, box 29, Area 8 File, RG 45, NARA; McCalla, "Marines at Guantanamo," p. 11.

27. Huntington to Heywood, June 17, 1898, Navy Dept. Annual Report, 1898, pp. 838–839.

28. McCalla, "Marines at Guantanamo," p. 5.

29. McCawley to Huntington, June 10, 1902, and Huntington to McCawley, June 14, 1902, 1898—June Folder, box 47, entry 42, RG 127, NARA. These two letters identify Lieutenant Draper as raising the first flag over Camp McCalla.

30. James McColgan and William Dumphy, entry for June 11, Huntington Journal, p. 9; Huntington to Heywood, June 17, 1898, Navy Dept. Annual Report, 1898, pp. 838–839. *Note:* In several sources Dumphy's name appears as Dunphy.

31. Clifford, *History of the First Battalion,* p. 13; "Engagements at Guantanamo, Cuba, Marine Battalion, North Atlantic Fleet, June 11 to 20, 1898," Bureau of Medicine and Surgery, Navy Dept. Annual Report, 1898, p. 798; Spanish-American War volume, entry 36A, Medical Certificates and Casualty Lists, 1828–1939, Records of the Bureau of Medicine and Surgery, RG 52, NARA. On June 12 McCalla states in report no. 86 that two privates and one sergeant were killed and that their bodies were mutilated.

32. Commandant's Report, p. 824, and Huntington to Heywood, June 17, 1898, Navy Dept. Annual Report, 1898, pp. 838–839.

33. John R. Spears, *Our Navy in the War with Spain* (1898), pp. 265–266; Clifford, *History of the First Battalion,* p. 15.

34. Huntington to Heywood, June 17, 1898, Navy Dept. Annual Report, 1898, pp. 838–839; Clifford, *History of the First Battalion,* p. 15; McCawley, "Marines at Guantanamo," p. 28; "First American Fortifications in Cuba, Playa del Este, Guantanamo Bay, July 9," *The New York Times Illustrated Magazine,* July 21, 1898, p. 4, clippings file, box 2, Huntington Collection, PC #276, MCHC.

35. Chaplain's letter of Aug. 29, 1898, from USS *Texas,* copied into Huntington Journal, pp. 294–296; Spears, *Our Navy in the War with Spain,* p. 267. Chaplain Jones returned to his launch accompanied by two reporters, George Coffin of the *Journal* and T. M. Dieuaide of the *New York Sun.* An account was published in the *New York Evening Sun* on July 18.

36. McCalla to commanding officer of *Panther,* June 12, 1898, *Marblehead,* box 3, North Atlantic Station, Correspondence with Commanders of Vessels, Dec. 1897–Dec. 1899, RG 313, NARA.

37. Commandant's Report, p. 824, and Huntington to Heywood, June 17, 1898, Navy Dept. Annual Report, 1898, pp. 838–839.

38. Elliott to Huntington, June 15, 1898, ibid., p. 845.

39. McCalla to Sampson, June 16, 1898, p. 846, and Huntington to Heywood, June 17, 1898, ibid., pp. 838–839.

40. McCalla to Sampson, June 16, 1898, ibid., p. 846.

41. First Indorsement by McCalla of Elliott's Report of June 18, 1898, ibid., p. 845.

42. Squadron Bulletin No. 4, Thursday, June 16, 1898, and Squadron Bulletin No. 8, Monday, June 20, 1989, box 461, OO, Subject File, RG 45, NARA; Spears, *Our Navy in the War with Spain,* pp. 270–271; McCalla, "Marines at Guantanamo," p. 13.

43. McCalla to Huntington, June 18, 1898, *Marblehead*, box 3, North Atlantic Station, Correspondence with Commanders of Vessels, Dec. 1897–Dec. 1899, RG 313, NARA.

44. Entry for June 20, Huntington Journal, p. 17; Sampson to Comdr. George C. Reiter, June 21, 1898, 1898—June 20–21 folder, Area 8 File, RG 45, NARA.

45. Entry for June 24, Huntington Journal, p. 18. Almost a year later the bodies were dis-interred and buried in the United States. On April 29, 1899, the remains were buried in the following locations: Dumphy and Good buried at Naval Cemetery, New York; McColgan buried at Stoneham, Mass.; Smith buried in Smallwood, Md.; and Taurman buried at Richmond, Va. See 1898—April folder, box 46, entry 42, Historical Division Letters Received, 1818–1915, RG 127, NARA.

46. Entry for June 25, Huntington Journal, p. 18; Squadron Bulletin No. 13, Saturday, June 25, 1898, box 461, OO, Subject File, RG 45, NARA. On June 28 William F. Ar-nold, U.S Navy, joined the battalion as P. Asst. Surgeon; see p. 278, June, 1898 Muster Rolls, RG 127, NARA.

47. Memos (three of July 4 and one of July 5) from *New York* to McCalla, *Marblehead*, and memo for Chief of Staff from McCalla, July 7, 1898, box 3, North Atlantic Station, Correspondence with Commanders of Vessels, Dec. 1897–Dec. 1899, RG 313, NARA.

48. General Order from McCalla, July 12, 1898, *Marblehead*, box 3, North Atlantic Sta-tion, Correspondence with Commanders of Vessels, Dec. 1897–Dec. 1899, RG 313, NARA; entries for July 23, 26–27, Huntington Journal, pp. 23–24.

49. Pages 24–25, July, 1898 Muster Rolls, RG 127, NARA.

50. Clifford, *History of the First Battalion*, p. 24.

51. Entries for Aug. 5 and Aug. 9, Huntington Journal, pp. 25–26.

52. Goodrich to McCalla, Aug. 13, 1898, Navy Dept. Annual Report, pp. 842–843.

53. Entries for Aug. 18–19, Huntington Journal pp. 28–29; *Correspondence Relating to Cuba, April 15 to September 1, 1898*, vol. 1, *Correspondence Relating to the War with Spai*n (1902), pp. 234 and 240.

54. Commandant's Report, Navy Dept. Annual Report, 1898, p. 825; Huntington was promoted to colonel, Elliott advanced three numbers, Lucas to brevet captain, Neville to brevet captain, Magill to first lieutenant and brevet captain, and Bannon to brevet first lieutenant. See Huntington Journal, entry for Aug. 29, p. 28; entry for Aug. 30, copy of letter received from the commandant, pp. 31–32; and entry for Sept. 19, p. 33. Order dated Sept. 17, 1898, Order Book No. 40, pp. 898–900, box 13, Letters and Telegrams Sent to Officers Conveying Orders ("Order Books"), entry 24, RG 127, NARA.

55. Huntington to commandant, Sept. 21, 1898, 1898–September folder, box 47, entry 42, RG 127, NARA.

56. "Report of Inspection of the Marine Battalion at Camp Heywood, Seaveys Island, Portsmouth, N.H., September 14, 1898," Maj. George C. Reid, Sept. 18, 1898, Navy Dept. Annual Report, p. 849.

57. McCawley to quartermaster, Sept. 27, 1898, ibid., pp. 884–888.

58. Clifford, *History of the First Battalion*, p. 26.

59. Commandant's Report, Navy Dept. Annual Report, 1898, pp. 825–826.

60. General Order 504, Navy Department, acting secretary, Dec. 13, 1898.

61. Special Order No. 254, U.S. Army Adjutant-General, Oct. 27, 1898, Extract, *Appen-dix to Report of Chief of Bureau of Navigation, 1898*, pp. 441–442.

62. Alan R. Millett, *Semper Fidelis: The History of the United States Marine Corps* (1991), pp. 134–135; Jack Shulimson, "Marines in the Spanish American War," in *Cruci-ble of Empire*, ed. James C. Bradford (1993), pp. 150–151; Nalty, *United States Marines in the War with Spain*, p. 17.

63. Millett, *Semper Fidelis*, p. 131.
64. General Order No. 494, Secretary of the Navy John D. Long, July 30, 1898, Commandant's Report, Navy Dept. Annual Report, 1898, p. 834.

THE MARINE BATTALION AT GUANTANAMO

The U.S. Navy cruiser Marblehead *was the flagship of Cdr Bowman H. McCalla, USN, who was the overall commander of the task force off Guantanamo that landed the 1st Marine Battalion ashore.*

Photograph of the irascible Bowman H. McCalla, the naval commander of the landing expedition at Guantanamo, who would have his differences with the Marine commander, LtCol Robert W. Huntington.

Photo courtesy of Naval Historical Center NH72745

Photo courtesy from the Henry Clay Cochrane Papers, MCHC

First Battalion Marines at Guantanamo, under 1stLt Herbert L. Draper, the battalion adjutant raise the American flag at newly named Camp McCalla. The Marines were the first American forces to land in Cuba.

A contemporary painting pictures Marines of the 1st Battalion repelling a Spanish night attack on their position. Searchlights and naval gunfire from the U.S. cruiser Marblehead support the troops ashore.

Photo courtesy National Archives 127-N-521285

Photo from the Henry Clay Cochrane Papers, MCHC

Captain Francis H. Harrington stands in a fortified position which includes a 3-inch naval landing gun and Marine infantry at Camp McCalla. A navy ship can be seen offshore in support of the Marines.

Marines continue to improve their position at Camp McCalla. One Marine takes a break and rests on a wheelbarrow while two Cuban irregulars, allied with the Marines, look on.

USMC Photo 515350

Photo courtesy of Naval Historical Center NH54531

The U.S. Navy gunboat USS Dolphin, originally built as a dispatch ship, provided naval gunfire support to the Marines under Capt George F. Elliott, who attacked the Spanish forces in the locality of Cuzco Well. Inadvertently the ship took a Marine platoon under fire, but redirected its guns after the Marines signaled the ship.

Sgt John H. Quick was awarded the Medal of Honor for his actions during the Spanish-American War when he signaled the USS Dolphin to cease fire. He is pictured below as a sergeant major, the rank he reached in World War I.

Photo History and Museums Division, USMC

Photo from Henry Clay Cochrane Papers, MCHC

Marines at Camp McCalla, Guantanamo rest behind three markers denoting the graves of Privates James McColgan and William Dumphy, and Navy Assistant Surgeon John B. Gibbs.

The officers of the 1st Marine Battalion pose for an official photograph at Guantanamo: Sitting left to right: IstLt James E. Mahoney; 1stLt Lewis C. Lucas; IstLt Herbert L. Draper; Lt Col Robert W. Huntington; Capt Charles L. McCawley, A.Q.M.; Capt Francis H. Harrington; Capt William F. Spicer; IstLt Wendell C. Neville. Standing left to right: 2dLt George C. Reid; IstLt Charles G. Long; 2dLt Edwin A. Jonas; Lt John M Edgar, (M. C.) U.S. Navy; 2dLt Newt H. Hall; IstLt Clarence L.A. Ingate; 1stLt William N McKelvey; Capt George F. Elliott; 2dLt Louis J. Magill; 2dLt Smedley D. Butler; 2dLt Philip M. Bannon; 2dLt Melville J. Shaw.

Defense Department (Marine) Photo 521218

Reprinted with permission from *The University of Virginia Edition of the Works of Stephen Crane, Vol. ix, Reports of War, War Dispatches, Great Battles of the World,* edited by Fredson Bowers (Charlottesville, Va.: The University Press of Virginia, 1971) pp. 134-42.

The Red Badge of Courage Was His Wig-Wag Flag
by Stephen Crane

GUANTANAMO CAMP, June 22.--It has become known that Captain Elliott's expedition against the guerillas was more successful than any one could imagine at the time. The enemy was badly routed, but we expected him to recover in a few days, perhaps, and come back to renew his night attacks. But the firing of a shot near the camp has been a wonderfully rare thing since our advance and attack.

Inasmuch as this affair was the first serious engagement of our troops on Cuban soil, a few details of it may be of interest.

It was known that this large guerilla band had its headquarters some five miles back from our camp, at a point near the seacoast, where was located the only well, according to the Cubans, within four or five leagues of our position. Captain Elliott asked permission to take 200 marines and some Cubans to drive the enemy from the well and destroy it. Colonel Huntington granted this request, and it was my good fortune to get leave to accompany it.

After breakfast one morning the companies of Captain Elliott and Captain Spicer were formed on the sandy path below the fortified camp, while the Cubans, fifty in number, were bustling noisily into some kind of shape. Most of the latter were dressed in the white duck clothes of the American jack-tar, which had been dealt out to them from the stores of the fleet. Some had shoes on their feet and some had shoes slung around their necks with a string, all according to taste. They were a hard-bitten, under-sized lot, most of them negroes, and with the stoop and curious gait of men who had at one time labored at the soil. They were, in short, peasants--hardy, tireless, uncomplaining peasants--and they viewed in utter calm these early morning preparations for battle.

And also they viewed with the same calm the attempts of their ambitious officers to make them bear some resemblance to soldiers at "order arms." The officers had an idea that their men must drill the same as marines, and they howled over it a good deal. The men had to be adjusted one by one at the expense of considerable physical effort, but when once in place they viewed their new position with unalterable stolidity. Order arms? Oh, very well. What does it matter?

Further on the two companies of marines were going through a short, sharp inspection. Their linen suits and black corded accoutrements made their strong figures very businesslike and soldierly. Contrary to the Cubans, the bronze faces of the Americans were not stolid at all. One could note the prevalence of a curious expression--something dreamy, the symbol of minds striving to tear aside the screen of the future and perhaps expose the ambush of death. It was not fear in the least. It was simply a moment in the lives of men who have staked themselves and have come to wonder which wins--red or black?

And glancing along that fine, silent rank at faces grown intimate through the association of four days and nights of almost constant fighting, it was impossible not to fall into deepest sympathy with this mood and wonder as to the dash and death there would presently be on the other side of those hills--those mysterious hills not far away, placidly in the sunlight veiling the scene of somebody's last gasp. And then the time. It was now 7 o'clock. What about 8 o'clock? Nine o'clock? Little absurd indications of time, redolent of coffee, steak, porridge, or what you like, emblems of the departure of trains for Yonkers, Newark, N.J., or anywhere--these indications of time now were sinister, sombre with the shadows of certain tragedy, not the tragedy of a street accident, but foreseen, inexorable, invincible tragedy.

Meanwhile the officers were thinking of business; their voices rang out.

The sailor-clad Cubans moved slowly off on a narrow path through the bushes, and presently the long brown line of marines followed them.

After the ascent of a chalky cliff, the camp on the hill, the ships in the harbor were all hidden by the bush we entered, a thick, tangled mass, penetrated by a winding path hardly wide enough for one man.

No word was spoken; one could only hear the dull trample of the men, mingling with the near and far drooning of insects raising their tiny voices under the blazing sky. From time to time in an hour's march we passed pickets of Cubans, poised with their rifles, scanning the woods with unchanging stares. They did not turn their heads as we passed them. They seemed like stone men.

The country at last grew clearer. We passed a stone house knocked to flinders by a Yankee gunboat some days previously, when it had been evacuated helter skelter by its little Spanish garrison. Tall, gaunt ridges covered with chaparral and cactus shouldered down to the sea, and on the spaces of bottom-land were palms and dry yellow grass. A halt was made to give the Cuban scouts more time; the Cuban colonel, revolver in one hand, machete in the other, waited their report before advancing.

Finally the word was given. The men arose from the grass and moved on around the foot of the ridges. Out at sea the *Dolphin* was steaming along slowly. Presently the word was passed that the enemy were over the next ridge. Lieutenant Lucas had meantime been sent with the first platoon of Company C to keep the hills as the main body moved around them, and we could now see his force and some Cubans crawling slowly up the last ridge.

The main body was moving over a lower part of this ridge when the firing broke out. It needs little practice to tell the difference in sound between the Lee and the Mauser. The Lee says "Prut!" It is a fine note, not very metallic. The Mauser says "Pop!"--plainly and frankly pop, like a soda-water bottle being opened close to the ear. We could hear both sounds now in great plenty. Prut--prut--pr-r-r-rut--pr-rut! Pop--pop--poppetty--pop!

It was very evident that our men had come upon the enemy and were slugging away for all they were worth, while the Spaniards were pegging away to the limit. To the tune of this furious shooting Captain Elliott with Lieutenant Bannon's platoon of C Company scrambled madly up the hill, tearing themselves on the cactus and fighting their way through the mesquite. To the left we could see that Captain Spicer's men had rapidly closed up and were racing us.

As we swung up to the crest we did not come upon Lucas and his men as we expected. He was on the next ridge, or rather this ridge was double-backed, being connected by a short transverse. But we came upon Mauser bullets in considerable numbers. They sang in the air until one thought that a good hand with a lacrosse stick could have bagged many.

Now the sound made by a bullet is a favorite subject for afternoon discussion, and it has been settled in many ways by many and eminent authorities. Some say bullets whistle. Bullets do not whistle, or rather the modern bullet does not whistle. The old-fashioned lead missile certainly did toot, and does toot, like a boy coming home from school; but the modern steel affair has nothing in common with it.

These Mauser projectiles sounded as if one string of a most delicate musical instrument had been touched by the wind into a long faint note, or that overhead some one had swiftly swung a long, thin-lashed whip. The men stooped as they ran to join Lucas.

Our fighting line was in plain view about one hundred yards away. The brown-clad marines and the white-clad Cubans were mingled in line on the crest. Some were flat, some were kneeling, some were erect. The marines were silent; the Cubans were cursing shrilly. There was no smoke; everything could be seen but the enemy, who was presumably below the hill in force.

It took only three minutes to reach the scene of activity, and, incidentally, the activity was considerable and fierce.

The sky was speckless; the sun blazed out of it as if it would melt the earth. Far away on one side were the white waters of Guantanamo Bay; on the other a vast expanse of blue sea was rippling in millions of wee waves. The surrounding country was nothing but miles upon miles of gaunt, brown ridges. It would have been a fine view if one had had time.

Then along the top of our particular hill, mingled with the cactus and chaparral, was a long, irregular line of men fighting the first part of the first action of the Spanish war. Toiling, sweating marines; shrill, jumping Cubans; officers shouting out the ranges, 200 Lee rifles crashing--these were the essentials. The razor-backed hill seemed to reel with it all.

And--mark you--a spruce young sergeant of marines, erect, his back to the showering bullets, solemnly and intently wigwagging to the distant *Dolphin!*

It was necessary that this man should stand at the very top of the ridge in order that his flag might appear in relief against the sky, and the Spaniards must have concentrated a fire of at least twenty rifles upon him. His society was at that moment sought by none. We gave him a wide berth. Presently into the din came the boom of the *Dolphin's* guns.

The whole thing was an infernal din. One wanted to clap one's hands to one's ears and cry out in God's name for the noise to cease; it was past bearing. And--look--there fell a Cuban, a great hulking negro, shot just beneath the heart, the blood staining his soiled shirt. He seemed in no pain; it seemed as if he were senseless before he fell. He made no outcry; he simply toppled over, while a comrade made a semi-futile grab at him. Instantly one Cuban loaded the body upon the back of another and then took up the dying man's feet. The procession that moved off resembled a grotesque wheelbarrow. No one heeded it much. A marine remarked: "Well, there goes one of the Cubans."

Under a bush lay a D Company private shot through the ankle. Two comrades were ministering to him. He too did not seem then in pain. His expression was of a man weary, weary, weary.

Marines, drunk from the heat and the fumes of the powder, swung heavily with blazing faces out of the firing line and dropped panting two or three paces to the rear.

And still crashed the Lees and the Mausers, punctuated by the roar of the *Dolphin's* guns. Along our line the rifle locks were clicking incessantly, as if some giant loom was running wildly, and on the ground among the stones and weeds came dropping, dropping a rain of rolling brass shells. And what was two hundred yards down the hill? No grim array, no serried ranks. Two hundred yards down the hill there was a--a thicket, a thicket whose predominant bush wore large, oily, green leaves. It was about an acre in extent and on level ground, so that its whole expanse was plain from the hills. This thicket was alive with the loud popping of the Mausers. From end to end and from side to side it was alive. What mysterious underbrush! But--there--that was a bit of dirty, white jacket! That was a dodging head! P-r-r-rut!

This terrific exchange of fire lasted a year, or probably it was twenty minutes. Then a strange thing happened. Lieutenant Magill had been sent out with forty men from camp to reinforce us. He had come up on our left flank and taken a position there, covering us. The *Dolphin* swung a little further on and then suddenly turned loose with a fire that went clean over the Spaniards and straight as a die for Magill's position. Magill was immensely anxious to move out and intercept a possible Spanish retreat, but the *Dolphin's* guns not only held him in check, but made his men hunt cover with great celerity. It was no extraordinary blunder on the part of the *Dolphin*. It was improbable that the ship's commander should know of the presence of Magill's force, and he did know from our line of fire that the enemy was in the valley. But at any rate, in the heat and rage of this tight little fight there was a good deal of strong language used on the hill.

Suddenly some one shouted: "There they go! See 'em! See 'em!" Forty rifles rang out. A number of figures had been seen to break from the other side of the thicket. The Spaniards were running.

Now began one of the most extraordinary games ever played in war. The skirmish suddenly turned into something that was like a grim and frightful field sport. It did not appear so then--for many reasons--but when one reflects, it was trap-shooting. The thicket was the trap; the *Dolphin* marked the line for the marines to toe. Coveys of guerillas got up in bunches of five or six and flew frantically up the opposite hillside.

There were two open spaces which in their terror they did not attempt to avoid. One was 400 yards away, the other was 800. You could see the little figures, like pieces of white paper. At first the whole line of marines and Cubans let go at sight. Soon it was arranged on a system. The Cubans, who cannot hit even the wide, wide world, lapsed into temporary peace, and a line of a score of marines was formed into a firing squad. Sometimes we could see a whole covey vanish miraculously after the volley. It was impossible to tell whether they were all hit, or whether all or part had plunged headlong for cover. Everybody on our side stood up. It was vastly exciting. "There they go: I See 'em! I See 'em!"

Dr. Gibbs, Sergeant-Major Goode, shot at night by a hidden enemy; Dunphy and McColgan, the two lads ambushed and riddled with bullets at ten yards; Sergeant Smith, whose body had to be left temporarily with the enemy--all these men were being terrifically avenged. The marines--raw men who had been harassed and harassed day and night since the first foot struck Cuba--the marines had come out in broad day, met a superior force and in twenty minutes had them panic-stricken and on the gallop. The Spanish commander had had plenty of time to take any position that pleased him, for as we marched out we had heard his scouts heralding our approach with their wooddove-cooing from hilltop to hilltop. He had chosen the thicket; in twenty minutes the thicket was too hot for his men.

The firing-drill of the marines was splendid. The men reloaded and got up their guns like lightning, but afterward there was always a rock-like beautiful poise as the aim was taken. One noticed it the more on account of the Cubans, who used the Lee as if it were a squirt-gun. The entire function of the lieutenant who commanded them in action was to stand back of the line, frenziedly beat his machete through the air, and with incredible rapidity howl: "Fuego! fuego! fuego! fuego! fuego!" He could not possibly have taken time to breathe during the action. His men were meanwhile screaming the most horrible language in a babble.

As for daring, that is another matter. They paid no heed whatever to the Spaniards' volleys, but simply lashed themselves into a delirium that disdained everything. Looking at them then one could hardly imagine that they were the silent, stealthy woodsmen, the splendid scouts of the previous hours.

At last it was over. The dripping marines looked with despair at their empty canteens. The wounded were carried down to the beach on the rifles of their comrades. The heaven-born *Dolphin* sent many casks of water ashore. A squad destroyed the Spanish well and burned the commander's house; the heavy tiles rang down from the caving roof like the sound of a new volley. The Cubans to the number of twenty chased on for a mile after the Spaniards.

A party went out to count the Spanish dead; the daylight began to soften. Save for the low murmur of the men a peace fell upon all the brown wilderness of hills.

In the meantime a blue-jacket from the *Dolphin* appeared among the marines; he had a rifle and belt; he had escaped from a landing party in order to join in the fray. He grinned joyously.

Possible stragglers were called in. As the dusk deepened the men closed for the homeward march. The Cubans appeared with prisoners and a cheer went up. Then the brown lines began to wind slowly homeward. The tired men grew silent; not a sound was heard except where, ahead, to the rear, on the flank, could be heard the low trample of many careful feet.

As to execution done, none was certain. Some said sixty; some said one hundred and sixty; some laughingly said six. It turns out to be a certain fifty-eight--dead. Which is many.

As we neared camp we saw somebody in the darkness--a watchful figure, eager and anxious, perhaps uncertain of the serpent-like thing swishing softly through the bushes.

"Hello" said a marine. "Who are you?"

A low voice came in reply: "Sergeant of the guard."

Sergeant of the guard! Saintly man! Protector of the weary! Coffee! Hard-tack! Beans! Rest! Sleep! Peace!

REPORT

OF THE

COMMANDANT OF UNITED STATES MARINE CORPS

––––––––

HEADQUARTERS U. S. MARINE CORPS,
Washington, D. C., September 24, 1898.

SIR: I have the honor to submit the following report of the condition and services of the United States Marine Corps for the past year . . . .

Shortly before war was declared between the United States and Spain Congress appropriated $50,000,000 for the national defense, of which the Secretary allotted to the Marine Corps, at different times, $106,529.64, for ammunition, equipments, clothing, etc., and careful preparations were immediately begun looking to the thorough equipment, in every respect, of the marines for war service.

In accordance with the verbal instructions of the Department of April 16, 1898, to organize a battalion at New York for service in Cuba, I issued orders on the 17th and 18th of April for the immediate assembling at New York of detachments of men from all the Eastern posts of the Corps and receiving ships. On the night of April 18, by direction of the Secretary, I proceeded to New York for the purpose of organizing the marine battalion for service. The battalion, as organized, consisted of 23 commissioned officers of the Marine Corps, 1 surgeon of the Navy, and 623 enlisted men, all under command of Lieut. Col. R. W. Huntington, U. S. M. C. The battalion was divided into six companies, one of which was an artillery company, having four 3-inch rapid-fire guns, received from the ordnance department, navy-yard, New York, and was composed of young, strong, and healthy men. The following is the organization of the battalion:

> Lieut. Col. R.W. Huntington, commanding.
> Maj. P. C. Pope.
> Maj. H. C. Cochrane.
> First Lieut. H. L. Draper, adjutant.
> Capt. C. L. McCawley, A. Q. M., quartermaster.
> Surg. John M. Edgar, United States Navy, surgeon.
> First Sergt. Henry Good, sergeant-major.
> First Sergt. W. J. Limerick, quartermaster-sergeant.

Company A: Capt. Allan C. Kelton, First Lieut. F. J. Moses, Second Lieut. L. J. Magill.
Company B: Capt. B. R. Russell, First Lieut. C. L. A. Ingate, Second

Lieut. M. J. Shaw.

Company C: Capt. G. F. Elliott, First Lieut. L. C. Lucas, Second Lieut. P. M. Bannon.

Company D: Capt. W. F. Spicer, First Lieut. W. C. Neville, Second Lieut. Newt. H. Hall

Company E: Capt H. K. White, First Lieut. J. E. Mahoney, First Lieut. A. S. McLemore.

Company F (artillery): Capt. F. H. Harrington, First Lieut C. G. Long, First Lieut. W. N. McKelvy.

Color guard: One sergeant, two corporals.

Each company consisted of 1 first sergeant, 4 sergeants, 4 corporals, 1 drummer, 1 fifer, and 92 privates; total, 103.

Total in battalion, 23 commissioned officers, 623 enlisted men.

Before leaving Washington for New York, I was informed by the Department that the commandant, navy-yard, New York, had been directed to fit out the *Panther*, formerly the *Venezuela*, for the transportation of a battalion of 400 men, the number decided upon by the Department, and that he had been instructed to render me all possible assistance in fitting out the ship as a transport, having regard for the health and comfort of the men . . . .

The vessel was ready in two days for the battalion of 400 men, which could have sailed then. When the battalion was ready to sail, two days after the arrival of the men at New York, orders were received from the Department directing that two companies be added to the battalion, and accommodations for these additional men had to be immediately provided. Work was proceeded with night and day to make the necessary provision for the increased number of men, and two days later, on April 22, the *Panther* sailed, with the battalion of 24 commissioned officers and 623 enlisted men, for Cuba.

As the men marched from the barracks to the ship they were greeted with great enthusiasm by the officers, sailors, and others on the vessels at the navy-yard, as well as those on shore. The band of the yard was loaned by the commandant to escort the battalion to the landing. As the *Panther* left the navy-yard and proceeded down the river she was repeatedly greeted with cheers and whistles from the vessels passed.

The greatest care was exercised in fitting out the battalion by the quartermaster of the Corps, Maj. F. L. Denny, U.S.M.C., the quartermaster of the battalion, Capt. C. L. McCawley, U.S.M.C., and myself, and when the *Panther* sailed the battalion was thoroughly fitted out with all the equipments and necessities for field service under the conditions prevailing in Cuba which experience and careful consideration could suggest, including mosquito netting, woolen and linen clothing, heavy and light weight underwear, three months' supply of provisions, wheelbarrows, push carts, pickaxes, shovels, barbed-wire cutters, wall and shelter tents, and a full supply of medical stores. Campaign suits of brown linen and campaign hats were ordered, but owing to the great demand for these articles at the time by the Army it was impossible to send them with the battalion. They were shipped later, however, and proved a great comfort to the men. Tent floors were purchased at Key West.

After orders were received to increase the strength of the battalion by two companies, making in all 623 men, it was found that the *Panther* would be very much crowded with this number on board. I reported the fact to the commandant of the station, and was informed by him that he had received orders to fit out the *Resolute*, formerly the *Yorktown*, as a permanent transport for the use of the battalion . . . . After the *Resolute* was fitted out and ready to sail and provisions placed on board for the battalion, the exigencies of the service required that she be taken for other purposes, and she was not available for the use of the battalion until it embarked at Guantanamo for the Isle of Pines.

After leaving New York the *Panther* proceeded to Hampton Roads for the purpose of awaiting a convoy to Cuba, arriving on April 23, 1898. Maj. P. C. Pope and First Lieut. J. E. Mahoney, who had been ordered to the battalion, joined it at Hampton Roads. The *Panther* left Hampton Roads April 26, under convoy of the U. S. S. *Montgomery*, arriving at Key West April 29. During the time the *Panther* remained at Key West, from the date last mentioned to June 7, the men were landed and went into camp there. The battalion received orders at 5:30 in the afternoon of May 24 to land, with all stores, by 3 o'clock the following morning, which was accomplished. Just before the *Panther* sailed from Key West, Maj. P. C. Pope was detached from the battalion. The *Panther* sailed from Key West for Cuba on June 7, 1898, and arrived at Santiago de Cuba on the morning of the 10th. On the same day, at 1 p.m., the ship arrived at Guantanamo Bay, Cuba, and at 2 p.m. of that day the battalion landed, with stores, and prepared to go into camp. On the 11th the camp was attacked by a much superior force of Spaniards, and from that time until the 14th the battalion was constantly under fire, and repulsed the enemy on every attack. The holding of the position at Guantanamo Bay was of the utmost importance to the Navy, as it was the only harbor where the vessels could seek shelter during the hurricane season. Owing to the dense undergrowth, affording safe shelter to the Spanish sharpshooters, it would have been impossible for the vessels, by shelling the shore, to keep the enemy from harassing those on board the ships with their Mauser rifles to such an extent as to make it dangerous for them to remain there . . . . Capt. Geo. F. Elliott, of the battalion, . . . was sent out on June 14 with a detachment of two companies of the battalion, and 50 Cubans, for the purpose of destroying a well at Cuzco, about 6 miles from the camp, which was the only water supply of the enemy within 12 miles. This small force attacked and defeated a body of about 500 Spaniards and accomplished the destruction of the well.

About 1 a.m. on the morning of the 12th of June, during a very severe attack on the camp, Asst. Surg. John Blair Gibbs, U. S. N., was killed by a Mauser bullet, reported by Surg. John M. Edgar, of the battalion, to have been fired at a range of from 600 to 800 yards. The death of Assistant Surgeon Gibbs cast a gloom over the whole command, as he was a most popular officer, liked by all, and his services were very much missed and the battalion could ill afford to lose them.

I regret to have to report the following list of the enlisted men of the Corps who lost their lives in the brave defense of the flag at Guantanamo Bay:

Killed: Sergt. Maj. Henry Good, Sergt. Charles W. Smith, Private Goode Taurman, Private William Dumphy, and Private James McColgan.

The following men of the battalion were severely wounded: Corpl. William B. Glass, Private Bartholomew McGowan, Private James D. Bourke, Private Robert J. Fleming, Private Albert E. Halvosa, Private Patrick Long, Private Charles C. Marley, Private Lewis L. Noonan, Private James Roxberry, Private Thomas Wallace, and Private Arthur Walker.

On the 5th of August the battalion embarked on the *Resolute*, which had been previously carefully fitted out as a transport as stated above, and on the 9th of the same month sailed for the Isle of Pines. After sailing, the destination of the vessel was changed to Manzanillo, where the ship arrived on August 12.

On August 13, news having been received of the signing of the peace protocol, the town surrendered, and on the 14th the *Resolute*, with the battalion on board, sailed for Playa del Este. On the 18th of the same month the *Resolute*, having taken on board certain officers and men of the artillery of the Army, sailed for Montauk Point, at which place she arrived on the 23d. Having landed the army detachment, and getting a clean bill of health, she proceeded to Portsmouth, N.H., where the battalion disembarked on August 26 . . . .

On the 16th, [September] the men having improved so much in condition as to make it safe to return them to their stations, some of which are in the South, and wishing to get them away from Portsmouth before the equinoctial storm, I issued orders to disband the battalion. The marked improvement in the condition of the officers and men shows that it was a wise provision to put them in camp in the healthful climate of the coast of New England, when they arrived from Cuba, instead of distributing them immediately to their respective stations. Colonel Huntington, in reporting the disbandment of the battalion, states his belief that the encampment has been of great benefit to the health of the officers and men . . . .

The Washington detachment, consisting of 3 officers and 164 men, arrived in the city September 22. The morning of the day of their arrival the President notified me that he desired to review the detachment. The honor thus tendered being unsolicited was highly appreciated, and the men upon their arrival were marched through quite a heavy downpour of rain to the White House and reviewed by the President. The men were enthusiastically greeted all along the line of march and many compliments upon their appearance were heard. The next morning, in spite of their long trip of the day before, and their march through the rain, every man of the detachment was reported well and present for duty . . . .

The fact that this battalion was attacked by overwhelming numbers, and for over three days and nights was under constant fire, and that the following day a portion of the battalion attacked and repulsed a superior force of Spaniards, shows that Colonel Huntington and his officers and men displayed great gallantry, and that all were well drilled and under the most effective discipline. The battalion has not lost a man by disease from the time it left for Cuba until its return, and the percentage of sickness was only 2 per cent, and in camp, after arrival at Portsmouth, only nine-tenths of 1 per cent, showing the good results of the extremely careful and complete preparation of the battalion for the service which devolved upon it, by the quartermaster of the Corps, Maj. F. L. Denny, the quartermaster of the battalion, Capt. C. L. McCawley, U.S.M.C., the medical officer, Surg. John M. Edgar, U.S.N., and myself, in procuring all the necessary clothing, medicines, and other necessaries for a tropical climate, and the care exercised by the officers for the health and comfort of the men, by the constant inspection of the camp, of provisions and meals before being served, as well as a rigid discipline always enforced in the Corps . . . .

The naval appropriation act, approved May 4, 1898, appropriated for 473 additional men for the Marine Corps, thus bringing the Corps up to its full authorized strength, as provided for in section 1596 of the Revised Statutes, viz, 3,073 enlisted men . . . .

During the war 57 vessels had marine guards, varying in strength from 80 down to 6 men, making a total of 2,055 enlisted men at sea. There were 623 in the battalion and 50 at Key West, making a total of 2,728. Deducting those on the Pacific coast, 275, this left only 71 enlisted men of the regular service available for duty at all eastern posts.

Thus it will be seen that if the additional 473 men had not been appropriated for, the Corps would have been unable to meet the demands for men required for the guards on board ship and men for the battalion and at Key West, and even after these 473 men were added to the Corps, it is shown that there were but 71 men of the permanent establishment available for duty at the different posts, and therefore, if the 1,500 additional men for service during the war had not been provided, the Corps would have been unable to furnish adequate guards for the various navy-yards and stations, where millions of dollars worth of public property is stored, which required most watchful guarding, on account of the many Spanish emissaries in the country. As the men enlisted for the war became sufficiently drilled, some of them were distributed among the various marine guards on board ship, relieving older men for positions as noncommissioned officers at the different posts. In addition to the men required at the navy-yards, guards composed of selected men were ordered to be established at the magazines at Norfolk and Philadelphia, as attempts had been made by Spanish spies to blow them up.

The men enlisted for the war were required to pass the same physical examination as those enlisted for the permanent establishment, except a reduction of 1 inch in height and the extension of the age limit to 35 years, as it was not thought advisable to reduce the general standard. For this reason the enlistments were somewhat slow, and upon the cessation of hostilities enlistments were stopped.

This act of May 4 also provided for a number of additional officers for service during the war, to be appointed from civil life, and from worthy noncommissioned officers of the Corps. Under the act, 40 second lieutenants were appointed from civil life and 3 from noncommissioned officers. These officers were very much needed, as there were but 4 line officers on shore for service at all the Eastern posts, and many of the guards on board ships were without officers before the act was passed. The newly appointed officers were hurriedly drilled and otherwise prepared for duty as rapidly as possible, and distributed among the auxiliary cruiser, the various posts, and the First Marine Battalion . . . .

In accordance with the order of the Secretary of the Navy, on account of the lawlessness in Key West of vicious persons congregating there as a result of the war, a number of men having been shot by desperate characters, a detachment, under command of Second Lieut. Henry C. Davis, consisting of 2 commissioned officers and 50 enlisted men, were sent from Washington to the naval base, Key West, Fla., for duty at that station. Capt. H. K. White was detached from the marine battalion before it sailed for Cuba and placed in command . . . .

Admiral Cervera and the other officers captured in the battle of July 3 off Santiago not confined at Portsmouth, were sent to Annapolis, Md. All the marines having been taken away from that station and sent to the front, a guard, under command of Maj. W. S. Muse, consisting of 2 officers and 60 enlisted men, was reestablished for the purpose of guarding these prisoners and performing guard duty at the Academy. On September 8 the prisoners left the Academy and returned to their country. Many of the Spanish wounded in the battle of July 3 were sent to the naval hospital, Norfolk, Va., and a guard was established there and camped in the hospital grounds. This guard was maintained until the prisoners were discharged from the hospital and was then returned to the barracks.

For some time after the establishment of the new Navy it was a question whether or not it would be advisable to station marines at the rapid-fire and secondary batteries. I maintained that the men of the Corps could do this work, and do it well, as the marines are thoroughly trained as sharpshooters, and it has been demonstrated that a good marksman with the rifle is a good gunner, and, furthermore, many of the men are thoroughly drilled at the small guns before going on board ship. I accordingly urged that the marines should be given a trial at these guns. After due consideration the Department accepted my suggestion, and included in the regulations orders to station them at the secondary batteries and rapid-fire guns. By the reports received after the battle of the 3d of July, when the Spanish fleet off Santiago was annihilated, and the reports of the Spanish officers who were on board these ships, it was shown that the greatest damage on the enemy's vessels resulted from the fire of the secondary batteries and the rapid-fire guns, this fire being so effective that the enemy were driven from their guns. As a great number of these guns on the ships engaged were manned by marines, I feel safe in asserting that the Department did not make a mistake when it directed that the small guns should be manned by marines. I have received reports from many commanding officers of marine guards of ships which took a prominent part in this action, indorsed very favorably by the commanding officers of the vessels, showing the stations and services of the marines . . . .

The marine battalion in Cuba was armed with the Lee straight-pull 6-millimeter rifle. Col. R. W. Huntington, who commanded the battalion, states concerning this arm: "The Lee straight-pull rifle has a few defects, which, I am informed, have been corrected. If this is the case the Lee will be a very superior military arm." . . .

The discipline and instruction of the Marine Corps have been maintained at a high standard, and to this is attributed in a large measure the efficiency of the services rendered by the marines in the war between the United States and Spain. One of the instances of discipline connected with the war, which attracted public attention, was the conduct of Private William Anthony in performing the very letter of his duty as orderly on the occasion of the destruction of the battle ship *Maine* in Havana Harbor by going below to the captain's cabin, irrespective of danger, and informing him that the ship had been blown up and was sinking. For his action on this occasion Private Anthony received commendatory letters from Capt. C. D. Sigsbee, of the *Maine*, and the Secretary of the Navy, and was promoted to the rank of sergeant by myself. The letters mentioned are appended, and I request that they be printed with this report . . . .

Although the corps has been restored to its statutory strength of 3,073 men, it seems certain that the demands which will probably be made upon it in the near future for foreign service, growing out of the present war, and on account of the growth of the Navy, will be greater than can be met by the corps with its present strength, and it is submitted that its enlisted strength should be increased by at least 1,000 men . . . .

As stated elsewhere in this report, 43 second lieutenants have been appointed under the authority contained in the act approved May 4, 1898, and their services have been of much value during the war. As these appointments are only temporary, being limited by the act to the emergency under which they were provided for, these officers will soon have to be mustered out, which will not leave enough officers to perform the required duties at the various posts and on the ships now in commission, and will leave none available for any additional ships which may be placed in commission or for any other duty which might be required.

The duty the officers are now performing at the posts of the corps requires an immediate increase of numbers, and the mustering out of the temporary officers at present in the service will make the duty on the regular officers extremely rigorous, requiring them to perform duty day on and day off at many of the posts, which should not be the case in any service.

This bill provides the rank of brigadier-general for the commandant of the corps. The authorized strength of the Marine Corps is at this time 116 officers and 4,700 men. There is no service in the world, except the Marine Corps, where a colonel has command of this number of men. The peace strength of the corps is over 3,000 men, which is an appropriate command for a brigadier-general. It is further submitted that the Marine Corps, as one of the coordinate military branches of the Government, is entitled to have as its head a brigadier-general, thus placing the commandant on an equality in this respect with the corresponding rank held by the heads of departments in the Army and bureaus of the Navy . . . .

It gives me pleasure to mention the fact that, notwithstanding the great increase in the strength of the corps, it being almost double its strength at the commencement of the war, and the consequent large increase of work in all departments, without any addition in the clerical force, the paymaster, adjutant and inspector, and quartermaster have rendered all assistance possible in every emergency, and have promptly and efficiently transacted all the business of their respective departments, the work having been at all times kept up to date. The great number of men enlisted in a short period of time at the beginning of the war devolved upon the Quartermaster's Department the duty of procuring material and manufacturing large quantities of clothing of all kinds, as well as the procuring of other supplies of various sorts, at very short notice. All of this work was performed in the most satisfactory manner, and the Department met all the demands made upon it without any delay. When orders were received to assemble the battalion at New York, it was necessary to procure large quantities of clothing, equipments, and various other stores for the use of the battalion in the tropics, and there were but four days in which to collect all the articles at New York, many of which had to be obtained from manufacturers and dealers at a considerable distance. By the energetic work of the quartermaster of the Corps, Maj. F. L. Denny, all the articles required arrived in ample time to be placed on board the *Panther* before the battalion sailed . . . .

The same strict recruiting regulations in force last year have been continued this year, with the exception that the authorized minimum height of men enlisted for the war was reduced 1 inch, and the age limit increased to 35 years, and an excellent class of men have been obtained. There are now 484 aliens in the Corps, and of these 179 have declared their intention to become citizens of the United States; 302 live in the United States but have not declared their intention to become citizens, and only 3 claim foreign residence.

There are 1,898 men on duty at the various shore stations and 1,678 on board ships in commission . . . .

Very respectfully,

CHARLES HEYWOOD,
Colonel Commandant.

THE SECRETARY OF THE NAVY.

REPORT OF COMMANDING OFFICER FIRST MARINE BATTALION

U. S. S. Panther,
Key West, Fla., April 30, 1898.

Sir: I have the honor to make the following report:

Before leaving New York on the 22d instant the force placed under my command was divided into five companies of infantry and one of artillery, the battery of artillery consisting of four 3-inch B. L. R. of the latest navy pattern.

The battalion marched aboard the transport *Panther* at 6:15 p.m. on that date, and sailed for Fort Monroe at 7:30 p.m., the departure being marked by intense enthusiasm in the navy-yard, docks, harbor front, and shipping of New York and Brooklyn.

At 8 p.m. on the 23d the ship anchored at Fort Monroe to await orders. Maj. P. C. Pope and First Lieut. J. E. Mahoney joined the battalion, reporting on board soon after the *Panther* dropped anchor.

At 8:05 a.m. on the 26th instant this ship sailed from Fort Monroe, under convoy of the U. S. S. *Montgomery*, and arrived at Key West at 11 a.m. on the 29th.

At the request of the commanding officer of the ship, six men were detailed for signal duty, and they have satisfactorily received and transmitted all signals and messages . . . .

The men of this command have been frequently and carefully instructed and drilled to such an extent as the limited facilities of the ship would permit; and, on the 26th instant, each of the six companies was practically instructed in loadings and firing at sea, each man firing ten rounds; and the battery of artillery received similar practical instruction, one round being fired from each gun.

The mechanism of the new rifle worked fairly well.

The accouterments have been marked in black, with the letter of the company and each man's company number.

Very respectfully,

R.W. Huntington,
Lieutenant-Colonel, United States Marine Corps,
Commanding First Battalion.

The Colonel Commandant United States Marine Corps,
Headquarters, Washington, D.C.

———

HEADQUARTERS, FIRST BATTALION,
Camp Sampson, Key West, Fla., May 25, 1898.

SIR: In obedience to your telegram of the 25th instant, I respectfully report that the battalion under my command was sent ashore from the *Panther* on the 24th instant, the order to this effect having been received about 5:30 p.m. on the 23d instant, this order being to land the battalion at 3 a.m.

We had permission to get out such stores as we could before 3 a.m. There was considerable delay in procuring the first lighter, and, it having been loaded, there was considerable more delay in getting the ship alongside the wharf. The ship was put alongside about 9:30 p.m.

Owing to my representations, Commodore Remey, commanding the base, extended the time allowed to take stores out and get out of the ship until the *Amphitrite*, which the *Panther* was to tow, should be ready to sail.

Subsequently I received orders from Commander Reiter that the battalion would leave the ship at 4:15 a.m. It was necessary to knock off work at 3:45 a.m. in order that the men might get ready to go ashore.

I was ordered by Commander Reiter, against my earnest plea, to leave on board the *Panther* one-half of our 6-millimeter ammunition (225,000 rounds) and one-half of the 3-inch ammunition (18 boxes), the *Panther* having two 3-inch guns and we having four. This 6-millimeter ammunition was retained, Commander Reiter informed me, to serve as ballast, as the *Panther* has no 6-millimeter rifles. This ammunition weighed about 14,000 pounds, and was stowed aft.

Commodore Remey modified this order so that we were able to take our 6-millimeter ammunition, but Commander Reiter retained one-half of the 3-inch.

Owing to the short time allowed for the removal of the stores, and notwithstanding the fact that the men worked hard and worked fast, considerable quantities of our property and part of the ten days' rations I requested were left on board.

Lieutenant Draper was present a part of the time when the matter of sending the battalion on shore was debated between Commodores Remey and Watson and Commander Reiter, and from his report of this conversation I am convinced that the order for the transfer of the battalion, and partially the extreme hurry in getting out of the ship, was due to the earnest solicitation and representations of Commander Reiter.

The battalion moved from the ship shortly after 4:15 a.m., and moved out to the beach, short 2 miles from the wharf, and after we had been there some time the *Panther* came out of the harbor and apparently lay to in the offing about two and one-half hours, waiting for the *Amphitrite*.

The *Saturn* was available for the service assigned the *Panther* and has much greater towing power, and was fitted for towing until her steel towing hawser was ripped out for the *Panther*.

The battalion is now strung out in camp along the beach for over half a mile.

About May 10 Commander Reiter attempted to get the battalion on shore, and an order was issued to that effect. I addressed a letter (copy annexed) to the commandant of the station against this transfer and the order was revoked. The same reasons that I then urged against the transfer held good on the 23d instant. In referring to this letter I find the expense for water is greater and for wood it is less than I had estimated. The expense for transportation is also greater than I had estimated.

The quartermaster has been compelled to hire a storehouse for the protection and preservation of the stores.

The battalion is established in camp, and the sick list shows a decided increase this morning, owing in part to the sun, heat, and exposure.

The usual routine of camp has been established, and a guard of 33 men and an officer has been sent into Key West for the protection of public property at the naval station, by order of the commandant of the base, this to continue daily.

Cooked meats have to be sent to these men, the transportation of which is paid by the Marine Corps.

Six men are on duty, two at a time, as orderlies for the commandant, from 8 a.m. to 10 p.m. daily.

I have no objection to these details except that the men are necessarily absent from their drill and from their places in squads and companies, and their military instruction at the present juncture is of great importance.

I think that, notwithstanding the annoyance, trouble, and expense this transfer has caused, the experience will be some value to the battalion.

Very respectfully,

R.W. HUNTINGTON,
Lieutentant-Colonel, United States Marine Corps,
Commanding Battalion

THE COLONEL COMMANDANT, UNITED STATES MARINE CORPS
Headquarters, Washington, D. C.

HEADQUARTERS FIRST MARINE BATTALION,
Guantanamo Bay, Cuba, June 17, 1898.

SIR: I have the honor to make the following report: The stores of this battalion were sent to the dock at Key West from Camp Sampson, on Sunday, June 5. We broke camp at 2 a.m. on June 6, and went on board the *Panther*, Major Pope going to Key West hospital.

On June 7 at 7:10 p.m., we sailed from Key West and arrived off Santiago de Cuba on the morning of the 10th; on the same day, at 1 p.m., we arrived in Guantanamo Bay; at 2 p.m. the battalion landed with stores. Company C was landed and deployed up the hill near the beach on the right of the entrance to the harbor. This hill is about 150 feet high and on top was formerly occupied by the Spanish troops, but when the position was vacated the day before our landing, the blockhouse on top of the hill was burned.

On the landing all houses and huts lately occupied by the Spanish forces were burned.

The hill occupied by us is a faulty position, but the best to be had at this point. The ridge slopes downward and to the rear from the bay; the space at the top is very small, and all the surrounding country is covered with thick and almost impenetrable brush. The position is commanded by a mountain, the ridge of which is about 1,200 yards to the rear.

On the afternoon of landing, tents were pitched and outposts established.

On the 11th, about 5 p.m., an attack was made upon one of the outposts and two privates, McColgan and Dumphy, of Company D, were killed, each receiving more than eight wounds, each of which would have caused death. These two men were patrols. A detachment was sent out from camp to support the outpost, and we found only faint traces of the enemy. After nightfall fire was opened upon our camp by small parties from different directions on five different occasions. The men turned out each time under arms with promptitude and courage. About 1 a.m. a more combined attack was made, and noisy fire from south, southeast, and southwest, was opened. During this attack Acting Assistant Surgeon John Blair Gibbs, United States Navy, was killed. From the best information attainable about 160 men were engaged in this attack.

On the morning of the 12th Sergeant C. H. Smith was killed and Corporal Glass, Privates McGowan and Dalton, all of Company D, were wounded--not dangerously.

On the morning of the 12th all tents and material were removed from the position and taken on the bay side of the hill, and a trench was dug on the south front, about 40 yards across, and a barricade made around the position, which would enable us to hold it, as I was informed that more troops were being assembled by the enemy in this immediate vicinity.

On the night of the 12th many persistent and trifling attacks were made, in reply to which we used a good deal of ammunition. About 2 a.m. Sergt. Maj. Henry Good was killed. On the 12th we were joined by 60 insurgent troops, and they, being acquainted with the country, and excellent woodsmen and fearless, were of the greatest assistance.

On the 13th, about 8 a.m., fire was opened upon the camp and subdued without loss or difficulty. About 8 a.m. of the 14th a rather smart fire was opened for a few moments on the camp and easily repelled. About 20 Cubans came from below the hill at this alarm, but their help was not needed. They opened fire.

At 9 a.m., 14th, a force consisting of Companies C and D, the native troops above mentioned, with about 25 more from Guantanamo, all under the direction of Colonel Tomas, Cuban army, proceeded through the hills about 6 miles and destroyed a well, said to be the only available water supply within 9 miles.

From the best information I can gather, this force was opposed by four regular companies of Spanish infantry and two companies of guerrillas, making a total of a little short of 500 men.

The engagement between these forces lasted from about 11 a.m. until 3.30 p.m. Our troops drove the enemy at every point, being obliged to make the first advance under fire, which, owing to the lay of the country, they could not return.

Captain Elliott reports that the men in many cases coolly estimated distances, borrowed his field glass to pick up parties of the enemy, and at a distance of 1,000 yards often inflicted damage and caused withdrawal.

Second Lieutenant Magill, with 50 men and 10 Cubans, joined Captain Elliott, climbing the mountain through cactus and brush; this advance was intended to cut off the retreat of the Spaniards, which unfortunately failed of its principal object, owing to the fact that his advance was stopped by the fire of the U. S. S. *Dolphin*.

Being apprehensive for the success of the movement, I ordered First Lieutenant Mahoney to be joined by First Lieutenant Ingate--these officers each having 50 men with them on picket--this combined force to proceed to Captain Elliott's assistance. Lieutenant Ingate failed to find his way to Lieutenant Mahoney, and Lieutenant Mahoney advanced alone, arriving too late to take an active part in the affair.

Our losses were 2 Cubans killed, 2 wounded, and 3 privates wounded, not dangerously; after the affair, while descending the mountain, Lieutenant Neville wrenched his hip and will probably be unfit for service for a month; about 10 or 12 of our men and 2 Cubans were overcome by the heat.

From information received from prisoners, which I believe to be reliable, about 60 of the Spanish force were killed and something more than 150 wounded, and 1 lieutenant and 17 privates were captured. The forces returned to camp at 8 p.m., exhausted by the long, hard march through this mountainous and tropical country.

This affair was planned by the Cubans, but too much praise can not be awarded to the coolness, skill, and bravery of our officers and men, by which alone its success was achieved.

Captain Elliott's cool advance up a rocky, steep mountain path, under fire for twenty minutes without being able to return it, and the gallantry and skill displayed by him throughout this affair were essential to the great success attained by the expedition, and are worthy of and I earnestly recommend that he be advanced in rank one grade. Captain Elliott mentions, in terms of high praise, the conduct of First Lieutenants Lucas and Neville, and Second Lieutenants Magill and Bannon.

Your attention is called to a report made by Captain Elliott, attached hereto.

Very respectfully,

R. W. HUNGTINGTON,
Lieutenant-Colonel, United States Marine Corps,
Commanding First Battalion.

COLONEL COMMANDANT CHARLES HEYWOOD,
United States Marine Corps, Headquarters, Washington, D.C.

[First indorsement.]

U. S. S. MARBLEHEAD (THIRD RATE)
June 19, 1898.

Respectfully referred to the commander in chief.

This report requires several corrections.

The blockhouse referred to on page 2 was burned by the gun fire from the *Yankee* on the 7th instant.

The position referred to on the same page was not occupied again after a small Spanish force had been driven away, when the *Marblehead* took permanent possession of the bay on the 8th instant.

Early on the morning of the 10th instant Captain Goodrell, with 40 marines from the *Oregon* and 20 marines from the *Marblehead*, examined the locality occupied by the marines, who arrived shortly after he had completed this duty. On the arrival of the *Panther* Captain Goodrell was sent on board to give Colonel Huntington the benefit of his observations.

Referring to paragraph 4, page 2, the position occupied by the marines has been pronounced by Major-General Perez, of the Cuban army, on the 17th instant, to be the only tenable position on the bay which could be successfully held by a small force. He also stated that 5,000 Spaniards could not take it.

If the marine position is commanded by a mountain ridge, that mountain ridge is commanded in turn by the ten 5-inch rapid-fire guns of the *Marblehead*, and of such other ships as may be here.

The mistake of locating the camp between the main position and the outpost was corrected on the 11th instant, at my suggestion.

The expedition was suggested by Colonel La Borde, and the *Dolphin* was sent to cover the sea front of our force.

Twenty-three marines overcome by the heat were brought back by the *Dolphin*.

This exhaustion was due, I believe, mainly to the fact that the campaign hats of the marines were on the *Resolute*, and not in the marine camp.

The behavior of the officers and men of the marine battalion generally has been most gallant, and is in general worthy of all praise.

Very respectfully,

B. H. McCALLA,
Commander, United States Navy, Commanding.

[Second indorsement.]

U. S. FLAGSHIP NEW YORK,
Off Santiago De Cuba, June 20, 1898.

Respectfully referred to the Secretary of the Navy.

W. T. SAMPSON,
Rear-Admiral, Commander In Chief U. S. Naval Force,
North Atlantic Station.

———

Headquarters First Marine Battalion,
Playa Del Este, Cuba, July 31, 1898.

SIR: I have the honor to make the following report: After the action of June 14 the enemy retreated farther up country and has never since annoyed us.

On June 25, at 3 a.m., Companies C and E and about 40 Cubans, under my command, crossed to the west side of Guantanamo Bay in small boats for the purpose of cutting off a body of the enemy who had been annoying small boats from the *Marblehead* in their search for mines. A landing was made and the troops disposed to cut off any retreat of the enemy on the point, while the *Marblehead* watched the isthmus leading from the mainland to our position.

A heavy patrol was then sent to search the point, but none of the enemy were found, although unmistakable signs showed that a force of 100 or 150 had occupied this point a day or two before.

This force reembarked at 7:30 a.m. and returned to the camp.

The regular pickets have been maintained--15 men by day and a full company with all its officers by night. This line of observation is about 800 yards to a mile from our position. One-half of this line--the left--is the same as that established on the 10th day of June, when we first landed. The right half of this line has been drawn back to easier supporting distance.

Sentries on each face of the fortified position occupied by us are maintained, but I have reduced these materially from the number which were kept on duty from the 10th to the 30th of June, inclusive.

Strong scouting parties, in addition to those sent out by the Cubans, have been sent out frequently to examine the surrounding country for the enemy.

During the past few days water has been reported in the well at Cuzco which was filled up by our force after the affair on the 14th ultimo, as reported to you in my communication of June 17, but inasmuch as rations have been sent from here to the Spaniards in Caimanara it does not seem necessary to fill up the well, but it is being closely observed by scouting parties from this camp.

The graves of our dead have been appropriately marked with headstones and a record placed in a bottle beneath the headstone in each case.

The strength of the battalion at this date is 515. Of this number 23 are commissioned and 482 enlisted; deducting 21 sick, leaves 484 available.

Your attention is invited to the reduction in the strength of the battalion as shown by the muster rolls forwarded herewith.

Very respectfully,

R. W. HUNTINGTON,
Lieutenant-Colonel, U.S. Marine Corps, Commanding Battalion.

THE COLONEL COMMANDANT UNITED STATES MARINE CORPS,
Headquarters, Washington, D.C.

————

HEADQUARTERS FIRST MARINE BATTALION,
Navy-Yard, Portsmouth, N.H., August 26, 1898.

SIR: I respectfully report that from the date of my last report, July 31, up to August 5, the battalion remained in camp at Playa del Este.

On the latter date we embarked on board the U. S. S. *Resolute*, and on the 9th instant sailed, under convoy of the U. S. S. *Newark*, bound for the Isle of Pines.

In an interview with the commander in chief before our departure, I asked if there was any military information available for my use there, and was told by him that there was a paper of which a copy should be sent to me.

This paper proved to contain certain general information relative to the island and the approaches to it. I had no information as to whether there was a hostile force in any part of the island.

The available draft of water at the principal port was, according to the above mentioned paper, 6 or 7 feet; as the *Suwanee* drew $8\frac{1}{2}$, and was the lightest draft of any vessel in the expedition, I suggested to Capt. C. F. Goodrich, who was in command, the great desirability of the addition of the *Maniti*, a captured tug drawing 4 feet, to his force, and by his direction and in his name applied to the chief of staff of the fleet for her.

My application was very positively and somewhat contemptuously denied, and I was told by him that the *Suwanee* could go anywhere, as she drew 8 feet.

By the chart 18 feet could be carried just into the Bay of Seguranca, but the *Newark* drew 21 feet and the *Resolute* $18\frac{1}{2}$. Two fathoms are marked on the chart several miles--8 or 10--from shore in the bay; the *Hist, Osceola*, and *Wompatuek* all drew more water than this.

Information received off Cape Cruz by Captain Goodrich induced him to resolve to demand the surrender of Manzanillo. I append herewith a copy of a report of Captain Goodrich, giving the details of his action under this resolve.

On the 14th instant the *Resolute*, with the battalion on board, sailed for Playa del Este.

On the 18th instant the *Resolute*, having taken on board certain officers and men of the United States artillery, sailed for Montauk Point, at which place she arrived on the 23d instant, and, having disembarked the detachment belonging to the Army proceeded to this place, where the battalion disembarked.

This report completes the history of the service for which the battalion was collected.

From May 24 to June 7 the battalion was in camp at Key West, and during this time--just previous to our departure for Cuba--diarrhea was very prevalent. The camping ground in Key West is bad and the water is bad.

Notwithstanding this the battalion disembarked at Play del Este in good condition, and during our stay there the sick list was at no time large. The gradual deterioration of the battalion was, however, clearly marked. The men seemed willing to work, but tasks that were comparatively easy at first became hard. The men seemed to have no reserve supply of strength, and, I doubt not, would during the last month of our stay there have yielded easily to any disease.

Campaign suits.--The material is not suitable, the color after washing being nearly as distinct as white at night, and not offering enough resistance to dews; and the cut is not desirable. The coat is too tight in the chest and back, and it should have more and larger pockets. These suits were, however, a great boon to officers and men during the scorching days.

Cartridge belts.--I respectfully recommend that the color of these belts be changed to that of the leggings or to conform to the color that may be selected for campaign suits.

Leggings.--These should be cut longer and, in my opinion, should be bound with leather, and fitted with rawhide laces.

Campaign hats.--The material of which they are made is very poor, and this kind of headgear is unsuitable for a very hot climate, as it is heavy and warm.

Shoes.--Those of the new issue, after hard wear, have proven very satisfactory.

Buzzicott cookers.-- These have given entire satisfaction.

The Lee straight-pull rifle has a few defects which, I have been informed, have been corrected. If this is the case, the Lee will be a very superior military arm.

I have also to recommend that canister be issued with the 3-inch navy rifle. The only ammunition issued to the battalion for these pieces was shrapnel, and it was very difficult to explode this projectile, with any certainty, at short ranges.

Water.--The battalion at Playa del Este was subjected to frequent inconvenience and discomfort owing to lack of fresh water.

Underclothting.--The so-called light-weight underclothes would be much better if they were lighter in weight.

After the *Resolute* had gotten under way for Manzanillo I received a telegraphic order from you to make recommendations for brevets of officers who were deserving of that honor.

In obedience to that order I have the honor to renew the recommendation made in my letter of June 17, 1898, in reference to Capt. George F. Elliott.

I also recommend that the following-named officers receive brevets of the next higher grade, viz: Capt. A. C. Kelton, First Lieuts. C. G. Long, A. S. McLemore, and W. N. McKelvy for gallant conduct on June 11, 12, and 13; also First Lieuts. L. C. Lucas and W. C. Neville, and Second Lieuts. L. J. Magill, M. J. Shaw, and P. M. Bannon for gallant conduct on June 11, 12, and 13, in the various attacks upon our position, and on the 14th for gallant conduct in our attack on the Spaniards, which resulted in their utter discomfiture.

First Lieut. James E. Mahoney succeeded to the command of Company E by the detachment of Capt. H. K. White at Key West; although Lieutenant Mahoney was not the senior lieutenant of the battalion, and as such entitled to succeed to this vacancy, the fact that I had received information from you that Captain Goodrell had been ordered to the battalion and my unwillingness to sever the association already formed between company officers and men led me to continue him in command of Company E.

This company was the last formed of the battalion; it was formed from recruits and from men who had been rejected for Company C, and under Lieutenant Mahoney, and owing to him, its efficiency increased remarkably. From regarding it as the worst company in the battalion I came to look upon it as among the best.

On the 11th, 12th, and 13th of June, Lieutenant Mahoney's coolness under fire and the excellent example he set for his men were conspicuous.

Lieutenant Mahoney's prompt and soldierly action, as set forth in my report of June 17, is deserving of high praise.

While under my command he has shown no tendency to commit the fault for which he was tried; and, deeming it for the best interests of the Government that he should receive promotion as soon as possible, I recommend that he be now advanced two numbers, so as to be placed in his original position upon the list, and also that he be brevetted captain.

From the time of the organization of the battalion to the present Lieutenant Draper, the adjutant of the battalion, has been untiring in assisting me. His duties have been performed with zeal and discretion. On June 11, 12, and 13 his conduct was marked by imperturbable coolness and courage, and I most heartily recommend that he be brevetted captain for his services on those days.

I have nothing but praise to award Capt. C. L. McCawley, A. Q. M. for the manner in which his duties have been performed, often under very trying circumstances. He has never seemed to consider his own ease in comparison with the service, and this means a great deal when the climate of Cuba is considered. During the various attacks on our position on June 11, 12, and 13 he was, a great part of the time, with me, and his deportment was becoming to a soldier. He acted often on those days as aid. I recommend that he be brevetted to the grade of major for gallant conduct.

I also recommend to the most favorable consideration of the Department Surg. John M. Edgar, U.S.N., for zealous and faithful performance of his duties under fire on June 11, 12, and 13.

Very respectfully,

R.W. Huntington,
Lieutenant-Colonel, United States Marine Corps,
Commanding First Battalion.

The Colonel Commandant, United States Marine Corps,
Headquarters, Washington, D.C.

————

Camp McCalla,
Guantanamo Bay, Cuba, June 15, 1898.

Sir: I have the honor to submit the following report:

In accordance with your verbal directions, I left camp at 9 a.m. yesterday with two companies of the battalion, C and D, commanded respectively by First Lieut. L. C. Lucas and Capt. William F. Spicer, with an aggregate of 160 men, and 50 Cubans under command of Lieut. Col. E. Eugene Tomas. Colonel Laborde, Cuban Army, was also present, but without command.

My orders were to destroy the well at Cuzco, about 6 miles from this camp, which was the only water supply of the enemy within 12 miles of this place, and the existence of which made possible the continuance of the annoying attacks upon our force in camp here.

Two miles and a half from Cuzco half the Cubans and the first platoon of C Company, under Lieutenant Lucas's command, passed over a mountain on our left, hoping to cut off the enemy's pickets. In this we failed, and our force was discovered by the Spanish outpost, which retreated immediately and gave the alarm to the main body, whose headquarters were in a house at Cuzco.

A high mountain separated the two forces at this point, and each attempted to gain its crest as a point of advantage. In this we were successful, but were fired on heavily by the enemy from the valley, at a distance of 800 yards. This fire was replied to by the Cubans of the main body. Lieutenant Lucas, with 32 men of his platoon and the remaining Cubans, came into the fight at 11:15. The other nine men of his platoon becoming exhausted were obliged to return to Camp McCalla. Lieutenant Bannon conducted the second platoon of C company just below the crest of the hill, out of fire from the enemy, leaving the narrow path, which was the only road, and making their way through the cacti. Just in rear of this platoon and following in single file was D company. The crest of the hill was in the shape of a horseshoe, two-thirds encircling Cuzco Valley and the well. The Cubans, C and D companies occupied one-half of this horseshoe ridge, while Second Lieut. L. J. Magill, with one platoon (50 men) of A company, came up from the valley on the opposite side, where he had been stationed as an outpost from Camp McCalla, having been attracted by the heavy fire, and believing his force necessary to our assistance, and occupied the left center of this horseshoe ridge. As soon as he saw our position he sent one of his men around the ridge to report to me. For fifteen minutes we were marching under a heavy fire, to which no reply was made, to gain this position. By the use of glasses and careful search by the men, individuals were discovered here and there, and, fire being opened upon them, they would break from cover to cover, and we were thus enabled to gain targets at which to fire, which had been heretofore impossible owing to the dense chaparral in which the enemy sought successful cover.

Many of the men fired as coolly as at target practice, consulting with each other and their officers as to the range. Among these were Privates Carter, Faulkner, and Boniface, all of whom did noticeable execution. This movement of the enemy gave Lieutenant Magill an opportunity to get in a cross fire, which was well taken advantage of.

Having reduced the enemy's fire to straggling shots, the U. S. S. *Dolphin*, Commander H. W. Lyon, U.S.N., which had been sent along the coast to cooperate with us if possible, was signaled to shell the house used as the enemy's headquarters and also the valley, but she was so far to the front, having mistaken the valley intended, that her fire was in Lieutenant Magill's direction, driving him to the reverse side of the ridge.

However, this shell fire started the enemy from his hiding places, which gave the other companies the opportunity to fire on them on the move.

Signal was made to the *Dolphin* to cease firing, and Lieutenant Magill was directed to form skirmish line and move down the valley in front of him toward the sea. This was defeated by renewed shell fire from the *Dolphin*.

The fight, which began at 11 a.m., was now drawing to a close, being over at 3 p.m. The enemy began a straggling retreat at 2 p.m., getting out of the valley as best they could.

The fire of the force under my command was at all times deliberate and aimed, sights being adjusted and volleys were fired when sufficiently large bodies of the enemy could be seen to justify it. The two platoons of Company C, under First Lieutenant Lucas and Second Lieut. P. M. Bannon, were handled with the best of judgment. D Company overcrowded on the firing line and men needlessly exposed themselves by standing in groups. First Lieut. W. C. Neville, commanding the first platoon, did his best with the men in front of him. Captain Spicer, commanding D Company, was overcome by the sun on the top of the hill and had to be sent on board the *Dolphin*. Lieutenant Neville injured his hip and ankle in catching his foot and falling down the mountain side after the fight was over. These accidents left Second Lieut. M. J. Shaw in command of D Company, which he handled with entire satisfaction. Forty men left the crest of the hill at 3.15 p.m. under Lieutenant Lucas and destroyed the well and burned the house lately occupied by the enemy. Canteens were taken from the men still holding the crest and filled with water required by signal from the *Dolphin*.

The marines fired on an average about 60 shots each, the Cubans' belts being filled during the action from the belts of the marines, each having to furnish 6 clips or 30 cartridges.

The loss to our force was 1 private of D Company wounded slightly, and 10 or 12 overcome by heat. These latter were kindly taken on board the *Dolphin* and cared for. This ship rendered every possible assistance to the expedition. Two Cubans were wounded during the fight on the hill, one being accidentally shot by Colonel Laborde by a pistol.

While destroying the well the Cubans were placed up the valley from which the enemy retreated and began a noisy and hot fight with guerrillas who had not been dislodged. In this fight the Cubans lost 2 killed and 2 wounded, but killed 5 of the enemy.

The march home began at 5:30 p.m., camp being reached at 8 p.m.

From the best information since obtained, which is believed to be reliable, 60 of the enemy, among whom were 2 officers, were killed. The wounded were numerous, but the wounds were probably light, owing to the range of 600 or 1,000 yards, at which distance all the explosive effect of the bullets are lost. Eighteen prisoners, including 1 lieutenant, were captured; about 30 Mauser rifles and a quantity of ammunition.

Lieutenant Magill also captured a complete heliograph outfit and destroyed the signal station. This had been used ever since our arrival here and could be seen at all times. Before closing I desire to commend Lieutenant Magill's good judgment in coming up and the excellent manner in which he handled his men.

Sergt. John H. Quick was obliged to stand on the open ridge under fire to signal the *Dolphin*, which he did with the utmost coolness, using his rifle with equal judgment while not thus engaged. My only regret is that E Company, under the command of First Lieut. James E. Mahoney, which had been sent to us from an outpost near Camp McCalla when the heavy firing was heard there, was unable to report to me until 4 p.m. Had he been an hour and a half sooner, I am satisfied that the entire force of the enemy, which was about 500 men, would have been captured. This delay was not due to any lack of zeal on his part.

I have the honor to be, sir, very respectfully, your obedient servant.

G. F. ELLIOTT,
Captain, United States Marine Corps,
Commanding C Company.

Lieut. Col. R. W. HUNTINGTON,
Commanding First Battalion of Marines,
Camp McCalla, Guantanamo Bay, Cuba.

———

HEADQUARTERS FIRST MARINE BATTALION,
Guantanamo, Cuba, June 18, 1898.

SIR: I desire to make the following supplementary report: Upon leaving camp you asked me if I wanted an adjutant. I declined to take one, the command being short of officers for duty; but having been notified that a Mr. Stephen Crane would be allowed to accompany the expedition, I requested him to act as an aid if one should be needed. He accepted the duty and was of material aid during the action, carrying messages to fire volleys, etc., to the different company commanders.

Very respectfully,

G. F. ELLIOTT,
Captain, United States Marine Corps, Commanding C.
Lieut. Col. R. W. HUNTINGTON, U.S.M.C.,
Commanding Battalion.

[First indorsement]

U. S. S. MARBLEHEAD, *June 19, 1898.*

Respectfully forwarded to the commander in chief.

The expedition was most successful, and I can not say too much in praise of the officers and men who took part in it.

B. H. McCALLA, COMMANDER, *S.O.P.*

———

U.S.S. MARBLEHEAD, (THIRD RATE)
Guantanamo, Cuba, June 16, 1898.

SIR: I have the honor to inform you that on the 14th instant, at the suggestion of Colonel Laborde, the Cubans under the command of himself and Lieutenant-Colonel Thomas, supported by two companies of marines under the command of Captain Spicer and Lieutenant Elliott, routed the force of about 300 Spaniards stationed in the pass between the marine camp and the south coast.

One portion of the command advanced by the cliffs so far as the well and blockhouse, which I referred to in my No. 88, supported by the *Dolphin.*

The other portion diverged from the coast line and advanced up the valley to the southeast, the two forces eventually uniting on the sides of the mountain in the vicinity of the blockhouse and well.

In this vicinity the Spaniards, numbering about 300, were encountered and driven from their position, sustaining a loss of between 40 and 60 killed and 1 officer and 17 soldiers captured.

As the day was well advanced, it was not possible for our force to make a search for the Spanish wounded, and I fear that many were left on the field uncared for.

We suffered a loss of 2 Cuban soldiers killed; 6 wounded, 4 of whom were Cubans. In addition, 23 marines were prostrated by the heat and, with the wounded, were transferred to the *Dolphin*, from which ship the force was also supplied with ammunition during the engagement.

The well and blockhouse referred to, on the south coast, were destroyed and a set of heliograph instruments taken.

The object of the movement was for the purpose of relieving the pressure on the marine camp by an offensive movement and it was, I believe, entirely successful.

I need hardly call attention to the fact that the marines would have suffered much less had their campaign hats not been on the *Resolute*.

I desire to call particular attention to the devotion of the Cubans to the cause of freeing their island, shown in so many ways, by stating that the last words of the Cuban who was shot through the heart and buried on the field were, "Viva Cuba Libre."

Inclosed, marked "A," is a list of the Spanish soldiers captured.

The second lieutenant, also captured, is Francisco Batista, of Guantanamo City.

The marines who were prostrated by the heat were nearly all able to return to their camp early in the evening.

Very respectfully,

B. H. McCALLA,
Commander, United States Navy, Commanding.

The COMMANDER IN CHIEF
North Atlantic Station.

————

HEADQUARTERS FIRST MARINE BATTALION,
CAMP HEYWOOD, SEAVEY ISLAND,
Navy-Yard, Portsmouth, N. H., September 19, 1898.

SIR: I inclose herewith a letter to myself from Capt. G. F. Elliott, U. S. M. C., relating to errors in the report of Commander B. H. McCalla, United States Navy, about the fight at Cuzco, Cuba, June 14, 1898, which letter I ask to be filed with the report referred to.

Upon the morning of June 14, 1898, Captain Elliott asked me who commanded the projected expedition to Cuzco. I told him that he was not under the command of the Cuban colonel, Laborde, but that he would consult with him, and if Laborde saw fit to issue orders he would obey them only if the movement approved itself to his judgment. I have cause to believe that Laborde's authority was not recognized by the officer in command of the Cubans.

Very respectfully,

R.W. Huntington,
Colonel Commanding First Marine Battalion.

The COLONEL COMMANDANT,
UNITED STATES MARINE CORPS.

———

HEADQUARTERS FIRST BATTALION OF MARINES,
CAMP HEYWOOD, SEAVEY ISLAND,
Kittery, Me., September 16, 1898.

SIR: I respectfully call your attention to the errors in the official report of Capt. B. H. McCalla, United States Navy, in regard to the military status taken by the battalion of marines under my command at the Cuzco fight, near Guantanamo Bay, June 14, 1898.

As this report will be filed for general publication with other archives of Government relating to the Spanish war, it should be correct.

Captain McCalla states in his report as follows:

"Cubans under the command of himself (Colonel Laborde) and of Lieutenant Colonel Tomas, supported by two companies of marines under the command of Captain Spicer and Lieutenant Elliott, routed a force of 300 Spaniards."

The facts are these: Two companies of marines formed a battalion under my command, and the companies were commanded, as stated in my report, by Captain Spicer and First Lieut. L. C. Lucas.

My command was not a supporting body for the Cubans, and before leaving camp, after conversation with you on the subject, I left with the understanding that I was to act with the Cubans so far as in my judgment it was for the good of the expedition, but that I was not under the command of either of the insurgent commanders.

This word "support," as used, is a military misnomer, for the marines numbered 225 and the Cubans 50 in the fight, and although the latter were brave enough, their quality as efficient fighting men was on a par with that of the enemy.

My report states that there were 500 of the enemy engaged, and it is now known that the force was a little larger, and not 300, as stated by Captain McCalla.

I believe Captain McCalla's report was made from the statements received from Colonel Laborde, and if he had believed mine, made to you and forwarded to him for his information, incorrect, he had many opportunities to call my attention to the facts at the time, but he left me for months believing it accepted unquestioned while controverting it in his own.

Very respectfully,

G. F. ELLIOTT
Captain, United States Marine Corps,

Col R. W. HUNTINGTON,
United States Marine Corps, Commanding First Battalion of Marines.

MARINE BATTALION AT GUANTANAMO

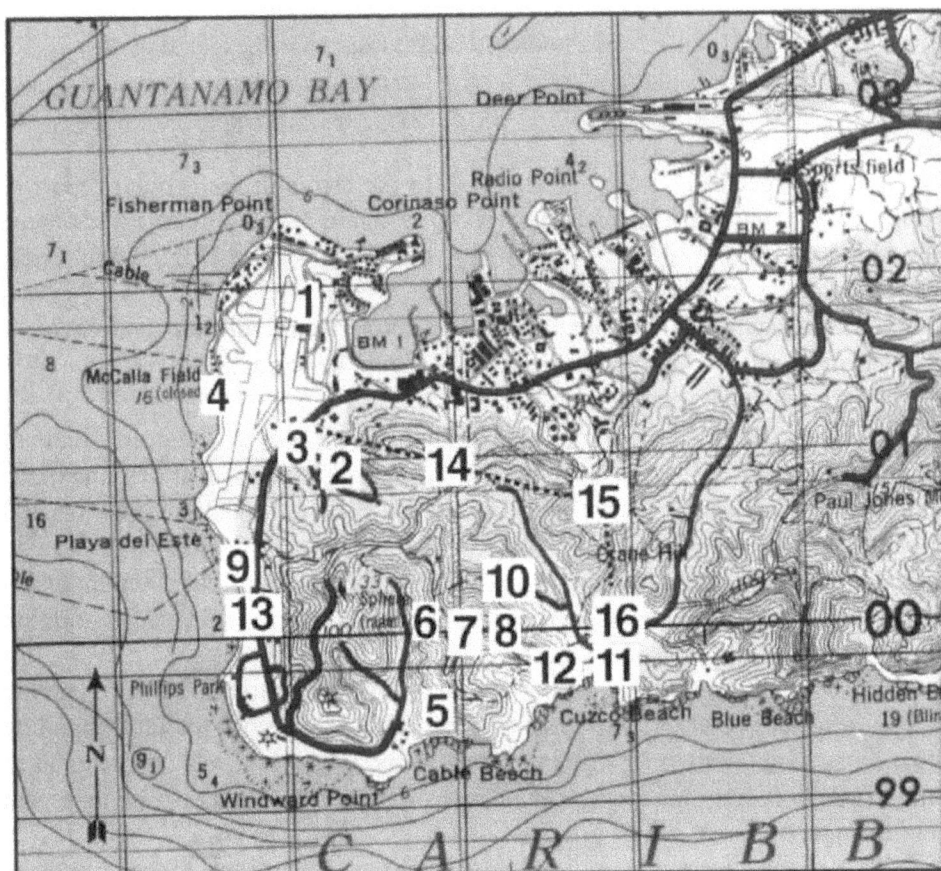

Legend

1. First Marine Battalion Headquarters
2. Dumphy/McColgan Monument
3. The Crossroads
4. The Old Stone Fort
5. Hill 350
6. Hill 400
7. Elliott's Position 14 June 1898
8. Quick Signaling Position 14 June 1898
9. Lieutenant Lucas' Starting Point
10. Lucas' Position when he rejoins Elliott 14 June 1898
11. Spanish Main Battle Position
12. Spanish Command Post on Cuzco Beach
13. Lieutenant Ingate's Objective (never reached)
14. Lieutenant Magill's Route
15. Spanish Signal Station overrun by Lieutenant Magill
16. Hill fired upon by the *Dolphin*

*Map taken from sketch map and locations provided by Colonel Robert R. Hull, USMC
(Ret). **NOTE**: 1898 locations are overlaid on present-day map of Guantanamo.

Published with the permission of the author.

Research Trip to Guantanamo Bay
by Colonel Robert R. Hull, USMC (Retired)

16 June, 1997

From: Colonel Robert R. Hull USMC (Ret)
To: Distribution

Subj: June 10-15 Research Trip to Guantanamo Bay, Cuba; Report of

Ref: (a) COMNAVBASE GUANTANAMO BAY 190520Z MAY97
          (b) Map Sheet GUANTANAMO BAY 1:25000 Series 824S
          (c) SECNAV/CMC Annual Report FY 1898
          (d) R. R. HULL Field Notes 11-14 JUN 1997

. . .

Summary

Historical - On 10 June 1898, the First Marine Battalion (Huntington's Battalion), commanded by Lt. Col. R. W. Huntington USMC landed at Fisherman's Point, Guantanamo Bay, Cuba and established a camp on the plateau area now called McCalla Field. From 11-13 June, Spanish forces launched numerous attacks against the Marines. The Marines held the position but not without sustaining casualties. On 14 June, a 2 company task force supported by a Cuban Army detachment attacked the main Spanish position at Cuzco Well causing the Spanish to retreat in the direction of Guantanamo City. From that day, the Spanish ceased to be a bother to the First Marine Battalion.
Research Trip - During the period 10-15 June 1997, field research was conducted in the area occupied and fought over by the First Marine Battalion. With the 1898 participant's accounts for guidance, and using a metal detector, efforts concentrated on discovering and/or verifying locations associated with the exploits of the First Marine Battalion. Areas of concentration included McCalla Field, Cuzco Hills and adjacent terrain features. Artifacts discovered in situ plus the contemporary narrative accounts aided the research team findings. Based on this, the team developed a conjectural reconstruction of key events, including the Battle of Cuzco Well. Significant terrain features and related areas of interest were identified by grid coordinates using a current military map (Ref B), providing a correlation with the eyewitness accounts of 1898. These efforts, including a description of the artifacts, and the team's findings and conjecture are discussed in detail.

1. Background

In accordance with the area clearance granted by ref (a), facilitated by CGMARFORLANT Liaison Element, Norfolk and with the concurrence of CO MARINE BARRACKS GD/SF Guantanamo Bay, Cuba, the undersigned accompanied by his son, Maj. Michael P. Hull USMC visited the Guantanamo Bay command during the period 10-13 June (for Maj. Hull) and 10-15 June (for the undersigned).

The purpose of the trip was to conduct field research of the Guantanamo Bay area in which the First Marine Battalion (Huntington's Battalion), commanded by Lt. Col. R.W. Huntington USMC, operated during the Spanish-American War. The field research concept included traversing the ground where the First Marine Battalion ("the Battalion") maintained its base of operations and further to critically examine the terrain associated with the battle of the campaign, the latter being known as the Battle of Cuzco Well. A prime objective of the research was, insofar as possible, to locate the Battalion's outposts, the routes to the Cuzco area, the main battle positions of both the Marines and the Spanish at Cuzco, and other locations significant to the Battalion's operations. Ideally, the discovery of war material in situ would assist in developing a conjectural reconstruction. The use of a metal detector was envisioned as an aid in discovering such items, particularly in the Cuzco Hills area.

2. A Team Approach.

A significant body of documentary evidence; both published and unpublished, had been assembled and consulted prior to the research trip. The two most important items were the contemporary reports by Lt. Col. Huntington and Capt. G. F. Elliott contained as enclosures to the Commandant's Annual Report to the Secretary of the Navy in 1898 (Ref C) . . . . These officer's reports have become the basis for most published accounts found as either articles or as included in general histories. However, located in various archives are numerous other items relating to the Battalion's operations. These include diaries, letters, sketches, photos, newspaper clippings and other unpublished official amounts.

Analysis of this material, prior to the conduct of the research trip, provided a reasonably clear and surprisingly detailed overview of the Battalion's operations, particularly in the vicinity of the camp established at McCalla Field. A notable exception to the documentation were contemporary maps or sketches of the Cuzco Well battle area. Narrative descriptions of this action were available and the general area was known. It remained to walk the ground in an effort to determine with some specificity the respective battle positions. Accordingly, most of the field research time was spent in the Cuzco Hills area including the hills overlooking Cuzco Beach and the Cuzco Beach area itself. The Battalion's initial base at Fisherman's Point, although greatly altered since 1898, was not neglected by the field research. This area, where most of the Battalion's casualties were incurred was visited on several occasions by the research team.

The findings below, include conjectural descriptions based [on] an analysis of extant documentation, a physical inspection of the area, and in the case of the Cuzco Well battle, analysis of material located by a metal detector.

In addition to the undersigned, the research team consisted of Maj. Michael P. Hull USMC, Capt. Tom Riordan USMC, Asst. Operations Officer MB Guantanamo, and Ssgt. P. W. Whitten, Minefield Maintenance Section MB Guantanamo. The enthusiasm and professionalism of these active duty Marines contributed materially to the findings in this report. Particularly noteworthy was Ssgt. Whitten's dedication to the effort. A highly motivated Marine, he was primarily responsible for the location of numerous artifacts in the Cuzco Hills area whose discovery provided convincing proof to the events which occurred there on 14 June, 1898.

3. Report Style.

The report's findings and conjectural reconstructions are presented below by phases. These phases coincide generally with the sequence with which the field research was conducted. The report is not intended to be a definitive account of the Battalion's operations. Rather it is presented to supplement and amplify the existing body of knowledge surrounding the Battalion's exploits during the period 10-14 June, 1898. Using this report and the existing documentation should permit the development of a reasonably accurate reconstruction of certain key events during this period. In order to aid this reconstruction, the key locations discussed below have been assigned grid coordinates based on the current military map (Ref B) . . . . Assuming the accuracy of the grid coordinates with relation to the 1898 activities described, these coordinates can be used by future researchers as a common base of data concerning the activities of the First Battalion from 10-14 June, 1898.

4. Findings and Conjectural Reconstructions.

A. Phase I--First Marine Battalion Base Camp encompassing area from Fisherman's Point to and including McCalla Field (inactive)

(1) First Marine Battalion Headquarters and Base of Supplies

McCalla Field and the surrounding plateau area was the site of the Battalion's Headquarters and its "base of supplies". It has been drastically altered by the construction of buildings, roads, and an airfield. Considerable quantities of earth were removed in the process which has also had an effect on the 1898 terrain contours. At the extreme northern end of this area, there is a small, well maintained park site upon which sits a large monument dedicated to the First Marine Battalion. Immediately adjacent to the monument is a tall flagpole. The grade at this location appears to be original and undisturbed. This location, coordinates **832021**, conforms to the descriptions, sketches and photographs depicting the Battalion's headquarters. On June 10, 1898, the Battalion, having landed at Fisherman's Point from the USS *Panther*, established a tent camp in this vicinity. Oriented in a north-south direction, it was rectangular in shape and measured approximately 25 by 125 yards. On 12 June, following the first Spanish attack on the camp the previous night, the tent camp was dismantled. In its place, the Battalion constructed a fortified position approximately 40 yards square with the north side resting close to the edge of the hill. Concurrently, a "base of supplies" was established on the beach just below the fortified position, and connected by a path to the hilltop position. The "base of supplies" was placed in charge of the Battalion's next senior officer, Maj. H. C. Cochrane. The main power station now covers the beach area where the "base of supplies" was located. The beach area of 1898 is now completely covered by concrete and industrial type structures and also serves as the site of the current ferry landing. The conjectural site of the Battalion's initial tent camp is in the vicinity of a rectangular multi-storied office building (unoccupied) and the nearby WWII era multi-storied square sided concrete blockhouse (disused).

(2) Memorial to Privates Dumphy and McColgan

In a flat valley floor, and adjacent to a dirt road running between two steep ridges is a small white memorial marking the site where Privates Dumphy and McColgan, both from D. Co. were killed in action. The two Marines, at the time of their deaths, were manning a sentinel post as part of the forward outpost that screened the Battalion's main position. As such, they marked the Battalion's front line. At approximately 1700 on 11 June they were killed by the Spanish at their post. The Spanish fire alerted the Battalion to an impending attack, launched later that night. The monument is located at coordinates **833010**.

From the memorial to the Battalion Headquarters measures approximately 1100 yards, on a direct line. The monument's current location was subject to evaluation by the research team to determine the plausibility that its current location did in fact occupy the exact position where the two Marines were killed. This evaluation considered primarily the surrounding terrain as well as reference to 19th century infantry doctrine. This doctrine prescribed the use of sentinel posts on a line covering the outermost approaches to a main position. In a position of support, and to the rear of this line of sentinels was positioned a small support force. ("Vedettes," term used to describe the sentinels; "Cossack Post", the support). It is probable that Dumphy/McColgan was only one of several posts established on a line in the small valley. About 300 yards south of the monument, lies a now obscured terrain feature, that in 1898 was known as the "crossroads." (See (3) below). Later that night (12th) somewhere between the memorial and the "crossroads", Sgt. Smith, also of D. Co. was killed in action.

The monument sits just next to an existing dirt road that begins near the current Sherman Road. Near the monument, the road veers toward the southeast. Both from a map study of the road's trace, and by viewing the site from the crest of nearby hills, it becomes apparent that the memorial lies astride the 1898 trail from Cuzco Well to Fisherman's Point. On the afternoon of 11 June, Pvts. Dumphy and McColgan were directly in the path of the lead elements of the 3rd *(Principe) Spanish Infantry Regiment.* Surprised while eating their evening meal of hardtack, and apparently unaware of the advancing Spanish, the two Marines were shot numerous times by the Spanish. The number of rounds each Marine received (21 in one and 15 in the other) led to early reports that the Spanish had mutilated them.

If Pvts. Dumphy and McColgan were two lone Marines on sentry duty with no support to back them up, the monument would appear to be in the wrong place. Assuming however, that the two Marines were part of a larger outpost with the center of their support located at the "crossroads" then their position (the monument) would be consistent with 19th [century] existing doctrine. A terrain analysis confirms the importance of the path through the valley. Given the importance of the "crossroads" position (it was a major outpost occupied by at least one platoon later that night as well as on the 13th and 14th) then the site of the monument appears to represent the approximate exact location of the two Marines when they were killed.

(3) The "Crossroads"

The "crossroads" appears in several contemporary narrative accounts. Extant sketch maps of the area also depict a confluence of trails labeled "crossroads". An early 1900s map shows a trail running from the vicinity of the current flagpole at McCalla Field, south across Sherman Road, then between two ridge lines where it veers to the southeast (site of Dumphy/McColgan memorial) through a saddle, then down the valley terminating at Cuzco Beach. Clearly, this was the main Spanish route between Cuzco Beach and Fisherman's Point in 1898. On the current map, trace the western leg of McCalla Road from the flagpole south. It veers to the southwest to avoid the old short east-west runway of McCalla Field. However, if the road instead of veering continues in a straight line to intersect with Sherman Road, the route would conform closely to the trail outlined on the early 1900s map. Further, the route, once across Sherman Road would neatly connect with the current dirt road where the Dumphy/McColgan monument sits. The other trail that defined the "crossroads" was a trail which started at water's edge in the basin to the east of McCalla Field, headed west, then south around the base of the hill toward the lighthouse at Windward Point. i.e. part of this trail is now Sherman Road.

Given the importance given to the "crossroads", it seemed important to discover its approximate 1898 position. After reviewing the earlier map and after a detailed walk over the area, it appears that the "crossroads" is located at coordinates **831012**. This places the "crossroads" approximately 700-800 yards south of the Battalion Headquarters. Another 200-300 [yards] southeast of this position lies the monument to Dumphy/McColgan.

The "crossroads" was recognized early by Lt. Col. Huntington as a critical piece of terrain. He had posted sentinels south of this location (Dumphy/McColgan). On the night of the 11th, he had Lt. Neville stationed here and Lt. Shaw stationed to the southwest of this location. That night, Shaw came under attack, withdrew to the "crossroads" where he joined Neville's platoon, and withstood all efforts by the Spanish to overrun the group. At dawn the next day the combined force returned to the Battalion Headquarters having been away from the main body for over 12 hours. The "crossroads" was the Lt. Mahoney's outpost position on the morning of 14 June. Lt. Magill, on that same day, had to pass through the "crossroads" on his way to reinforce Capt. Elliott's force in battle with the Spanish at Cuzco. In addition to the deaths of Dumphy and McColgan at their post just south of the "crossroads", Sgt. Smith D. Co. was killed late on the night of the 11th in this vicinity. Like the dirt path near where Dumphy/McColgan were killed, the crossroads lay astride the main trail Fisherman's Point-Cuzco Well.

(4) The "Old Stone Fort"

Virtually silent on the subject in the official contemporary accounts are a series of night patrol actions on 11 and 12 June. The actions on 11 June are discussed above in (3) where Lt. Shaw's platoon initially operated southwest of the "crossroads" and later joined forces with Lt. Neville at the "Crossroads" position, where they remained until daylight. The 11 June night attack on the Battalion's main position came from a southwest direction.

On the night of 12 June, the Battalion's position was attacked several times from a number of directions. While these attacks were in progress, Lt. Neville's platoon was operating in the plateau area (McCalla Field) southwest of the Battalion's position. At some point in time, he came under fire from a group of Spaniards located near the remains of an old stone building. Lt. Neville ordered his force to spread out in the prone position on a line at the cliff edge. After a series of rifle volleys, he led his group in a charge against the building driving out the Spanish. During the preparations for the attack one Marine, Pvt. Taubman fell from the cliffs to the rocks below and was killed. His body was recovered the next day by a ship's boat. During the exchange of fire three Marines were wounded.

On the 14th, Elliott's route to Cuzco followed the cliff trail towards Windward Point. Along this route, Stephen Crane noted that they had passed the Spanish stone fort. Today this area is either covered with McCalla Field runway, or by structures along the cliff edge. In an effort to locate the approximate location of the "Old Stone Fort", the team worked along the existing roads until coming upon two concrete batteries erected in 1906 as coast artillery emplacements. Now minus their guns, the emplacements, a light yellow color, are in near pristine condition otherwise. They are sited to cover the sea approaches to the harbor and are directly opposite the harbor's first entrance buoy. From the flagpole at McCalla Field, the twin emplacements bear roughly southwest at a distance of approximately 750 yards. Conjecturally, the research team places the "Old Stone Fort", at coordinates **827016**, or about where a short circular stub of the old runway is located.

B. Phase II--Cable Beach-Cuzco Hills-Cuzco Beach.

(1) Elliott's Approach March 14 June 1898.

Shortly after breakfast on 14 June 1898, Capt. G. F. Elliott (Co. C), Capt. W. F. Spicer (Co. D) and a supporting force of Cubans, Lt. Col. Tomas departed the "Base of Supplies" on the beach below the Battalion's fortified position. (Coordinates **832022**). Elliott, the senior, was in command of the force. Its mission was to "destroy the well at Cuzco". Following the coastal path and passing the" Old Stone Fort" (See A (4) above), they continued toward Windward Point. At sea, the USS *Dolphin* was providing escort duty. Prior to reaching Windward Point, Elliott ordered Lt. Lucas' platoon to scale the hills, head eastward upon reaching the crest line, and attempt to surprise the Spanish sentinels believed to be screening the Spanish main position at Cuzco Well. (See B (3) below for Lt. Lucas' route to the battlefield.) Rounding Windward Point, Elliott's force came to Cable Beach (the paved road turns abruptly north at the beach). Looking north at this point, he was able to look up the valley to the top of the crest where be observed Lt. Lucas group heading eastward.

(2) Hill 350 (in feet)--Elliott's first view of Cuzco Beach.

To Elliott's immediate front, rose a steep hill which seemed to start its ascent almost from the sea which was then on his right. The massive hill continued on in a north-south direction. To get to Cuzco meant a steep climb up the west face of the hill, which was soon accomplished. Reaching the top of the hill, Hill 350, coordinates **839996,** and looking east Elliott now had a view of Cuzco Beach and the main Spanish position. The battle may have started here but the range to Cuzco Beach is about 1000 yards. Initially, the undersigned had presumed this location as Elliott's command post for the entire battle. This was based on a map study. Upon actually viewing the terrain from this location, it became obvious that Hill 350 was not the primary battle position of the battle. Nevertheless, a sweep of the hill top and the terrain leading north to Hill 400, coordinates **839001,** was conducted but with negative results. It should be noted that at the crest of Hill 350 is a circular concrete gun position probably dating from WWII. Also, fragments of old field communication wire was in the vicinity. Obviously, this location had been worked over in modern times. From Hill 350 and looking both north and east one can easily see how the intervening terrain could be described as a "horseshoe" in shape, as Elliott did in his report. From the top of Hill 350 to the next peak in the ridge system, which trends north at this point, is a peak labeled Hill 400. From that peak, part of the hill mass turns east in a gently curving arc. Between these two peaks, the ground was searched thoroughly by the metal detector with negative results. This ground was eliminated by the team as the site of the Marine's main battle position. The Team now continued from Hill 400 following the ridge line as it trended easterly and slightly southerly.

(3) Elliot's Main Battle Position--Lucas rejoins Elliott.

From just below the Crest of Hill 400, the team continued along the crest line in a generally east slightly southerly direction. Almost immediately, the metal detector recorded buried metal. At this point, 6mm cartridge cases and cartridge clips began to be recovered. On the cartridge bottom were stamped letters and numbers. All had stamped 6mm USN on the lower half of the rim. Some had WRA CO stamped above this, others UMC. (WRA CO was the Winchester Repeating Arms company; UMC the Union Metallic Cartridge company, the forerunner of Remington Arms company.) The initial find of these items began at coordinates **840000** and continued along the ridge line for about 300 yards to coordinates **843000**. Usually, they were found just beneath the surface, although a few were discovered on top of the ground. Often, clusters of cartridges were found in a small area near one of the small (12-18 inch) rocks littering the hillside. This would indicate that an individual Marine chose this location as his firing position

As the ridge line continues east/south it begins to slope more directly in a southeastern direction. At this point, at about the 250 foot contour level, the nose of the hill refuses to a fairly sharp angle heading northeast. At about this position, metal indication ceases. This point appears to conform with the flank of Elliott's force nearest the enemy. It measures approximately 500-600 yards from the old building at Cuzco Well (See C (2) below). The entire Marine position is at an angle to the Spanish position. Consequently, the other flank of the position is farther from the Cuzco Well by about 200-250 yards. i.e. about 700-850 yards from Cuzco Well. Using the traces of metal found on the ridge leads to the conjecture Elliott's main battle position on the ridge line, consisting of D Co. and one platoon of C Co. (Lt. Bannon) plus Cubans is occupying a battle line 300 yards in length at a distance from the enemy of between 500 to 850 yards. This line is traced by coordinates **840000-843001**.

As Elliott's force engaged the Spanish below, Lt. Lucas "now rejoined the fight". When last seen by Elliott, Lucas was on the skyline having climbed the steep hill by the coast road in order to cut off any Spanish outposts. The first part of the climb was strenuous and cost him several heat casualties. Once on the peaks, the route became easier as he followed the ridge lines in that area. (Power lines on that ridge line may be following his route). In any event, when he rejoined Elliott he most likely came around in view from the northern side of the ridge, coordinates **843002**, where the rest of the force was now engaged with the Spanish. The Marine position now had more depth on the nose of that ridge line.

The team selected this position as the most likely CP for Elliott. (Final CP until beginning of Spanish retreat.) This conjectural CP would have given him the needed visibility and control. Accordingly, Elliott's CP is fixed at coordinates **843000**. At this point, the terrain over looks the Cuzco valley toward the east and also begins to slope rapidly to the south where it then levels off at 200 feet before sloping again sharply in the sea. This latter piece of terrain is about 500 yards from the Cuzco Well position at its top, and is almost parallel to the position. Early speculation on the part of the team had made this a possible Marine battle position. However, a thorough sweep of this terrain registered no metallic hits whatsoever, and this terrain was ruled out as a, battle position. It may have been a position used by the Spanish in the opening stage of the battle. Coming off the slope, a small brass buckle usually associated with a harness was discovered.

Based on the material evidence discovered in this location, we place the Marine main battle position along the trace of the ridge defined by coordinates 84000 to 843001. On this firing line was D. Co. commanded by Capt. Spicer, Lt. Bannon's platoon from C. Co. plus a number of Cubans. Elliott commanded from this position with his probable final CP at coordinates **843000**. Lt Lucas' platoon came up on the other (north) side of this ridge and came into view (by the Marines) as the ridge line narrows and forms the nose overlooking Cuzco valley. As he came into this position at coordinates **843002** Elliott was able to communicate with him by messenger, thus Elliott's original force was together for the first time since Lucas was detached on his scouting mission, during the force's approach march.

(4) Signaling Position of Sgt. Quick and Pvt. Fitzgerald

A prime objective of the research team was to determine the possible location from which Sgt. Quick and Pvt. Fitzgerald signaled to the USS *Dolphin*. Both Marines received the Medal of Honor for these exploits. All contemporary accounts agree that in order for the *Dolphin* to see the signals (Elliott's force did not have the standard issue signal flags used for "WigWag" signaling; the Marines tied cloth neckerchiefs to the end of their rifles and waved these to and fro in the approved manner), the Marines had to stand on the top of the ridge line, which put them in full view of the Spanish. Some accounts note that Sgt. Quick had his back to the enemy while facing the ship.

An early assumption based on a prior map study suggested that Hill 350, coordinates 839996, served as Elliott's CP throughout the battle and also would have served as the signal location for Quick and Fitzgerald. As noted above in B. (2), this location was rejected as the CP after the field visit to the area. At this location, the range to the Spanish was over 1000 yards.

The key to discerning the Quick/Fitzgerald signaling location then depended on finding the Marine's main battle position, and with that, Elliott's probable CP in the final moments prior to the Spanish retreat. As noted in (3) above we place Elliott's CP in the vicinity of coordinates **843000**. Building on that data, the probable location of both Quick and Fitzgerald as they signaled the *Dolphin* is also in this vicinity. They probably needed to move around this point to find the right location for the ship to see them. This location is also sufficiently close to the Spanish in the valley below (estimate between 500-600 yards) such that their bravery would be specifically noted by those around them. Accordingly, we estimate their position to have been in the same general vicinity as Elliott's CP at coordinates **843000**.

C. Phase III The Spanish position at Cuzco Beach-Magill's Hill

(1) Cuzco Beach--Naval Cemetery

The team returned to the Cuzco area the following day, this time approaching the area by the road (Magazine Road) to the Naval Cemetery. The objective was to find evidence of the Spanish position. A related objective was to determine if the hill rising north and overlooking the Cuzco valley would reveal evidence of naval gunfire. At the first peak of this hill (in fact the hill extends further northward as part of a ridge complex) is located a monument erected in 1988 to commemorate Sgt. Quick's and Pvt. Fitzgerald's exploits.

The flat terrain that defines the cemetery and the adjacent terrain that leads to the beach has been worked over both by manmade works as well as the effects of nature. Specifically, evidence includes concrete block construction of field heads plus strands of early model field communication wire. From the beach inland, evidence exists of tidal storm surges that have on occasion swept inland. In short, a thorough sweep of the level area south of the cemetery road revealed nothing of interest attributable to the late 19th century. It should be noted that the small hills south of the cemetery and overlooking the water were not swept. The area swept south of the road is in the vicinity of coordinates **849998**.

(2) The Old Foundation at Cuzco Beach

At the foot of the hill where the monument is located, Magazine Road makes a sharp turn to the north, bisecting Cuzco Valley and leading into the magazine area. Here, the north edge of the road is bounded by the beginning of a hill trending north. In this immediate vicinity were the ruins of yellow brick steps. There was no above ground evidence of the building to which these steps led. As one climbed the steps, immediately to the right was an old concrete water reservoir, rectangular in shape and about the size of a good sized backyard swimming pool. A fairly elaborate system of pipes and valves were part of this structure. Clearly, this had been a significant source of well water at an earlier time in this century.

About 30 feet to the right (east) of the concrete tank was a relatively level patch of ground overgrown with small trees and cactus. In one corner of this area was a large number of red curved roof tiles, many in near perfect condition. Their quantity, condition and location suggested modern manufacture. They were probably the roof tile to the demolished building related to the yellow brick steps. At one edge of this relatively flat area, were the remains of a stone foundation. It was dry laid, constructed of rubble (local rocks) material, and chinked with the peculiarly oval local coral found in the vicinity. Although only one corner was obvious to visual inspection, a closer look at the outlines revealed the shape and size of the foundation. The outside dimensions were measured. The structure size was 35 feet 3" (east-west and facing the beach) by 27 feet 9". This was certainly an important early structure in the area.

The foundation's perimeter was carefully swept. Located by the detector were a quantity of framing nails, cut nails and a few wire nails plus the remains of an iron door hinge. Small fragments that might have been part of a jar or similar vessel were located. The framing nails, cut nails, and door hinge were consistent with 19th century building materials. The team concluded that this was the foundation to one of the important 19th century ranch buildings at Cuzco, and probably served as the Spanish headquarters during the Cuzco Well battle. Its location is coordinates **847998**.

(3) Magill's Route to Cuzco Well

On the morning of 14 June, Lt. Col. Huntington not only dispatched the two company task force under Capt. Elliott to Cuzco Well, but also established three platoon size outposts to screen his main position at Fisherman's Point, and to be prepared to assist Elliott. To the southwest was Lt. Ingate's platoon from Co. B, augmented by a corpsman and a correspondent. His instructions were to take up a screening position at coordinates **828002**, where the cliff trail is constricted by the hills. Here he was to wait for Elliott's column to arrive and then to take his orders from Elliott. Unfortunately, this was Ingate's first experience away from the main headquarters. He wandered around the plateau area, missed Elliott, ended up back at the main position. He was then ordered to join Lt. Mahoney at the "crossroads" (coordinates **831012**) and then reinforce Elliott at Cuzco. The shooting from that location now noticeable at the main camp. He missed this landmark also, Mahoney waited for him, finally departed for Cuzco and arrived after the battle was essentially over.

Also near the "crossroads" was the third force sent out by Huntington to screen/reinforce. This was the Co. A. platoon led by Lt. Magill. Based on his subsequent actions, Magill's platoon was probably "leaning" into the direction of Cuzco, probably at the saddle beginning just southeast of the location of the memorial to Dumphy/McColgan. Assuming this as his start point, coordinates 835008, Magill, keeping to the ridge lines north and east of the Cuzco Valley trail (Magazine Road) led his force toward the Spanish position. On the way, he overran a Spanish signal station (Heliograph). The reflections from this station had been noted by the Marines at Fisherman's Point. A logical location for this station would be the hill at coordinates **848007**. For the Marines at Fisherman's Point to see the reflected signals, which were essentially "line of sight", the Spanish were most likely communicating with a Spanish outpost near Conde Beach, coordinates **808042**.

As Magill continued on the ridge line, it now turned south and led directly to a hill overlooking the Cuzco Well area. The trace of Magill's path from the "crossroads" area to the Cuzco Well location is described by the coordinates **831012-835008-848007-848003**. At this latter point (site of the Quick/Fitzgerald monument), Magill was nearly in a position to seal off the Spanish retreat from Cuzco Well.

(4) Magill's Hill/Monument Hill

An early conjecture, based on a map study and analysis of the contemporary accounts, made the hill mass coordinates **848998-848001** the logical location of the hill into which the USS *Dolphin* fired on the afternoon of 14 June. The naval gunfire precipitated the Spanish retreat. Lt. Magill was reported in a position to seal off the Spanish retreat until the *Dolphin's* shells impacting on a hill drove his force back up the ridge line out of the line of fire. It remained to discover evidence of naval shells on this hill to positively identify this position. As discussed in (2) above, the old stone foundation was at the foot of this hill at coordinates **847998**.

An old fire break traces a straight line up the face of the hill for about 300 yards to where the Quick/Fitzgerald monument is located. Reasoning that the bulldozer had disturbed the original soil, the detector began to sweep a path to the immediate left of the fire break. In the course of the sweep which continued up to and past the monument, numerous items were recovered. These included fragments of a 4-inch naval shell (verified by EOD [Explosive Ordnance Disposal] Gtmo detachment), suspected 6 and 3 pounder naval shell fragments, and numerous cartridge cases and clips.

The latter were identified as 6mm with markings identical to those found previously on the opposite ridge line. Several larger cartridge cases were discovered, initially thought to be used in the Spanish Mauser rifles. On further analysis, they turned out to be 30-06 cartridge cases from the Frankfort Arsenal and manufactured in . . . 1905-1906 (Probably used by U.S. Army personnel on a hunting expedition; note the coastal artillery positions previously discussed were constructed in 1906).

The USS *Dolphin's* log for his period is in the National Archive[s]. On 14 June, 1898, the log records expenditures of 14 rounds of 4"-Common, 11 rounds of 6 pounder, and 12 rounds of 3 pounder ammunition in the support of the Marines at Cuzco. Based on this evidence, Magill's final position just prior to the battle's end is located at coordinates **848003** (site of Quick/Fitzgerald monument). Several 6mm rounds were found beyond the monument (at this point . . . [there] is a saddle in the ridge line) an indication that the enemy position extended around the base of the hill facing west (across the valley was Elliott's main body with Lt. Lucas on Elliott's northern flank facing east).

On this particular day, the team had brought a thermometer to the field. At 1030 on 12 June, the reading on the thermometer as it was taken from the backpack read 99 degrees. When place [d] in the shade, it eventually settled at only 90 degrees.

5. Conclusions.

The above findings were based on three factors.
1) analysis of the existing body of accounts by 1898 participants
2) physical study of the terrain
3) identification of material discovered at particular locations.

As the field research progressed, and in particular as physical evidence was located, the team soon developed a consensus opinion. This opinion is reflected in the findings and discussion in paragraph 4 above. At the same time, the members recognized that reconstructing the operations of the First Marine Battalion (Huntington's Battalion), events that occurred nearly 100 years ago, could not be done with 100% certainty. While the team is confident of its findings, it is recognized that future researchers may come to different conclusions. As a minimum, it is hoped that this report will add to the existing body of knowledge concerning the subject events and serve as a guide to any future research efforts.

6. Acknowledgments.

My thanks to Capt. Larry E. Larson USN, COMNAVBASE Guantanamo for granting "permission to come aboard" and for the courtesies of his command. Also, a thank you to Col. Bob Mauskapf USMC, who provided initial encouragement and though his efforts helped to make it happen. Colonel Reno Bamford II USMC, C.O. Marine Barracks Guantanamo added his gracious hospitality in addition to his full support of the research effort. To both Capt. Tom Riordan USMC and to Ssgt. P.W. Whitten USMC, both of whom are Marines in the finest tradition, my thanks not only for your dedication to the project but also for the major contributions you made. Finally, to my son Mike, aka Maj. M. P. Hull USMC, my sincerest thanks for his assistance, but more importantly, for his company.

Robert R. Hull

Colonel, U.S. Marine Corps (Ret)

Initial Distribution:

COMNAVBASE Guantanamo Bay, Cuba
C.O. Marine Barracks Guantanamo Bay, Cuba
Col. Robert Mauskapf, USMC MarForLant Liaison Element Norfolk
Maj. Michael P. Hull, USMC
Capt. Thomas J. Riordan, USMC
SSgt. T. P. W. Whitten, USMC

VICTORY ON LAND AND SEA

Photo courtesy of Naval Historical Center NH85346

The armored cruiser USS New York, *the flagship of Rear Admiral William T Sampson, is shown after the decisive battle of Santiago Bay. In the battle, the American fleet destroyed the seven ships of the Spanish squadron without the loss of any U.S. ships. The Spaniards suffered casualties of over 350 dead, and over 150 wounded. More than 1,600 Spaniards including Admiral Pascual Cervera y Topete, the Spanish commander, were taken prisoner. American losses were 1 man killed and 10 wounded.*

An American sailor poses before the former Spanish fort Santa Cruz, on the island of Guam. On 20 June 1898, the American cruiser USS Charleston *entered Apra harbor and took the surrender of the Spanish forces on Guam.*

Photo courtesy of National Archives 127-N-521890

Photo courtesy of Naval Historical Center

Marine IstLt John T. Myers landed on 21 June 1898 with 30 Marines from the USS Charleston *on the island of Guam and disarmed the small Spanish garrison there. In the above photograph, taken in December 1899, Myers is shown as a Marine captain commanding the Marine Barracks, Subic Bay, in the Philippines.*

Marine 1stLt John A. Lejeune commanded the Marine detachment from the American cruiser Cincinnati, *which landed on 9 August 1898 at Cape San Juan, Puerto Rico, to relieve a U.S. naval force under attack by Spanish forces.   Pictured above as a Major General, Lejeune was the commander of the U.S. 2d Division in World War I and in 1920 became Commandant of the US. Marine Corps.*

Photo History and Museums Division, USMC

Photo History and Museums Division, USMC

Marine 1stLt Wendell C. Neville served with the 1st Marine Battalion at Guantanamo. Like Lejuene, Neville served in World War I and became Commandant of the Marine Corps, in 1929. He is photographed above as Commandant of the Marine Corps.

Charles Heywood was Commandant of the Marine Corps during the Spanish-American War.   He retired in 1903 as a major general. Heywood zealously protected the traditional mission of the Marine Corps while at he same time seizing the opportunity to form a Marine battalion to be deployed with the fleet.

Department of Defense (Marine) Photo A413182

Photo History and Museums Division, USMC

Captain George F. Elliott (pictured above as a brigadier general) commanded the Marine attack on 14 June 1898 on the Spanish forces in the Cuzco Well area. With the destruction of the well which was the only source of fresh water in the sector, Spanish forces withdrew and no longer presented a viable threat to the Marine battalion on Guantanamo. In 1903, Elliott succeeded MajGen Charles Heywood as Brigadier General Commandant of the Marine Corps (the rank of the Commandant reverted by law to brigadier general upon the retirement of Heywood).

In September 1898, the 1st Marine Battalion is seen marching through the streets of Portsmouth, New Hampshire. On 22 September 1898, the Marines paraded before President William McKinley at the White House in a driving rainstorm.

Photo courtesy of Naval Historical Center NH 46345

Photo courtesy of Col Robert R. Hull, USMC (Ret)

A photograph taken in June of 1997 shows the flagpole at the US Marine Barracks Guantanamo marking the 1st Marine Battalion's command post in June 1898. The view is north and overlooking Guantanamo beach and harbor.

Chronology of Events Involving the Spanish-American War

1895

12 June--President Grover Cleveland issues proclamation of neutrality concerning the revolt in Cuba.

15 July--Cuban insurgents declare that the Cuban Republic is independent of Spain.

1896

10 February--Spanish General Valeriano Weyler y Nicolau takes over the Spanish effort to end the revolt in Cuba.

6 April--United States Congress passes joint resolution calling for Executive to recognize Cuban independence.

1897

4 March--President William McKinley takes office.

16 June--Annexation Treaty with the Hawaiian Republic signed at the White House on 16 June. However, President McKinley was unable to gain the two-thirds majority in the Senate for ratification.

8 August--Spanish Prime Minister Antonio Canovas del Castillo assassinated by an Italian anarchist, leading eventually to a change of government in Spain.

13 September--General Stewart Lyndon Woodford arrives in Spain as U.S. Minister to put pressure on Spanish government for an early and certain peace in Cuba.

23 October--Spanish government announces to Woodford that Spain would grant autonomy to Cuba.

4 November--Assistant Navy Secretary Theodore Roosevelt convenes special board "to consider the reorganization of the Navy." Suggestion made to transfer officers and men of the Marine Corps to the line of the Navy. Colonel Commandant Charles Heywood argues to keep Marine Corps separate.

December--U.S. State Department announces arrangements for contributions to those suffering due to the Spanish policy of reconcentration in Cuba. Spain had agreed to permit entry of food, clothing, and medicines into Cuba free of duty.

1898

January--Spain declares autonomy for Cuba and Puerto Rico.

12 January--Anti-American riots occur in Havana, led by pro-Weyler Spanish army officers.

25 January--USS *Maine* anchors in Havana harbor on port visit.

9 February--Letter of Enrique de Lome, Spanish Minister to the U.S., critical of President McKinley is published by the *New York Journal*.

15 February--USS *Maine* explodes in Havana Harbor, 28 Marines die along with 238 sailors.

21 February--U.S. Navy Court of Inquiry begins session in Havana.

25 February--Acting Secretary of the Navy Theodore Roosevelt orders Commodore George Dewey to move squadron to Hong Kong and "Keep full of coal."

26 February--Secretary of Navy John Davis Long orders naval units in Pacific and Caribbean to take on coal.

9 March--President McKinley's "50 Million Dollar Bill" for national defense passes 311 to 0 in the House and 76 to 0 in the Senate.

21 March--Navy Court of Inquiry declares that USS *Maine* blown up by external agency, believed to be a submarine mine.

29 March--President McKinley sends ultimatum to Spain calling for abandonment of reconcentration, the declaration of an armistice between Spain and Cuba, and that Spain accept U.S. mediation.

10 April--Spanish Captain General Ramon Blanco y Arenas announces an unconditional armistice with Cuba, but refused to submit to U.S. mediation upon Cuban sovereignty.

16 April--Colonel Commandant Charles Heywood USMC, receives orders to organize two Marine battalions to serve in Cuba.

17 April--Colonel Heywood issues orders to assemble men from all East Coast ports and stations at the Brooklyn Navy Yard under the command of Lieutenant Colonel Robert Huntington, USMC.

19 April--Congress passes resolution that Cuba is free and independent, and authorizes the President to employ U.S. troops to force Spain to relinquish control over the island.

22 April--President McKinley declares a blockade of Cuban ports. Also, at the Brooklyn Navy Yard, Huntington's Battalion parades to the transport USS *Panther* and sails south.

23 April--President McKinley calls for 125,000 volunteers.

24 April--Spain declares war on U.S.

25 April--U.S. recognizes that a state of war has existed between the U.S. and Spain since 21 April.

25 April--Commodore Dewey moves his squadron into Mirs Bay (Tai Pang Han), thirty miles up the coast from Hong Kong.

26 April--Huntington's battalion sails for Key West, Florida from Fortress Monroe, Virginia.

27 April--Commodore Dewey's squadron leaves Mirs Bay for Philippines.

29 April--Spanish squadron under Vice Admiral Pascual Cervera y Topete departs Cape Verde Islands, headed west.

30 April--Commodore Dewey and naval squadron enter Manila Bay at 11:30 p.m.

1 May--Commodore Dewey opens fire on Spanish fleet near Cavite Naval Station. Spanish fleet destroyed by 12:30 p.m., and signals surrender at 12:37 p.m.

3 May--Lieutenant Dion Williams USMC and Marines from USS *Baltimore* take Cavite Naval Station unopposed.

4 May--Congress authorizes USMC to increase strength by 24 officers and 1,640 enlisted men.

11 May--Sailors and Marines from USS *Marblehead* and USS *Nashville* cut two (of three) transoceanic cables off Cienfuegos, Cuba. Twelve Marines receive Medal of Honor.

19 May--Filipino insurgent leader Emilio Aguinaldo returns to the Philippines from Hong Kong to rally the people against the Spanish. On the same date, Admiral Cervera's squadron anchors in Santiago Harbor, Cuba.

3 June--U.S. Navy sinks the collier *Merrimac* in Santiago Harbor in an attempt to bottle up the Spanish squadron.

5 June--A U.S. naval force of three ships under Commander Bowman H. McCalla enters Guantanamo Harbor to destroy a blockhouse above Fisherman's Point.

6 June--U.S. warships of the North Atlantic Fleet under Rear Admiral William T. Sampson bombard fortifications at Santiago Harbor.

7 June--Forty Marines from USS *Oregon* and 20 from USS *Marblehead* check for a suitable landing area in Guantanamo at Fisherman's Point, destroy cable station at Playa del Este, and withdraw.

10 June--Huntington's Battalion of Marines lands at Fisherman's Point.

11-14 June--Huntington's Battalion holds off Spanish regulars and Cuban loyalist troops at Guantanamo.

14 June--Marines at Guantanamo under Captain George F. Elliott destroy Cuzco Well. Sergeant John Quick and Private John Fitzgerald, USMC, both win Medal of Honors signaling USS *Dolphin* to shift fire.

20 June--USS *Charleston* under Captain Henry Glass, USN, captures Guam. Lieutenant John T. Myers, USMC, and 30 Marines accept the surrender of the Spanish garrison.

22 June--U.S. Army V Corps under General William Shafter, USA, lands off Daiquiri to begin drive on Santiago, Cuba.

30 June--First U.S. troops land at Luzon, Philippines.

1 July--Emilio Aguinaldo proclaims the Philippine Republic.

1 July--U.S. Army captures El Caney outside Santiago, Cuba.

3 July--Spanish Admiral Cervera's squadron attempts to break out of Santiago Harbor and is destroyed by the American fleet.

17 July--Spanish garrison at Santiago, Cuba, surrenders to General Shafter.

27 July--USS *Dixie* arrives at Playa del Ponce, Puerto Rico and seizes Ponce. Lieutenant Henry C. Haines orders U.S. flag raised over city hall.

28 July--U.S. troops under Army General Nelson Miles come ashore in Puerto Rico.

31 July--BGen Arthur MacArthur USA, arrives at Manila with 4000 soldiers.

5 August--Huntington's Battalion departs Guantanamo for another objective area in Cuba.

9 August--Spanish attack lighthouse manned by U.S. sailors overlooking San Juan Passage, Puerto Rico.

10 August--1st Lieutenant John A. LeJeune USMC and 37 Marines from USS *Cincinnati* and USS *Amphitrite* reinforces sailors at San Juan Lighthouse.

12 August--U.S. Navy squadron bombards Manzanillo, Cuba, to prepare for Marine landing.

12 August--Peace Protocol between Spain and U.S. suspends Caribbean operations. Landing of Huntington's Battalion at Manzanilla, Cuba, called off.

12 August--The United States officially annexes the Hawaiian Islands.

13 August--Admiral Dewey's fleet and U.S. Army under Major General Wesley Merritt make simultaneous attacks on Manila, Philippines. Spanish authorities surrender and 7,000 Spanish troops taken prisoner.

15 August--Huntington's Battalion ordered to return to U.S.

26 August--Huntington's Battalion arrives at Portsmouth, New Hampshire.

10 December--Treaty of Paris signed to end war with Spain.

1899

1 January--Spain transfers Cuba to U.S. control.

6 February--Senate ratifies Treaty of Paris, which formally ends the war with Spain, and the U.S. annexes the Philippines, Guam, and Puerto Rico.

3 March--Congress passes Navy and Marine Corps Personnel Bill, doubling the size of USMC to 225 officers and 6,000 enlisted.

23 May--Colonel Percival C. Pope USMC arrives at Cavite Naval Station, Philippines with the First Battalion of Marines.

Spanish-American War
Marine Corps Medal of Honor Awardees

11 May 1898, Cable-cutting expedition off Cienfuegos, Cuba:

from USS *Nashville*:

Private Frank Hall
Private Joseph H. Franklin
Private Joseph F. Scott
Sergeant Philip Gaughn
Private Pomeroy Parker
Private Oscar W. Field
Private Michael L. Kearney

from USS *Marblehead*:

Private Herman Kuchneister
Private Walter S. West
Private James Meredith
Private Edward Sullivan
Private Daniel Campbell

14 June 1898, Action against Spanish at Cuzco Well, Cuba

Sergeant John Henry Quick
Private John Fitzgerald

3 July 1898, On USS *Brooklyn* during actions off Santiago, Cuba

Private Harry Lewis MacNeill

Selected Annotated Bibliography

Spanish-American War

Compiled by LtCol David E. Kelly, USMCR

Books with * indicate titles in Marine Corps Historical Center library. Updated versions of this bibliography to be available on the History and Museums Division Web Site or on diskette from the Historical Center's library.

General Marine Corps History

*Heinl, Jr., Col, Robert D., USMC. *Soldiers of the Sea: The United States Marine Corps, 1775-1962.* Annapolis, MD: U.S. Naval Institute Press. 1962. Reprint, Baltimore, MD: Nautical & Aviation Publishing Co. of America, 1991.

Chapter 4, "The Expeditionary Years," covers Spanish-American War and discusses the development of the Advance Base Force.

*Leonard, John W., and Fred F. Chitty. *The Story of the United States Marines, 1740-1919.* New York, NY: United States Marine Corps Publicity Bureau, 1919?.

An early general history of the Corps.

*Metcalf, LtCol, Clyde. *A History of the United States Marine Corps.* New York, NY: G. P. Putnams's Sons, 1939.

A valuable general history of the Marine Corps, written on the eve of World War II. Chapter 10, "The War with Spain and Operations in the Far East," gives succinct coverage of that era. Lacks a bibliography and footnotes.

*Millett, Allan R. *Semper Fidelis: The History of the United States Marine Corps.* New York, NY: Macmillan Publishing Co., Inc., 1980.

Chapter 5, "The Marine Corps and the New Navy 1889-1909," and Chapter 10, "The Creation of the Advance Base Force 1900-1916," in well-documented accounts explain the origins of the Advance Base Force, and how the Navy and Marine Corps began to practice fleet landing exercises on a regular basis. The book also discusses how the experiences of the Marine battalion at Guantanamo led to the Navy realizing the utility of using its own Marines for landing operations.

*Moskin, Robert J. *The U.S. Marine Corps Story*. New York, NY: McGraw-Hill, 1977.

Chapter VII, "The Four Month War With Spain 1898," has a general discussion of the war, together with several good photos of the First Battalion of Marines at Guantanamo.

*Simmons, BGen Edwin H., USMC, Ret. *The United States Marines: The First Two Hundred Years 1775-1975*. Quantico, VA: Special edition published for Marine Corps Association by arrangement with the Viking Press, 1976.

Marines in the Spanish-American War

*Clifford, John H. *The History of the First Battalion of U.S. Marines*. Portsmouth, NH, 1930.

A self published, rare booklet. A firsthand account by a Marine from his enlistment in 1898, through the fighting at Guantanamo, Cuba and the return to the United States after the war. Has listing of every Marine in the battalion.

*Keeler, Frank. *The Journal of Frank Keeler, 1898*. Edited by Carolyn A. Tyson. Quantico, VA: Marine Corps Museum. 1968.

A personal account of Frank Keeler's service in the Marine Corps during the Spanish-American War.

*Nalty, Bernard C. *The United States Marines in the War with Spain* . (Marine Corps Historical Reference Series, no.3) Washington D.C.: Historical Branch, G-3 Division, Headquarters, U.S. Marine Corps, 1959.

Small mimeographed monograph of the War. One sketch map of Cuba.

*Shulimson, Jack. *The Marine Corps Search for a Mission, 1880-1898*. Lawrence, KS: University Press of Kansas, 1993.

Early chapters deal with reform and professionalism issues in the Marine Corps at the time. Chapter 6 deals with the "new" Navy. Lots of information on Navy Lieutenant William Fullam's pressure to remove Marines from modern naval ships. Chapter 9 discusses the Spanish American War and its aftermath. Comprehensive discussions of reforms, roles, development of postwar roles for Marine Corps.

*U.S. Marine Corps. *Annual Report of the Commandant of the Marine Corps, 1898*.

Includes copies of reports from Colonel Robert Huntington and the Battalion at Guantanamo.

Sources Located at the Marine Corps Historical Center

Subject Files. Reference Section. Washington, D.C.

Personal Papers Collection, Marine Corps Historical Center, Washington, D.C.

Cochrane, Henry C. Papers: Diaries and letters contain firsthand account of the Guantanamo battle.

Huntington, Robert W. Papers: Contemporary letters by the commanding officer of the 1st Marine Battalion relative to the war.

Spanish-American War History

Bradford, James C., ed. *Crucible of Empire: The Spanish-American War and Its Aftermath.* Annapolis, MD: U.S. Naval Institute Press, 1993.

Section by Dr. Jack Shulimson, pp. 127-151, "Marines in the Spanish-American War."

*Chadwick, French E. *The Relations of the United States and Spain: The Spanish-American War.* New York, NY: Russell & Russell, 1968.

*Dierks, Jack Cameron. *A Leap to Arms: The Cuban Campaign of 1898.* Philadelphia, PA: Lippincott, 1970.

A concise, general history of the war. Diplomatic background, Army and Navy operations.

*Freidel, Frank Burt. *The Splendid Little War:* Boston, MA: Little, Brown, and Co., 1958.

Extensively illustrated general history of the war. Photos emphasize Army actions, also includes paintings and illustrations from the time, and many Navy photos. A few Marines appear on board ship in some photos.

Johnston, William A. *History Up to Date: A Concise Account of the War of 1898 Between the United States and Spain: Its Causes and the Treaty of Paris.* New York, NY: A. S. Barnes & Co., 1899.

*Lodge, Henry Cabot. *The War with Spain.* New York, NY: Harper & Brothers, 1899.

*Millis, Walter. *The Martial Spirit: A Study of Our War with Spain*. Boston, MA: Houghton Mifflin Co., 1931.

A general history of the conflict, written during the anti-war period between World Wars I and II, questions the motives for, conduct of, and results of the war. Critical of Army preparations and actions. Brief mention of Marines at Guantanamo in three paragraphs on page 259.

*Musicant, Ivan. *Empire by Default: The Spanish-American War*. New York, NY: H. Holt, 1997.

Musick, John R. *Lights and Shadows of Our War with Spain*. New York, NY: J. S. Ogilvie, 1898.

O'Toole, G. J. A. *The Spanish-American War: An American Epic, 1898*. New York, NY: Norton W. W. & Co., Inc., 1984.

Russell, Henry B. *An Illustrated History of Our War with Spain*. Hartford, CT: A. D. Worthington and Co., 1898.

Outlines preparations of Navy Department in the late 1890's; the building of new war ships and President McKinley's efforts to avoid war by undertaking negotiations with Spain. Discusses Battle of Manila Bay, and explains why Admiral George Dewey could not take control of the city of Manila until reinforcements arrived from the United States.

Sargent, Herbert Howland. *The Campaign of Santiago de Cuba*. Chicago, ILL: A. C. McClurg & Co., 1907.

Keller, Allan. *The Spanish-American War: A Compact History*. New York, NY: L. Hawthorn Books, 1969.

Staff Correspondents. *The Chicago Record's War Stories*. Chicago, Ill: Chicago Record. 1898

Articles filed by newspaper reporters covering the War. Includes coverage of the prelude to the war; speech from a U.S. senator describing conditions in Cuba under "Reconcentration;" Stephen Crane's description of Marines fighting at Guantanamo and night time signaling from shore to ship for gunfire from the ships while under attack; and Hobart Billman's story of night attack on western shore of harbor at Guantanamo by two companies of Huntington's First Battalion of Marines.

Trask, David F. *The War with Spain in 1898*. New York, NY: Macmillan, Co., Inc., 1981.

Excellent overview of the War. Lots of information on background to the war, pressures by the Cuban Junta on U.S. public opinion, Spanish General Valeriano Weyler's policy of "reconcentration" in Cuba, outcry by U.S. newspapers demanding action, mobilization of U.S. Army, and destruction of the USS *Maine*.

*Wagner, Arthur L. *Our Country's Defensive Forces in War and Peace*. Akron, OH: The Werner Co., 1899.

Watterson, Henry. *History of the Spanish-American War*. Hartford, CT: American Publishing Co., 1898.

Wright, Marcus J. *Leslie's Official History of the Spanish-American War*. Washington?. War Records Office, 1899.

Bibliographies/Reference Works

Beede, Benjamin R., ed. *The War of 1898 and U.S. Interventions, 1898-1934. An Encyclopedia*. New York, NY: Garland Publishing, 1994.

Dyal, Donald. *Historical Dictionary of the Spanish-American War*. Westport, CT: Greenwood Publishing Group Inc., 1996.

Venzon, Anne C. *The Spanish-American War: An Annotated Bibliography*. New York, NY: Garland, 1990.

Biography/Memoirs

*Buel, James. W. *Hero Tales of the American Soldier and Sailor as Told by the Heroes Themselves*. New York, NY: W. W. Wilson, 1899.

*Jeffers, Paul H. *Colonel Roosevelt: Theodore Roosevelt Goes to War, 1897-1898*. New York, NY: J. Wiley & Sons, 1996.

*LeJeune, MajGen John A., USMC. *Reminiscences of a Marine*. New York, NY: Arno Press, 1979.

*Schmidt, Hans. *Maverick Marine: General Smedley Butler and the Contradictions of American Military History*. Lexington, KY: University Press of Kentucky, 1987.

Serious examination of Butler's career as a Marine officer and his controversial post-retirement career as an anti-war and anti-imperalist activist. Early chapter covers his first eight months as one of the officers commissioned for the duration of the war, and his reentry into active service as the Corps expanded in colonial conflicts in the Philippines and the Caribbean area.

*Thomas, Lowell J. *Old Gimlet Eye: The Adventures of Smedley Butler*. New York, NY: Farrar & Rinehart, Inc., 1933.

A glowing, almost hagiographic biography of Butler's career written for the popular press which romanticizes Butler's colorful time in the Corps until his forced retirement in 1931.

Young, Hon James Rankin. *Reminiscences and Thrilling Stories of the War By Returned Heroes*. In collaboration with J. Hampton Moore. Washington, D.C.: R. A. Dinsmore. 1898.

Related Topics of Interest

Uniforms, Weapons, Etc.

Field, Ron. *The Spanish-American War 1898*. New York, NY: Brassey's. 1998.

Illustrates uniforms, arms, and flags.

U.S. Army

*Cosmas, Graham. *An Army for Empire: The United States Army in the Spanish-American War*. Columbia, MO: University of Missouri Press, 1971.

Describes problems for U.S. Army in the 1890's, political difficulties during mobilization for war between regular Army units, volunteers, and state militias, effects of this on the fighting at Santiago, Cuba, and how the American public perceived these problems. Also outlines problems between the Army and the Navy at Santiago.

*Adjutant-General. *Correspondence Relating to the War With Spain*. 2 vols. Washington D.C.: Government Printing Office, 1902.

African-American Units

*Johnson, E. A. (Edward Austin). *History of Negro Soldiers in the Spanish-American War: and Other Items of Interest.* New York, NY: Johnson Reprint Corp., 1970.

Naval Operations

The Battleship Indiana and Her Part in the Spanish-American War, 1898. Edited by W. G. Cassard. United States: N.p., 1898.

*Cervera y Topete, Pascual. *Views of Admiral Cervera Regarding the Spanish Navy in the Late War; November, 1898.* Washington, D.C.: Government Printing Office, 1898.

Short booklet, the English translation of the Spanish naval commander's outline of the Spanish Navy's deficiencies in the war due to lack of proper funding in the 1890's.

Cervera y Topete, Pascual. *The Spanish-American War: A Collection of Documents Relative to the Squadron Operations in the West Indies.* Washington, D.C.: Government Printing Office, 1899.

Concas y Palau, Victor M. *The Squadron of Admiral Cervera.* Washington, D.C.: Government Printing Office, 1900.

The Development of the Modern Navy and the Spanish War. Newport, RI: Naval War College, 1936.

*Feuer, A. B. *The Spanish-American War at Sea: Naval Action in the Atlantic.* Westport, CT: Praeger, 1995.

Clearly written account of naval actions in the Atlantic and Caribbean. Chapter 6, "The Cable Cutting at Cienfuegos" describes the action where Marines won their first Medal of Honor in the war. Chapter 10, "The Capture of Guantanamo," is a very complete account of the actions of the First Battalion of Marines in Cuba, with a thorough description of the three days of defensive fighting which led to the decision to attack the Spanish-held well at Cuzco, and operations in the harbor to clear Spanish mines. Chapter 16, "Captain Littleton Waller Tazwell Waller's Story", gives Waller's account of Marines on the USS Indiana during the 3 July naval battle off Santiago, Cuba.

Gannon, Joseph C. *The USS Oregon and the Battle of Santiago.* New York, NY: Comet Press Books, 1958.

*Graham, George Edward. *Schley and Santiago: An Historical Account of the Blockade and Final Destruction of the Spanish Fleet.* Chicago, Ill: W. B. Conkey Co., 1902.

Long, John D. *The New American Navy.* 2 vols. New York, NY: Outlook Co., 1903.

*Miller, Nathan. *The U.S. Navy an Illustrated History.* Annapolis, MD: U.S. Naval Institute Press, 1976.

General Navy history, includes photos of Navy and Marines during the war.

*Rickover, Hyman. G. *How the Battleship Maine Was Destroyed.* Washington, D.C.: U.S. Government Printing Office, 1976.

Results of Admiral Rickover's study on physical causes of the explosion which sunk the ship. He concludes that it was due to spontaneous combustion of the coal on board the ship, not an external mine.

U.S. Navy Department. *Annual Report of the Navy Department, 1898.* 2 vols. The second volume is the *Appendix to the Report of the Chief of the Bureau of Navigation: Naval Operations of the War with Spain.*

Literature

*Crane, Stephen. *Wounds in the Rain: War Stories.* New York, NY: Frederick A. Stokes, 1900.

Crane's versions of events involving Marines, Army personnel, and correspondents during the war. Also has other stories from war in Turkey.

The War Dispatches of Stephen Crane. Edited by R. W. Stallman and E. R. Hagemann. New York, NY: NYU Press, 1964.

Works of Stephen Crane, vol. ix, *Reports of War, War Dispatches, Great Battles of the World,* edited by Fredson Bowers (Charlottesville, VA.: The University Press of Virginia, 1971)

Pictorial Works

*King, Lt Nephew, W., USN, with MajGen O. O. Howard, USA, and Capt Robley D. Evans, USN. *The Story of the War of 1898 and the Revolt in the Philippines.* New York: Peter Fenelon Collier, 1899.

A rare, out of print, oversized picture book. Photographs, drawings and some full color lithographs, concentrate on Army and Navy operations, but includes several pages on Huntington's First Battalion of Marines.

Pictures: Spanish-American War. United States?: N.p., 1898.

*Wright, Marcus J. *The Official and Pictorial Record of the Story of American Expansion.* Washington: M. J. Wright, 1904.

Diplomacy

Benton, Elbert J. *International Law and Diplomacy of the Spanish-American War.* Baltimore, MD: Johns Hopkins University Press, 1908.

Offner, John L. *An Unwanted War: The Diplomacy of the United States and Spain Over Cuba, 1895-1898.* Chapel Hill, NC: University of North Carolina Press, 1992.

Imperialism

Foner, Philip S. *The Spanish-Cuban-American War and the Birth of American Imperialism, 1895-1902.* New York, NY: Monthly Review Press, 1972.

Morgan, Wayne H. *America's Road to Empire: The War with Spain and Overseas Empire.* New York, NY: Wiley, 1965.

Intelligence

Corson, William R. *The Armies of Ignorance: The Rise of the American Intelligence Empire.* New York, NY: Dial Press, 1977.

Dorwort, Jeffrey M. *The Office of Naval Intelligence: The Birth of America's First Intelligence Agency, 1881-1918.* New York, NY: Naval Institute Press, 1979.

Jeffrey-Jones, R. *American Espionage from Secret Service to CIA.* New York, NY: Free Press, 1977.

Powe, Marc B. *The Emergence of the War Department Intelligence Agency 1885-1918.* Manhattan, KS: Military Affairs, 1975.

Public Opinion

Brown, Charles H. *The Correspondent's War: Journalists in the Spanish-American War*. New York, NY: Scribner, 1967.

Linderman, Gerald F. *The Mirror of War: American Society and the Spanish-American War*. Ann Arbor, MI: University of Michigan Press, 1974.

Wilkerson, Marcus M. *Public Opinion and the Spanish-American War*. Baton Rouge, LA: Louisiana State University Press, 1932.

Casualties

Roddis, Louis H. *Naval and Marine Corps Casualties in the Wars of the United States*. N.p.,1946?.

www.ingramcontent.com/pod-product-compliance
Lightning Source LLC
Chambersburg PA
CBHW080507110426
42742CB00017B/3021